# Foundation Gatsby Projects

## Create Four Real Production Websites with Gatsby

Nabendu Biswas

Apress®

*Foundation Gatsby Projects: Create Four Real Production Websites with Gatsby*

Nabendu Biswas
Bangalore, India

ISBN-13 (pbk): 978-1-4842-6557-4
https://doi.org/10.1007/978-1-4842-6558-1

ISBN-13 (electronic): 978-1-4842-6558-1

Managing Director, Apress Media LLC: Welmoed Spahr
Acquisitions Editor: Louise Corrigan
Development Editor: James Markham
Coordinating Editor: Nancy Chen

Cover designed by eStudioCalamar

Cover image designed by Freepik (www.freepik.com)

Distributed to the book trade worldwide by Springer Science+Business Media New York, 1 New York Plaza, New York, NY 10004. Phone 1-800-SPRINGER, fax (201) 348-4505, e-mail orders-ny@springer-sbm.com, or visit www.springeronline.com. Apress Media, LLC is a California LLC and the sole member (owner) is Springer Science + Business Media Finance Inc (SSBM Finance Inc). SSBM Finance Inc is a **Delaware** corporation.

For information on translations, please e-mail booktranslations@springernature.com; for reprint, paperback, or audio rights, please e-mail bookpermissions@springernature.com.

Apress titles may be purchased in bulk for academic, corporate, or promotional use. eBook versions and licenses are also available for most titles. For more information, reference our Print and eBook Bulk Sales web page at http://www.apress.com/bulk-sales.

Any source code or other supplementary material referenced by the author in this book is available to readers on GitHub via the book's product page, located at www.apress.com/9781484265574. For more detailed information, please visit http://www.apress.com/source-code.

Printed on acid-free paper

*To my wife and kid. This book is affectionately dedicated.*

# Table of Contents

# About the Author

**Nabendu Biswas** is a full-stack JavaScript developer who has
been working in the IT industry for the past 15 years.
He has worked for some of the world's top development
firms and investment banks. He currently works as an
Associate Architect at Innominds. He is also a passionate
tech blogger who publishes on thewebdev.tech and is an
all-round nerd, passionate about everything JavaScript,
React, and Gatsby. You can find him on Twitter @nabendu82.

# About the Technical Reviewer

**Alexander Chinedu Nnakwue** has a background in Mechanical Engineering from the University of Ibadan, Nigeria and has been a frontend developer for over three years. He has worked on both web and mobile technologies. He also has experience as a technical author, writer, and reviewer. He enjoys programming for the web, and occasionally, you can find him playing soccer. He was born in Benin City and is currently based in Lagos, Nigeria.

# Introduction

I have done quite a bit of freelance work in WordPress development since 2011. The three things that I didn't like about WordPress at that time were that little coding knowledge was required, the sites were slow, and they were easily hacked.

The awesome static site generator GatsbyJS solves all of these problems. It is built with React, so you can utilize all your React knowledge. Plus, it uses the in-demand GraphQL, so you will work with that also. The sites are blazing fast and completely secure. You need a bit of ReactJS knowledge to work with Gatsby, but it adds so much to the React ecosystem. It has a large plugin system like WordPress, which adds functionality. It can be used with a wide range of backend systems, like CMS, Firebase, and many more. In this book, we will first create a simple site using only Gatsby. After that, we will use Stackbit to quickly build a Gatsby site. Then we will build a complex site with all features using the Contentful CMS. The last chapter shows you how to build a video chat site, similar to Skype but using the Twilio service.

# CHAPTER 1

# Creating an Agency Site

In this chapter, we will build a simple demo agency site (known as a *service company* in India). Although I could use one of the many starter kits available at the Gatsby site that offer complete CSS, I've decided to use a starter kit with minimal CSS so you can learn how to write your own. We are going to do the setup first, and then move on to the basic styles. After that, we will create the sections and pages on the site. Finally, we will deploy the site using Netlify.

## The Setup

In this project you can use any IDE like VS code. Everything else we will install through npm. Let's start with Gatsby.

First install Gatsby globally by running the following command in your terminal.

```
npm install -g gatsby-cli
```

To create a new Gatsby site, run the following command in the terminal. This is the most basic Gatsby starter kit, with minimal Gatsby plugins installed (more on that later).

```
gatsby new agencyDemo https://github.com/gatsbyjs/gatsby-starter-hello-world
```

Now, go to the directory and run `gatsby develop`. The commands are shown in Listing 1-1.

***Listing 1-1.*** The gatsby develop Command

```
cd agencyDemo
gatsby develop
```

The basic site is now up and running,[1] as shown in Figure 1-1.

---

[1]http://localhost:8000/

© Nabendu Biswas 2021

N. Biswas, *Foundation Gatsby Projects*, https://doi.org/10.1007/978-1-4842-6558-1_1

Hello world!

***Figure 1-1.*** *Gatsby is up and running*

We will start by creating the home page.

# Creating the Home Page

In Gatsby, everything is React-based, so we will create the home page component. We will first create a set of global styles.

So, first create a folder called styles inside src. Then create a file called global.css inside it. We will put the generic global CSS shown in Listing 1-2 inside this file.

***Listing 1-2.*** The global.css File

```css
html {
    box-sizing: border-box;
    font-size: 10px;
    font-weight: 400;
    letter-spacing: 0.075em;
    margin:0;
}
*, *:before, *:after {
  box-sizing: inherit;
}
body {
  font-family: "Open Sans", Helvetica, sans-serif;
  padding: 0;
  margin: 0;
}
a {
  text-decoration: none;
}
```

Next, create a file called `gatsby-browser.js` in the root directory and include this `global.css` file by adding the following:

```
import "./src/styles/global.css"
```

We will use the extremely popular CSS-in-JS library *styled component* to style the rest of the project.

We need to install some dependencies for `styled-components`. So, open the terminal and type the following command. We have to stop the `gatsby develop` running on the terminal by pressing Ctrl+C.

```
npm install--save gatsby-plugin-styled-components styled-components babel-
plugin-styled-components
```

Next, include the following code in the `gatsby-config.js` file. This file should already be in the root folder.

```
module.exports = {
  plugins: [`gatsby-plugin-styled-components`],
}
```

Then restart `gatsby develop` in the terminal. Next, we will create our index or home page.

## Creating the Index Page

We will now start with the index page. We will have a full-page image and some centered text on top of it. First change your `index.js file`, as shown in Listing 1-3.

*Listing 1-3.*  The index.js File

```
import React, { Component } from "react";
import { Link } from "gatsby";
import { Banner, TextWrapper, MoreText } from "../styles/IndexStyles";

export default () => (
    <div style={{position: 'relative'}}>
        <Banner></Banner>
        <TextWrapper>
            <div>
```

```
                <h2>GeekyHacker</h2>
                <p>One Stop for<br/>
                All your development<br />
                And design needs</p>
                <Link to="/works">Our Works</Link>
            </div>
        </TextWrapper>
        <MoreText>Learn More</MoreText>
    </div>
)
```

Now, we will start to write the styled components. Create a file called IndexStyles.js inside the styles directory.

First we will write styles for the banner. We will show the banner.jpg file as a background image, so we will use the :after pseudo element.

Also, upload the banner.jpg image to the static folder. From the static folder in a Gatsby project, we can directly use an image (see Listing 1-4).

***Listing 1-4.*** The IndexStyles.js File

```
import styled from "styled-components"
const Banner = styled.div`
 &:after {
   content: "";
   display: block;
   height: 100vh;
   width: 100%;
   background-image: url('banner.jpg');
   background-size: cover;
   background-repeat: no-repeat;
   background-position: center;
   filter: grayscale(100%) blur(2px);
 }
```

Next, we will center the text. We need to use the positioning system, as we are showing the text over an image. We already made the parent a `position: relative` and we are making this `div position: absolute`. Then we are using left, top, and transform (see Listing 1-5).

***Listing 1-5.*** The position: absolute Setting

```
const TextWrapper = styled.div`
 position: absolute;
 z-index: 1;
 left: 50%;
 top: 50%;
 transform: translate(-50%, -50%);
 color: white;
 div {
   display: flex;
   justify-content: center;
   align-items: center;
   flex-direction: column;
 }
`;
```

Make sure you have the following at the bottom of the `IndexStyles.js` file or you will get an error.

```
export { Banner, TextWrapper, MoreText }
```

The result is shown in Figure 1-2.

***Figure 1-2.*** *Centered text with the image in the background*

Let's now add some styles to the h2, p, and a tags (a is a link tag that converts to an anchor tag). See Listing 1-6.

***Listing 1-6.*** Link to the Anchor Tag

```
h2 {
    font-size: 5rem;
    opacity: 1;
    padding: 0.35em 1em;
    border-top: 2px solid white;
    border-bottom: 2px solid white;
    text-transform: uppercase;
    margin: 0;
}
p {
    text-transform: uppercase;
    text-align: center;
    letter-spacing: 0.225em;
```

```
  font-size: 2.5rem;
}
a {
  background-color: #ed4933;
  box-shadow: none;
  color: #ffffff;
  border-radius: 3px;
  border: 0;
  cursor: pointer;
  font-size: 1.5rem;
  font-weight: 600;
  letter-spacing: 0.225em;
  padding: 1.8rem 0.8rem;
  text-align: center;
  text-decoration: none;
  text-transform: uppercase;
}
```

Let's add the style for the Learn More text. For this, we also use the position: absolute logic, as shown in Listing 1-7.

***Listing 1-7.*** The Learn More Text

```
const MoreText = styled.div`
 position: absolute;
 color: #ffffff;
 text-align: center;
 text-transform: uppercase;
 letter-spacing: 0.225em;
 font-weight: 600;
 font-size: 1.2rem;
 z-index: 1;
 left: 50%;
 bottom: 10%;
 transform: translate(-50%, -50%);
```

```
&:after {
    content: "";
    display: block;
    height: 2rem;
    width: 2rem;
    left: 50%;
    position: absolute;
    margin: 1em 0 0 -0.75em;
    background-image: url("arrow.svg");
    background-size: cover;
    background-repeat: no-repeat;
    background-position: center;
  }
`;

export { Banner, TextWrapper, MoreText };
```

This code will result in the beautiful page shown in Figure 1-3.

***Figure 1-3.*** *The beautiful page*

# Creating the Sections

Let's start by creating section two.

## Creating Section Two

This section will contain a header, a quotation, and three icons. Update the index.js file to include Listing 1-8. The new part is shown in bold.

*Listing 1-8.* Adding a Header to index.js

```
import React, { Component } from "react";
import { Link } from "gatsby";
import { Banner, TextWrapper, MoreText, SectionTwo } from "../styles/
IndexStyles";

export default () => (
   <>
   <section style={{position: 'relative'}}>
      <Banner></Banner>
      <TextWrapper>
         <div>
            <h2>GeekyHacker</h2>
            <p>One Stop for<br/>
            All your development<br />
            And design needs</p>
            <Link to="/works">Our Works</Link>
         </div>
      </TextWrapper>
      <MoreText>Learn More</MoreText>
   </section>
   <SectionTwo>
      <div>
         <h2>Our Passion</h2>
         <p>Most good programmers do programming not because they expect
         to get paid,
         but because it's fun to program.</p>
```

```
        <h5>- Linus Torvalds</h5>
    </div>
  </SectionTwo>
```

```
)
```

Now, let's add some styled components to SectionTwo, as shown in Listing 1-9.

***Listing 1-9.*** Adding Styled Components to index.js

```
const SectionTwo = styled.section`
 background-color: #21b2a6;
 text-align: center;
 padding: 10rem 0;
 div {
   width: 66%;
   margin: 0 auto;
 }
 h2 {
   font-size: 3rem;
   padding: 1.35em 0;
   color: #ffffff;
   border-bottom: 2px solid #1d9c91;
   text-transform: uppercase;
   letter-spacing: 0.6rem;
   margin: 0;
 }
 p {
   text-transform: uppercase;
   color: #c8ece9;
   text-align: center;
   letter-spacing: 0.225em;
   font-size: 1.5rem;
 }
 h5 {
   font-size: 1.4rem;
   line-height: 2rem;
```

```
color: #ffffff;
border-bottom: 2px solid #1d9c91;
font-weight: 800;
letter-spacing: 0.225em;
text-transform: uppercase;
padding-bottom: 0.5rem;
margin-bottom: 5rem;
}
`
```

We will now use some font-awesome icons to give this section a nice finish. Open the terminal and install these dependencies.

```
npm install @fortawesome/react-fontawesome @fortawesome/fontawesome-svg-core
@fortawesome/free-solid-svg-icons
```

Then import the libraries in index.js, as shown in Listing 1-10.

***Listing 1-10.*** Adding Icons to index.js

```
import { FontAwesomeIcon } from '@fortawesome/react-fontawesome';
import { library } from '@fortawesome/fontawesome-svg-core';
import { faHeart, faCode, faGem, fas } from '@fortawesome/free-solid-svg-
icons';

library.add(faHeart, faCode, faGem, fab, fas);
```

Add the code in Listing 1-11, to the div and after the h5, and you will get the result shown in Figure 1-4.

***Listing 1-11.*** Completing Section Two for index.js

```
<span>
    <FontAwesomeIcon icon="gem" color="#04F5C6" size="6x"
    style={{marginRight: '3rem'}} fixedWidth border />
    <FontAwesomeIcon icon="heart" color="#00F0FF" size="6x"
    style={{marginRight: '3rem'}} fixedWidth border />
    <FontAwesomeIcon icon="code" color="#73DBFD" size="6x"
    fixedWidth border />
</span>
```

11

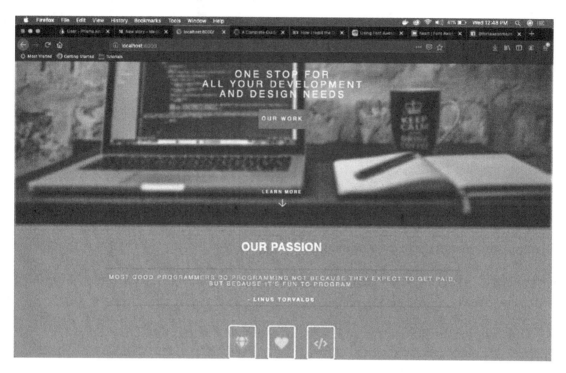

***Figure 1-4.*** *Our passion*

We also need some padding in this section. Let's add it. It is shown in bold in Listing 1-12.

***Listing 1-12.*** Adding Padding to IndexStyles.js

```
const SectionTwo = styled.section`
  background-color: #21b2a6;
  text-align: center;
  padding: 10rem 0;
  div {
    width: 66%;
    margin: 0 auto;
  }
...
...
`
```

Next, we will create Section Three.

# Creating Section Three

This section will include an image and text, so we will use Flexbox. Add the code in index.js, as shown in Listing 1-13, after SectionTwo.

*Listing 1-13.* Adding Section Three to index.js

```
<SectionThree>
    <FlexBoxIndex>
        <div className="image">
            <img src="pic01.jpg" alt="pic01" />
        </div>
        <div className="text__section3">
            <h2>Website Development</h2>
            <p>
                We hand code beautiful websites using HTML5,
                CSS3, JS because they are fully customizable and
                efficient. No WordPress websites here.
            </p>
        </div>
    </FlexBoxIndex>
    <FlexBoxIndex inverse>
        <div className="text__section3">
            <h2>Website Design</h2>
            <p>
                We have talented and experienced Web Designers, who
                can design beautiful and usable websites.
            </p>
        </div>
        <div className="image">
            <img src="pic02.jpg" alt="pic02" />
        </div>
    </FlexBoxIndex>
```

```
<FlexBoxIndex>
    <div className="image">
        <img src="pic03.jpg" alt="pic03" />
    </div>
    <div className="text__section3">
        <h2>Mobile App Development</h2>
        <p>
            We develop Mobile apps in Reactive Native, which can
            be used in both ios and Android.
        </p>
    </div>
</FlexBoxIndex>
</SectionThree>
```

Now, let's add the code in Listing 1-14 to IndexStyles.js, just below SectionTwo.

***Listing 1-14.*** Adding Section Three to the IndexStyles.js File

```
const SectionThree = styled.section`
 background-color: #2b343d;
 color: #ffffff;

`

const FlexBoxIndex = styled.div`
 display: flex;
 .image {
   width: ${props => (props.inverse ? "60%" : "40%")};
 }
 img {
   width: 100%;
 }
 .text__section3 {
   width: ${props => (props.inverse ? "40%" : "60%")};
   display: flex;
   justify-content: center;
```

```
    align-items: center;
    flex-direction: column;
  }
h2 {
    font-size: 3rem;
    color: #ffffff;
    text-transform: uppercase;
    letter-spacing: 0.225rem;
    margin: 0;
  }
p {
    text-transform: uppercase;
    color: #c8ece9;
    text-align: center;
    letter-spacing: 0.075em;
    font-size: 1.5rem;
  }
`
```

Let's do some housekeeping. In Listing 1-15, remove **p** from TextWrapper, SectionTwo, and FlexBoxIndex. Then create a new styled component component, called props.

*Listing 1-15.* Housekeeping in IndexStyles.js

```
const GenereicPara = styled.p`
 text-transform: uppercase;
 text-align: center;
 letter-spacing: ${props => (props.lessSpacing ? "0.075em" : "0.225em")};
 font-size: ${props => (props.lessSize ? "1.5rem" : "2.5rem")};
 line-height: ${props => (props.lessSize ? "2rem" : "3rem")};
 color: ${props => (props.grey ? "#c8ece9" : "#ffffff")};
```

Now replace all the p tags with GenericPara. The updated code is highlighted in bold in Listing 1-16.

***Listing 1-16.***  The index.js File

```
<section style={{ position: 'relative' }}>
    <Banner></Banner>
    <TextWrapper>
        <div>
            <h2>GeekyHacker</h2>
            <GenereicPara>One Stop For<br />
                All your development<br />
                And design needs</GenereicPara>
            <Link to="/works">Our Work</Link>
        </div>
    </TextWrapper>
    <MoreText>Learn More</MoreText>
</section>
<SectionTwo>
    <div>
        <h2>Our Passion</h2>
        <GenereicPara lessSize grey>Most good programmers
        do programming not because they expect to get
        paid,<br />
            but because it's fun to program.</GenereicPara>
        <h5>- Linus Torvalds</h5>
    </div>
    <span>
        <FontAwesomeIcon icon="gem" color="#04F5C6"
        size="6x" style={{marginRight: '3rem'}} fixedWidth
        border />
        <FontAwesomeIcon icon="heart" color="#00F0FF"
        size="6x" style={{marginRight: '3rem'}} fixedWidth
        border />
        <FontAwesomeIcon icon="code" color="#73DBFD"
        size="6x" fixedWidth border />
    </span>
</SectionTwo>
<SectionThree>
```

16

```
<FlexBoxIndex>
    <div className="image">
        <img src="pic01.jpg" alt="pic01"/>
    </div>
    <div className="text__section3">
        <h2>Website Development</h2>
        <GenereicPara lessSize lessSpacing>We hand code
        beautiful websites using HTML5, CSS3, JS because
        they are fully customizable and efficient. No
        WordPress websites here.</GenereicPara>
    </div>
</FlexBoxIndex>
<FlexBoxIndex inverse>
    <div className="text__section3">
        <h2>Website Design</h2>
        <GenereicPara lessSize lessSpacing>We have
        talented and experienced Web Designers, who
        can design beautiful and usable websites.
        </GenereicPara>
    </div>
    <div className="image">
        <img src="pic02.jpg" alt="pic02"/>
    </div>
</FlexBoxIndex>
<FlexBoxIndex>
    <div className="image">
        <img src="pic03.jpg" alt="pic03"/>
    </div>
    <div className="text__section3">
        <h2>Mobile App Development</h2>
        <GenereicPara lessSize lessSpacing>We develop
        Mobile apps in Reactive Native, which can be
        used in both ios and Android.</GenereicPara>
    </div>
</FlexBoxIndex>
</SectionThree>
```

Let's do the same song and dance for the h2 tag. Remove h2 from SectionTwo and FlexBoxIndex. Then add a styled component called GenericH2 to the IndexStyles.js file, as shown in Listing 1-17.

***Listing 1-17.*** Adding a Generic h2 Tag

```
const GenericH2 = styled.h2`
 font-size: 3rem;
 padding: ${props => (props.none ? "0" : "1.35em 0")};
 color: #ffffff;
 border-bottom: ${props => (props.none ? "0" : "2px solid #1d9c91")};
 text-transform: uppercase;
 letter-spacing: 0.6rem;
 margin: 0;
`
```

Now replace all the h2 tags with GenericH2. The updated code is highlighted in bold in Listing 1-18.

***Listing 1-18.*** Adding GenericH2

```
<SectionTwo>
    <div>
        <GenericH2>Our Passion</GenericH2>
        <GenereicPara lessSize grey>Most good programmers
        do programming not because they expect to get
        paid,<br />
            but because it's fun to program.</GenereicPara>
        <h5>- Linus Torvalds</h5>
    </div>
    ...
</SectionTwo>
<SectionThree>
    <FlexBoxIndex>
        <div className="image">
            <img src="pic01.jpg" alt="pic01"/>
        </div>
```

```
    <div className="text__section3">
        <GenericH2 none>Website Development</GenericH2>
        <GenereicPara lessSize lessSpacing>We hand
        code beautiful websites using HTML5, CSS3,
        JS because they are fully customizable and
        efficient. No WordPress websites here.
        </GenereicPara>
    </div>
</FlexBoxIndex>
<FlexBoxIndex inverse>
    <div className="text__section3">
        <GenericH2 none>Website Design</GenericH2>
        <GenereicPara lessSize lessSpacing>We have
        talented and experienced Web Designers, who
        can design beautiful and usable websites.
        </GenereicPara>
    </div>
    <div className="image">
        <img src="pic02.jpg" alt="pic02"/>
    </div>
</FlexBoxIndex>
<FlexBoxIndex>
    <div className="image">
        <img src="pic03.jpg" alt="pic03"/>
    </div>
    <div className="text__section3">
        <GenericH2 none>Mobile App Development
        </GenericH2>
        <GenereicPara lessSize lessSpacing>We develop
        Mobile apps in Reactive Native, which can be
        used in both ios and Android.</GenereicPara>
    </div>
</FlexBoxIndex>
</SectionThree>
```

The result is shown in Figure 1-5.

19

***Figure 1-5.*** *Section three*

We have two more sections to go for the Home page; then we will create the Our Works and About Us pages. We will use a Layout component for the header and footer.

## Creating Section Four

We will start with Section Four now. We have the usual heading and paragraph, followed by six sections containing some details about the technologies. We are adding SectionFour to the index.js file using the code shown in Listing 1-19.

***Listing 1-19.*** Adding SectionFour to index.js

```
<SectionFour>
    <div className="header__section4">
        <div className="title__section4">Our Technologies</div>
        <GenereicPara lessSize grey>
        We use modern and latest technologies which helps our clients
        <br />
```

```
        as they are highly scalable and maintainable.
        </GenereicPara>
      </div>
    </SectionFour>
```

Now, let's add CSS for this code to the IndexStyles.js file, as shown in Listing 1-20. Also, don't forget to export the newly created styled component.

*Listing 1-20.* Adding CSS to IndexStyles.js

```
const SectionFour = styled.section`
 background-color: #505393;
 color: #ffffff;
 text-align: center;
 .header__section4 {
   width: 66%;
   margin: 0 auto;
 }
 .title__section4 {
   font-size: 3rem;
   padding: 1.35em 0;
   color: #ffffff;
   border-bottom: 2px solid #464981;
   text-transform: uppercase;
   letter-spacing: 0.225em;
   margin: 0;
 }
```

Now we will create the grid, which will contain the six sections.

# Creating the Grid

The six sections will be exactly the same, only the background will be different. Put the code in Listing 1-21 under header__section4.

***Listing 1-21.*** Changing the Background in index.js

```
<div className="grid__section4">
 <div className="item1" style={{ backgroundColor: "#4D508E" }}>
    <div className="flex__section4">
       <FontAwesomeIcon icon={faReact} color="#00FFCC"
       size="3x" fixedWidth />
       <GenericH2 none>React</GenericH2>
    </div>
    <GenereicPara lessSize lessSpacing grey>
       Modern JavaScript framework which will make your web
       application
       extremely fast and, at the same time, handy for every
       user.
    </GenereicPara>
 </div>
 <div className="item2" style={{ backgroundColor: "#4A4D89" }}>
 <div className="flex__section4">
       <FontAwesomeIcon icon="code" color="#00FFCC" size="3x"
       fixedWidth />
       <GenericH2 none>React Native</GenericH2>
 </div>
    <GenereicPara lessSize lessSpacing grey>
       Cross-platform for mobile app development based on
       JavaScript,
       whose resulting code is compiled to Android and iOS.
    </GenereicPara>
 </div>
    <div className="item3" style={{ backgroundColor: "#484A83" }}>
    <div className="flex__section4">
       <FontAwesomeIcon icon={faJs} color="#00FFCC" size="3x"
       fixedWidth />
       <GenericH2 none>JavaScript</GenericH2>
    </div>
    <GenereicPara lessSize lessSpacing grey>
```

```
        JavaScript is the language of the web. It is used for
        Web development, mobile development and app development
        and everything else.
</GenereicPara>
</div>
<div className="item4" style={{ backgroundColor: "#45477E" }}>
<div className="flex__section4">
    <FontAwesomeIcon icon={faHtml5} color="#00FFCC"
    size="3x" fixedWidth />
    <GenericH2 none>HTML5</GenericH2>
</div>
<GenereicPara lessSize lessSpacing grey>
    HTML, a standardized system for tagging text files to
    achieve font, colour, graphic, and hyperlink effects on
    World Wide Web pages.
</GenereicPara>
</div>
<div className="item5" style={{ backgroundColor: "#424479" }}>
<div className="flex__section4">
    <FontAwesomeIcon icon={faCss3} color="#00FFCC" size="3x"
    fixedWidth />
    <GenericH2 none>CSS3</GenericH2>
</div>
<GenereicPara lessSize lessSpacing grey>
    CSS is a style sheet language used for describing the
    presentation of a document written in a markup language
    like HTML.
</GenereicPara>
</div>
<div className="item6" style={{ backgroundColor: "#3F4174" }}>
<div className="flex__section4">
    <FontAwesomeIcon icon={faGalacticSenate} color="#00FFCC"
    size="3x" fixedWidth />
    <GenericH2 none>Gatsby</GenericH2>
</div>
```

23

```
    <GenereicPara lessSize lessSpacing grey>
        Gatsby is a free and open source framework based on
        React that helps developers build blazing fast websites
        and apps
    </GenereicPara>
    </div>
  </div>
```

Now, we will add the CSS in Listing 1-22 to our IndexStyles.js file, inside the SectionFour styled component.

***Listing 1-22.*** Adding CSS to IndexStyles.js

```
.grid__section4 {
   display: grid;
   grid-template-columns: 1fr 1fr;
   width: 66%;
   margin: 0 auto;
   padding: 3rem 0;
}
.grid__section4 > * {
   padding: 3rem;
}
.flex__section4 {
   display: flex;
   justify-content: center;
   align-items: center;
   padding: 1rem;
}
.flex__section4 > h2 {
   margin-left: 1rem;
}
```

We also need to install a new fontawesome library, as we are using some brand icons here. So, in the terminal, stop Gatsby and install this via npm:

```
npm install @fortawesome/free-brands-svg-icons
```

The changes made to the header of the index.js file are marked in bold in Listing 1-23.

***Listing 1-23.*** Changing the Header in index.js

```
import React from "react"
import { Banner, TextWrapper, MoreText, SectionTwo, SectionThree,
SectionFour, FlexBoxIndex, GenereicPara, GenericH2 } from "../styles/
IndexStyles"
import { FontAwesomeIcon } from "@fortawesome/react-fontawesome"
import { library } from "@fortawesome/fontawesome-svg-core"
import { fab, faHtml5, faJs, faReact, faCss3, faGalacticSenate } from
"@fortawesome/free-brands-svg-icons"
import { faHeart, faCode, faGem, fab, fas } from "@fortawesome/free-solid-
svg-icons"
library.add(faHeart, faCode, faGem, fab, fas)
```

Now, our Section Four looks like Figure 1-6.

***Figure 1-6.*** *Section Four page*

# Creating the Contact Us Form

The next section will have a parallax image with a Contact Us form. We will be reusing the banner styled component used on the Index page here. Add the code in Listing 1-24 after SectionFour.

***Listing 1-24.*** Parallax Image in index.js

```
<section style={{ position: "relative" }}>
    <Banner parallax></Banner>
</section>
```

We need to update the banner styled component to include the parallax effect. Update the bold text shown in Listing 1-25.

***Listing 1-25.*** IndexStyles.js

```
const Banner = styled.div`
 &:after {
   content: "";
   display: block;
   height: ${props => (props.parallax ? "80vh" : "100vh")};
   width: 100%;
   background-image: url('banner.jpg');
   background-size: cover;
   background-repeat: no-repeat;
   background-position: center;
   background-attachment: ${props => (props.parallax ? "fixed" : "scroll")};
   filter: grayscale(100%) blur(2px);
 }
`
```

Next, let's add a form to the top of the image. The code is shown in Listing 1-26, which we need to put after banner.

*Listing 1-26.* Form in index.js

```
<FormFive>
 <form name="contact" method="post" data-netlify="true">
 <div className="fields">
     <GenericH2 none>Contact Us</GenericH2>
     <input type="text" name="name" id="name" placeholder="Name" />
     <input type="email" name="email" id="email" placeholder="Email" />
     <textarea name="message" id="message" placeholder="Message" rows="7">
     </textarea>
     <div className="actions">
         <input type="submit" value="Send Message" className="button__
         primary" />
     </div>
 </div>
 </form>
</FormFive>
```

Next, let's add the styles for FormFive to IndexStyles.js, as shown in Listing 1-27.

*Listing 1-27.* Styles for Form Five in IndexStyles.js

```
const FormFive = styled.div`
 position: absolute;
 z-index: 1;
 width: 80%;
 top: 50%;
 left: 50%;
 transform: translate(-50%, -50%);
 color: white;
 form > .fields {
   display: grid;
   grid-template-columns: 1fr;
   grid-gap: 1rem;
 }
 input[type="text"],
 input[type="email"],
```

```css
textarea {
  appearance: none;
  font-size: 2rem;
  background-color: rgba(144, 144, 144, 0.75);
  border-radius: 3px;
  border: none;
}
input[type="text"],
input[type="email"] {
  height: 2.75em;
  padding: 0.75em 1em;
}
textarea {
  padding: 0.75em 1em;
}
.button__primary {
  background-color: #ed4933;
  box-shadow: none;
  color: #ffffff;
  border-radius: 3px;
  border: 0;
  cursor: pointer;
  font-size: 1.5rem;
  font-weight: 600;
  letter-spacing: 0.225em;
  padding: 1.8rem 0.8rem;
  text-align: center;
  text-decoration: none;
  text-transform: uppercase;
}
```

This will result in the section shown in Figure 1-7.

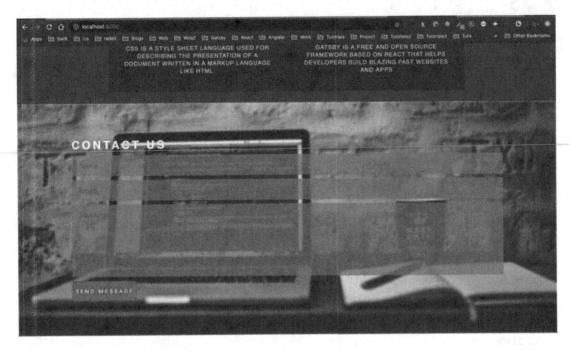

*Figure 1-7.*  *The Contact Us page*

# Creating the Footer Section

Now, we will create the footer section. This footer will be common to all our pages, so we will put it in the Layout component.

Create a folder called components inside src and a file called layout.js inside that. The file contains a simple footer with different icons. Here, the {children} will show the components, which we will soon use to wrap the Layout component. The code is shown Listing 1-28.

*Listing 1-28.*  Footer Section of layout.js

```
import React from "react"
import { FontAwesomeIcon } from '@fortawesome/react-fontawesome'
import { faTwitter, faFacebook, faInstagram, faLinkedin, faYoutube,
faPinterest } from '@fortawesome/free-brands-svg-icons'
import { Footer } from '../styles/IndexStyles';
export default ({ children }) => (
    <div>
```

```
      {children}
      <Footer>
          <div class="icons">
              <FontAwesomeIcon icon={faTwitter} size="2x" fixedWidth />
              <FontAwesomeIcon icon={faFacebook} size="2x" fixedWidth />
              <FontAwesomeIcon icon={faInstagram} size="2x" fixedWidth />
              <FontAwesomeIcon icon={faLinkedin} size="2x" fixedWidth />
              <FontAwesomeIcon icon={faYoutube} size="2x" fixedWidth />
              <FontAwesomeIcon icon={faPinterest} size="2x" fixedWidth />
          </div>
          <div class="copyright">
              <span>&copy; 2019, GeekyHacker | </span>
              <span>Made with ♥ and ☕ in India</span>
          </div>
      </Footer>
    </div>
)
```

Let's put some styles in IndexStyles.js for the footer. These styles can be placed anywhere, as the order doesn't matter. But don't forget to export it at the end. The code is shown in Listing 1-29.

***Listing 1-29.*** Styles for the Footer in IndexStyles.js

```
const Footer = styled.footer`
 padding: 6em 0 4em 0;
 background-color: #1d242a;
 text-align: center;
 .icons > * {
   cursor: pointer;
   margin-right: 1rem;
   color: rgba(255, 255, 255, 0.5);
 }
 .copyright {
   color: rgba(255, 255, 255, 0.5);
   font-size: 1.2rem;
```

```
  letter-spacing: 0.225em;
  padding: 0;
  text-transform: uppercase;
  margin-top: 1rem;
}
```

Now, let's wrap our home page with this Layout component. The updated code is marked in bold in Listing 1-30.

***Listing 1-30.*** The Updated index.js File

```
import React, { Component } from "react"
import { Link } from "gatsby"
import { Banner, TextWrapper, MoreText, SectionTwo, SectionThree,
SectionFour, FlexBoxIndex, GenereicPara, GenericH2 } from "../styles/
IndexStyles"
import Layout from "../components/layout"
import { FontAwesomeIcon } from "@fortawesome/react-fontawesome"
import { library } from "@fortawesome/fontawesome-svg-core"
import { fab, faHtml5, faJs, faReact, faCss3, faGalacticSenate } from
"@fortawesome/free-brands-svg-icons"
import { faHeart, faCode, faGem, fas } from "@fortawesome/free-solid-svg-icons"

library.add(faHeart, faCode, faGem, fab, fas)

export default () => (
<Layout>
   <section style={{ position: "relative" }}>...
   <SectionTwo>...
   <SectionThree>...
   <SectionFour>...
   <section style={{ position: "relative" }}>...
</Layout>
)
```

Our home page now has a footer, as shown in Figure 1-8.

***Figure 1-8.*** *The footer*

We have one more thing left to do to the home page, and that is to add a menu.

# Creating the Menu

The menu is also created in the Layout component, as it will be shared with the Our Works and About Us pages. Let's first create a header with navigation by adding the bold text in Listing 1-31 to the layout.js file.

***Listing 1-31.*** Header in layout.js

```
import React from "react"
import { FontAwesomeIcon } from '@fortawesome/react-fontawesome'
import { faTwitter, faFacebook, faInstagram, faLinkedin, faYoutube,
faPinterest } from '@fortawesome/free-brands-svg-icons'
import { Header, Footer, GenericH2, GenereicPara } from '../styles/
IndexStyles';
import { Link } from "gatsby";
```

```
export default ({ children }) => (
  <div>
    <Header>
      <GenericH2 none>
        <Link to="/" style={{color: '#fff'}}>GeekyHacker</Link>
      </GenericH2>
      <div className="menu__items">
        <Link to="/works"><GenereicPara lessSize lessSpacing grey>
        Works</GenereicPara></Link>
        <Link to="/about"><GenereicPara lessSize lessSpacing grey>
        About</GenereicPara></Link>
      </div>
    </Header>
    {children}
    <Footer>
      ...
      ...
    </Footer>
  </div>
)
```

Let's add some styles to styled-components, as shown in Listing 1-32.

*Listing 1-32.* Header Styles in IndexStyles.js

```
const Header = styled.header`
 display: flex;
 justify-content: space-between;
 align-items: center;
 width: 100%;
 height: 30px;
 background-color: #1d242a;
 color: #ffffff;
 padding: 3rem 0;
 .menu__items {
   display: flex;
 }
```

```
.menu__items > * {
  margin-right: 1rem;
}
`
```

We now get a header with a menu, as shown in Figure 1-9.

***Figure 1-9.***  *The menu*

# Creating the Our Works and About Us Pages

Next, we will create the Our Works page. Create a new file called works.js inside the pages folder. The content is shown in Listing 1-33.

***Listing 1-33.***  The works.js File

```
import React from "react";
import { Works, GenericH2 } from "../styles/IndexStyles";
import Layout from "../components/layout";
import Project from "../components/Project";

const projects = []
```

```
export default () => (
  <Layout>
    <Works>
      <GenericH2 none dark style={{textAlign: 'center'}}>Our Works
      </GenericH2>
      <section class="gallery__flex">
        { projects && projects.map(proj => <Project key={proj.title}
        project={proj} />)}
      </section>
    </Works>
  </Layout>
)
```

Let's add some styles to the IndexStyles.js file, as shown in Listing 1-34.

*Listing 1-34.* Works Styles in IndexStyles.js

```
const Works = styled.div`
 background-color: #ffffff;
 color: #4e4852;
 padding: 2em 0 1em 0 !important;
 .gallery__flex {
   display: grid;
   grid-template-columns: repeat(auto-fit, minmax(300px, 1fr));
   grid-gap: 20px;
   justify-items: center;
 }
`
```

We will now create a new component called project to which we will pass each project. Let's create an array called objects that contains some projects, which we pass to the project component by mapping over it. The content is shown in Listing 1-35.

*Listing 1-35.* Array in works.js

```
const projects = [
  {image: "printbill.png", title: "PrintBill", link: "https://www.
  printbill.in/"},
```

```
{image: "sprung.png", title: "Sprung", link: "https://sprung.us"},
{image: "orange.png", title: "Orange Health", link: "https://whispering-
bastion-31600.herokuapp.com/"},
{image: "billing.png", title: "Billing Restro", link: "https://
billingrestro-react-prod.herokuapp.com/"},
{image: "ferrarisports.png", title: "Ferrari Sports", link: "http://
ferrarisports.com/"},
{image: "pregnancy.png", title: "Pregnancy info", link: "http://
pregnancy.info/"},
{image: "jaagastudy.png", title: "Jaaga Study", link: "https://
nabendu82.github.io/incognosco/index.html"},
{image: "responsive1.png", title: "Responsive Site- POC", link:
"https://shikhacorps.in/corps/"},
{image: "responsive2.png", title: "Responsive Site2- POC", link:
"https://shikhacorps.in/cssgridresponsive/"},
{image: "styleconferences.png", title: "Style Conferences", link:
"https://nabendu82.github.io/shayhowe/index.html"},
{image: "itunes.png", title: "iTunes Clone - POC", link: "https://
shikhacorps.in/mytunes/"},
{image: "parallax.png", title: "Parallax Site - POC", link: "https://
shikhacorps.in/parallaxsite/"},
{image: "photography.png", title: "PhotoGraphy Site-POC", link:
"https://shikhacorps.in/photographysite/"},
{image: "yelpcamp.png", title: "YelpCamp", link: "https://hidden-
coast-48928.herokuapp.com/"},
{image: "blogsite.png", title: "Blog Site", link: "https://serene-
wildwood-22136.herokuapp.com/blogs"},
{image: "portfolio.png", title: "Portfolio Site", link: "https://
nabendu82.github.io/"},
]
```

Next, let's create the project component inside the components folder. First create a new Project.js file inside the components folder. The content is shown in Listing 1-36.

***Listing 1-36.*** The Project.js File

```
import React from 'react';

const Project = ({ project }) => {
    return (
        <div class="card">
            <img class="card__img" src={project.image} alt="" />
            <div style={{marginTop: '1rem'}}>
                <h5 class="card-title">{project.title}</h5>
                <a class="card-link" href={project.link} target="_blank">Link</a>
            </div>
        </div>
        )
}

export default Project;
```

Let's add some styles for this component in `global.css`. Enter the code in Listing 1-37 after the existing styles.

***Listing 1-37.*** Styles in global.css

```
.card {
    background: lightgray;
    padding: 10px;
    width: 300px;
    height: 200px;
    margin: 10px 10px;
    color: white;
    text-align: center;
}
.card-link{
    color: blue;
    border-bottom: dotted 1px;
    font-size: 1.5rem;
    line-height: 2rem;
    font-weight: 600;
}
```

```
.card-title{
  color: black;
  margin:0;
  padding:0;
  font-size: 1.6rem;
  line-height: 2.2rem;
  font-weight: 800;
  letter-spacing: 0.225em;
  text-transform: uppercase;
}
.card__img {
  width: 100%;
  height: 120px;
  object-fit: cover;
}
```

The Our Works page will look as shown in Figure 1-10.

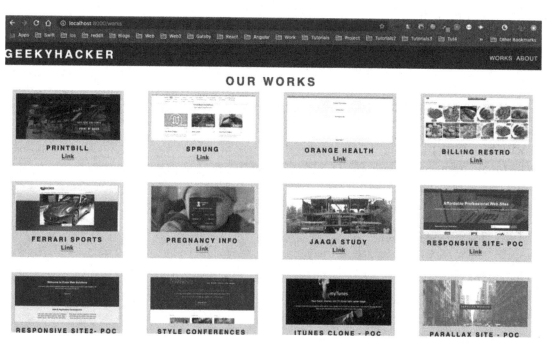

***Figure 1-10.*** *Our Works page*

We missed one thing and that is to make the header *fixed*, which means that if we scroll down the page, the header still remains at the top. To do this, add the code marked in bold in Listing 1-38 to the `IndexStyles.js` file.

***Listing 1-38.*** Fixed Header in IndexStyles.js

```
const Header = styled.header`
 display: flex;
 justify-content: space-between;
 align-items: center;
 width: 100%;
 height: 30px;
 background-color: #1d242a;
 color: #ffffff;
 padding: 3rem 0;
 z-index: 1000;
 position: fixed;
 top:0;
 left:0;
 .menu__items {
   display: flex;
 }
 .menu__items > * {
   margin-right: 1rem;
 }
`
```

The code causes issues with the Our Works text, because of the `margin: 0` set for `GenericH2`. Let's edit it using `props`, so that it can be used in `works.js` without affecting other files. The updated code is marked in bold in Listing 1-39.

***Listing 1-39.*** Header Styles in IndexStyles.js

```
const GenericH2 = styled.h2`
 font-size: 3rem;
 padding: ${props => (props.none ? "0" : "1.35em 0")};
 color: ${props => (props.dark ? "#4E4852" : "#ffffff")};
 border-bottom: ${props => (props.none ? "0" : "2px solid #1d9c91")};
```

39

```
text-transform: uppercase;
letter-spacing: 0.6rem;
margin: ${props => (props.some ? "5rem 0 0 0" : "0")};
`
```

Now, in works.js, we just need to add some props, as shown in Listing 1-40.

***Listing 1-40.*** Adding Some Props to works.js

```
export default () => (
  <Layout>
    <Works>
        <GenericH2 none dark some style={{textAlign: 'center'}}>Our
        Works</GenericH2>
        <section class="gallery__flex">
         { projects && projects.map(proj => <Project key={proj.title}
         project={proj} />)}
        </section>
    </Works>
  </Layout>
)
```

We will next create a new page called about.js inside the pages folder. The content is shown in Listing 1-41.

***Listing 1-41.*** The about.js File

```
import React from 'react';
import Layout from "../components/layout";
import { Link } from "gatsby";
import { Banner, TextWrapper, GenereicPara, GenericH3 } from "../styles/
IndexStyles";

const about = () => {
  return (
      <Layout>
      <section style={{ position: 'relative' }}>
          <Banner different></Banner>
          <TextWrapper>
```

```
            <div>
                <GenericH3 none>Who are we</GenericH3>
                <GenereicPara lessSize grey>GeekyHacker is an experienced and
                passionate group of designers, developers, and artists. Every
                client we work with becomes part of the team. Together we
                face the challenges and celebrate the victories.
                </GenereicPara>
                <Link to="/works">Our Work</Link>
            </div>
        </TextWrapper>
    </section>
    </Layout>
  )
}

export default about
```

Here, we are reusing most of the index.js file, but using a different banner image. We are doing this again with the help of props of styled components. The changes are marked in bold in Listing 1-42.

*Listing 1-42.*  Banner Image in IndexStyles.js

```
const Banner = styled.div`
 &:after {
   content: "";
   display: block;
   height: ${props => (props.parallax ? "80vh" : "100vh")};
   width: 100%;
   background-image: ${props => (props.different ? "url('developer.jpg')" :
   "url('banner.jpg')")};
   background-size: cover;
   background-repeat: no-repeat;
   background-position: center;
   background-attachment: ${props => (props.parallax ? "fixed" : "scroll")};
   filter: grayscale(100%) blur(2px);
 }
```

Let's create SectionTwo now, which we are going to place after `</section>`. The code is shown in Listing 1-43.

***Listing 1-43.*** Section Two in about.js

```
<SectionTwo white>
<div>
    <GenericH3 dark none>About Us</GenericH3>
    <GenereicParaAbout lessSize grey>Founded in 2016, <b>GeekyHacker</b> is
    a small web design & development company based in Bangalore, India.
    Over the last few years we've made a reputation for building websites,
    mobile apps, and web apps that look great and are easy-to-use.</
    GenereicParaAbout>
    <GenereicParaAbout lessSize grey>We originated from futuristic
    technology and progressing toward success with a great desire. We work
    with self-derived strategies, as we have experienced everything on our
    own. We are equipped with the state-of-the-art work station in the
    website development and testing. So, results delivered on time, every
    time! Your success is our bread and butter!</GenereicParaAbout>
    <GenereicParaAbout lessSize grey>We always happy to say loudly, we smell
    & feel the success every day because of the ShikhaCorps experts in
    execution planning with website design and digital marketing. They
    are always adopting with our valuable clients to satisfy on their
    requirement in each perspective, so our valuable clients make us more
    valuable in our success. While you work with us you feel, we are in
    right place & right time.</GenereicParaAbout>
    <GenereicParaAbout lessSize grey>Our Vision is to make our self
    as India's most valuable corporation through ultimate performance
    and uniqueness in every single project that we do!. Our Mission is
    to enhance the wealth generating capability of the enterprise in a
    globalizing environment by exhibiting our efficiency and adopting the
    innovative "more-than-enough" methodology in our work.
    </GenereicParaAbout>
</div>
</SectionTwo>
```

We have made changes to the `SectionTwo` styled component, to include a white background. These changes are shown in bold in Listing 1-44.

***Listing 1-44.*** White Background in IndexStyles.js

```
const SectionTwo = styled.section`
  background-color: ${props => (props.white ? "#ffffff" : "#21b2a6")};
  text-align: center;
  padding: 10rem 0;
  ...
  ...
  `
```

We also added two new styled components, as shown in Listing 1-45.

***Listing 1-45.*** New Styled Components in IndexStyles.js

```
const GenericH3 = styled.h3`
  font-size: 3rem;
  padding: ${props => (props.none ? "0" : "1.35em 0")};
  color: ${props => (props.dark ? "#4E4852" : "#ffffff")};
  border-bottom: ${props => (props.none ? "0" : "2px solid #1d9c91")};
  text-transform: uppercase;
  letter-spacing: 0.6rem;
  margin: 0;
  `

const GenereicParaAbout = styled.p`
  text-transform: uppercase;
  text-align: center;
  letter-spacing: ${props => (props.lessSpacing ? "0.075em" : "0.225em")};
  font-size: ${props => (props.lessSize ? "1.5rem" : "2.5rem")};
  line-height: ${props => (props.lessSize ? "2rem" : "3rem")};
  color: ${props => (props.grey ? "#4E4852" : "#ffffff")};
  `
```

Now the About Us page looks like Figure 1-11.

ABOUT US

**Figure 1-11.** *The About Us page*

It's time to deploy the site to Netlify.

# Deploying the Site

We already set up a form submission in the `index.js` page with Netlify. If you want to see the form submission setup details, watch this[2] YouTube video by Traversy Media. I have pushed all my code to GitHub, so open your Netlify account. If you are using Netlify for the first time, you need to register through your GitHub account (see Figure 1-12).

---

[2]https://www.youtube.com/embed/6ElQ689HRcY

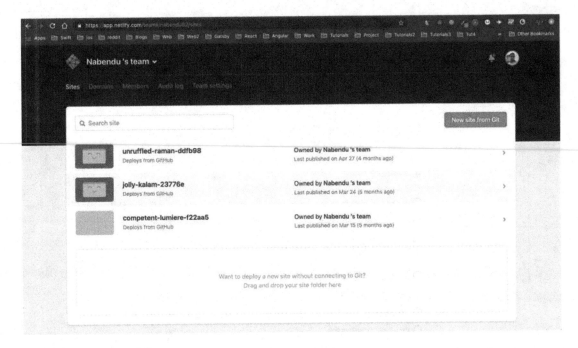

***Figure 1-12.***  *Netlify*

Next, click on New Site from Git and then choose the provider. I chose GitHub, since my code is there. Once you authorize it, it will show you a list of all your GitHub repositories (see Figure 1-13).

***Figure 1-13.*** *All the repos are listed*

Click on the repo to deploy it. In my case, the repo is called AgencyDemo (see Figure 1-14).

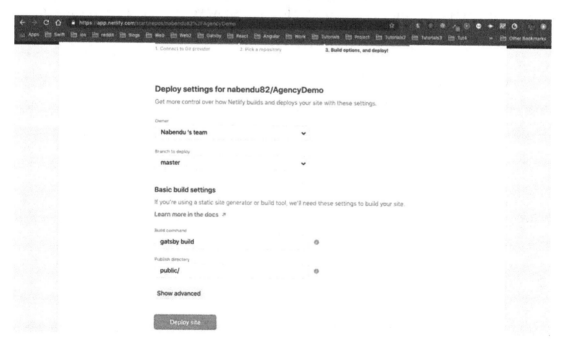

***Figure 1-14.*** *Defaults*

Keep the defaults and click on Deploy Site. The site will be deployed within minutes (see Figure 1-15).

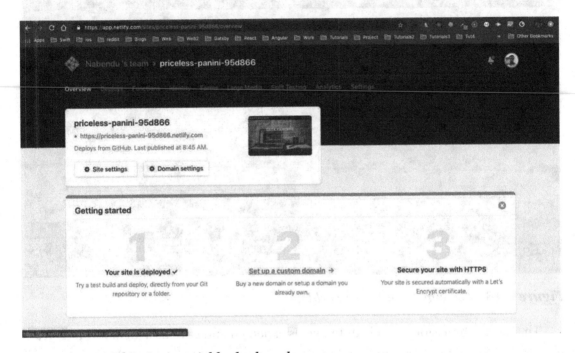

***Figure 1-15.***  *The site is quickly deployed*

Our site has been deployed. It's time to check the form submission feature of Netlify. Go to the form on the home page and add content (see Figure 1-16).

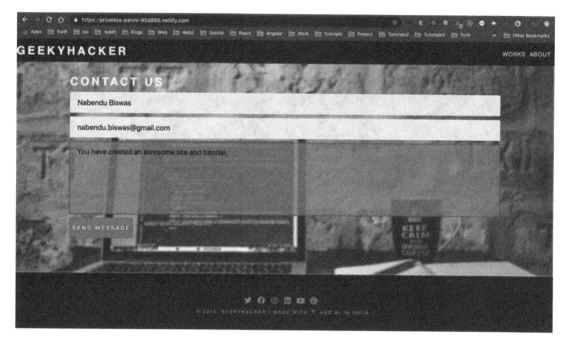

***Figure 1-16.*** *The content has been added*

The form submission initially didn't go as expected and gave us a lot of errors. After searching, I found that the form handling in sites generated through Gatsby is a bit different in Netlify. I found these two links to solve the issue:

https://www.netlify.com/blog/2017/07/20/how-to-integrate-netlifys-form-handling-in-a-react-app/#form-handling-with-static-site-generators[3]

https://github.com/sw-yx/gatsby-netlify-form-example-v2[4]

So, we will change our functional component to a class-based component and make the changes shown in bold in Listing 1-46.

***Listing 1-46.*** Functional to Class-Based Component: The index.js File

```
import React, { Component } from "react";
import { Link } from "gatsby";
import { Banner, TextWrapper, MoreText, SectionTwo, SectionThree, SectionFour,
FormFive, FlexBoxIndex, GenereicPara, GenericH2 } from "../styles/IndexStyles";
```

---

[3]https://www.netlify.com/blog/2017/07/20/how-to-integrate-netlifys-form-handling-in-a-react-app/#form-handling-with-static-site-generators

[4]https://github.com/sw-yx/gatsby-netlify-form-example-v2

```
import Layout from "../components/layout"
import { FontAwesomeIcon } from '@fortawesome/react-fontawesome';
import { library } from '@fortawesome/fontawesome-svg-core';
import { fab, faHtml5, faJs, faReact, faCss3, faGalacticSenate } from
'@fortawesome/free-brands-svg-icons'
import { faHeart, faCode, faGem, fas } from '@fortawesome/free-solid-svg-icons';
import { navigate } from 'gatsby-link';

library.add(faHeart, faCode, faGem, fab, fas);

const encode = (data) => {
    return Object.keys(data)
        .map(key => encodeURIComponent(key) + "=" + encodeURIComponent(data[
        key]))
        .join("&");
}

class IndexPage extends Component {
    constructor(props) {
        super(props)
        this.state = { name: "", email: "", message: "" };
    }

    handleSubmit = e => {
        e.preventDefault();
        const form = e.target
        fetch("/", {
            method: "POST",
            headers: { "Content-Type": "application/x-www-form-urlencoded" },
            body: encode({ 'form-name': form.getAttribute('name'),
            ...this.state })
        })
            .then(() => navigate(form.getAttribute('action')))
            .catch(error => alert(error));
    };

    handleChange = e => this.setState({ [e.target.name]: e.target.value });
```

We also need to make these changes to the index.js file, marked in bold in Listing 1-47.

*Listing 1-47.* More Changes to index.js

```
render() {
 const { name, email, message } = this.state;
   return (
     <Layout>
         <section style={{ position: 'relative' }}>...
         <SectionTwo>...
         <SectionThree>...
         <SectionFour>...
         <section style={{ position: 'relative' }}>
             <Banner parallax></Banner>
             <FormFive>
                 <form name="contact" method="post" action="/thanks/" data-
                 netlify="true"              onSubmit={this.handleSubmit}
                 >
                     <div className="fields">
                         <GenericH2 none>Contact Us</GenericH2>
                         <input type="text" name="name" id="name"
                         placeholder="Name" value={name} onChange={this.
                         handleChange} />
                         <input type="email" name="email" id="email"
                         placeholder="Email" value={email} onChange={this.
                         handleChange} />
                         <textarea name="message" id="message"
                         placeholder="Message" rows="7" value={message}
                         onChange={this.handleChange}></textarea>
                         <div className="actions">
                             <input type="submit" value="Send Message"
                             className="button__primary" />
                         </div>
                     </div>
                 </form>
```

```
            </FormFive>
         </section>
      </Layout>
  )
}
}
```

```
export default IndexPage;
```

We also need to add a thanks.js file inside the pages folder. The content is shown in Listing 1-48.

***Listing 1-48.*** The thanks.js File

```
import React from 'react'
import Layout from "../components/layout";
import { GenericH2, GenereicParaAbout } from "../styles/IndexStyles";

export default () => (
 <Layout>
   <GenericH2 none dark some style={{textAlign: 'center', padding:
   '3rem'}}>Thank you!</GenericH2>
   <GenereicParaAbout lessSize grey>Form submission has been successful</
   GenereicParaAbout>
 </Layout>
)
```

Now, when we submit the form, we receive the message shown in Figure 1-17 in our Netlify console.

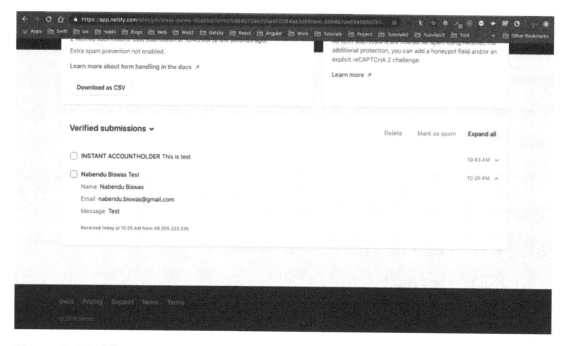

***Figure 1-17.*** *The message was received*

You can find the complete code for the project at `https://github.com/nabendu82/AgencyDemo`.[5]

The Netlify deployment is at `https://priceless-panini-95d866.netlify.com/`.[6]

# Summary

This completes Chapter 1 and our `AgencyDemo` project. You can use this site whenever you want to start your freelancing business. We covered the following topics in this chapter.

- Creating a Gatsby site with the most basic starter kit

- Using styled components in the project

- Adding a contact form to the project

- Deploying a site with Netlify

In the next chapter, we are going to learn how to convert our existing `dev.to` blogs to a personal blog site.

---

[5]`https://github.com/nabendu82/AgencyDemo`
[6]`https://priceless-panini-95d866.netlify.com/`

# CHAPTER 2

# Creating a Blog Site Using Stackbit

I have written 200 blogs at the time of this writing. It had become a habit to write technical articles. I had good traction on Medium, but once dev.to was launched, I started republishing my articles there as well. I got a lot of followers and views in dev.to.

I decided it is time for me to create my own blog site and I considered using GatsbyJS to do it. There are many ways to create a blog site with GatsbyJS, but I found an article[1] by Ben Halpern[2] (creator of dev.to) about its collaboration with Stackbit.

You need to follow the very simple process in this[3] article and your personal blog site will be ready in no time.

## The Setup Process

You need to follow four steps:

1.   Visit the Stackbit Creation Workflow[4] site and choose a theme.
     I chose Fjord, as shown in Figure 2-1.

---

[1]https://dev.to/devteam/you-can-now-generate-self-hostable-static-blogs-right-from-your-dev-content-via-stackbit-7a5

[2]https://twitter.com/bendhalpern

[3]https://dev.to/connecting-with-stackbit

[4]https://app.stackbit.com/edit/5dcc19f8ef1bec0017ec0910/theme

© Nabendu Biswas 2021
N. Biswas, *Foundation Gatsby Projects*, https://doi.org/10.1007/978-1-4842-6558-1_2

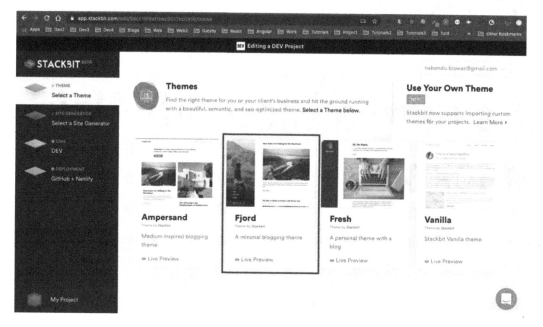

***Figure 2-1.***  *Choose a theme*

2.  Then you need to choose your static site generator. Here I chose
    Gatsby, as shown in Figure 2-2.

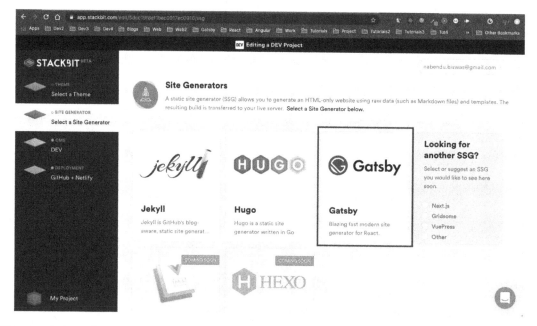

***Figure 2-2.***  *Choose Gatsby for the site generator*

3.   Then you need to connect to your GitHub and DEV accounts, as
      shown in Figure 2-3.

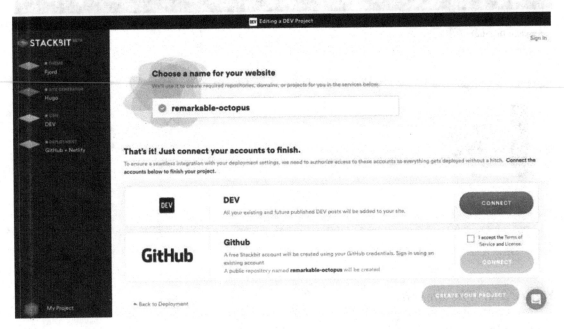

***Figure 2-3.*** *Connect to DEV and GitHub*

4.   Next, you need to click Create Your Project. Stackbit will create a
      new blog site for you.

Then you need to connect to a Netlify account to keep the site live, as shown in
Figure 2-4.

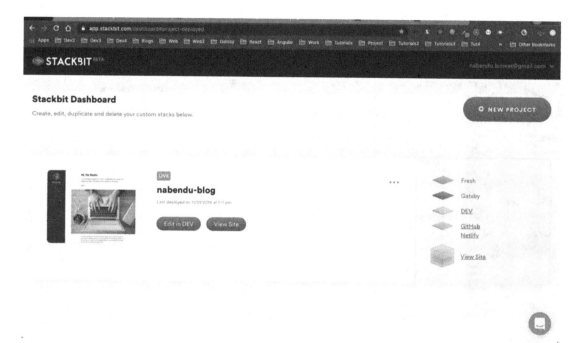

***Figure 2-4.*** *The site is live*

By following these simple steps, I took my blog site live, as shown in Figure 2-5. It's found at https://nabendu-blog-d8fee.netlify.com/.[5]

---

[5]https://nabendu-blog-d8fee.netlify.com/

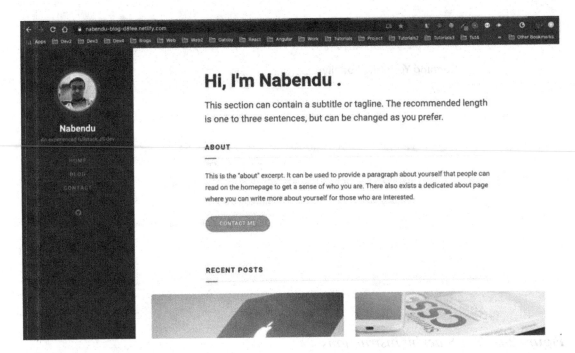

***Figure 2-5.***  *The live site*

Now, whenever I publish a post in DEV (`dev.to`), it will be reflected on this site. This makes DEV a headless CMS for my site.

As you can see in Figure 2-5, there is some work to be done, like editing the home page, buying a good domain name, connecting in Netlify, and adding some Gatsby plugins.

Stackbit created a repository on GitHub[6]. So, I am heading over there and following the instructions shown in Figure 2-6.

---

[6]https://github.com/nabendu82/nabendu-blog

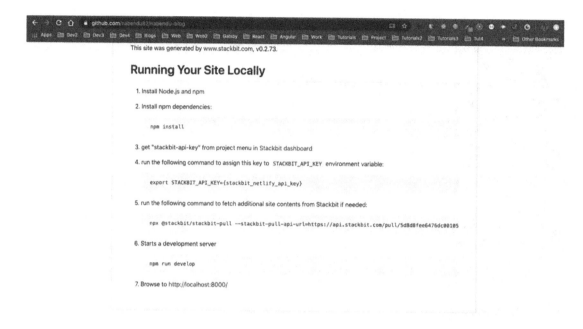

**Figure 2-6.** *The Stackbit instructions*

First I will git clone my repository in my desktop with the following command:

git clone https://github.com/nabendu82/nabendu-blog.git

Next, I will change to the directory and run npm install, with this command:

cd nabendu-blog
npm install

Now, we need to go to the Stackbit dashboard[7] to get our API keys, as shown in Figure 2-7.

---

[7]https://app.stackbit.com/dashboard

*Figure 2-7.* *The API keys*

Then we need to assign this key to STACKBIT_API_KEY:

export STACKBIT_API_KEY=your_api_key

Then, as per the GitHub instruction, run the following command. It seems to fetch all posts.

```
npx @stackbit/stackbit-pull --stackbit-pull-api-url=https://api.
stackbit.com/pull/5d8d8fee6476dc00105e91ac
```

Then, as per the instructions, run npm run develop. Once it compiles successfully, open http://localhost:8000/[8]. Figure 2-8 shows that we successfully created our local development environment.

---

[8]http://localhost:8000/

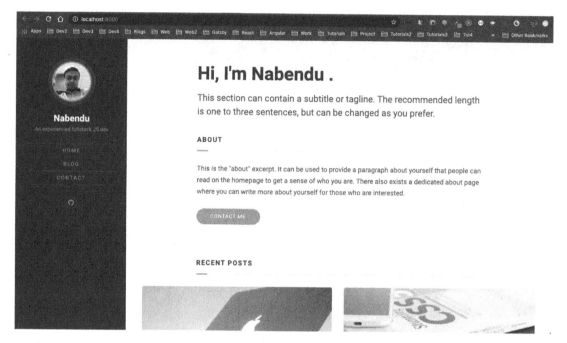

***Figure 2-8.***  *The localhost*

Now, let's open the project in VSCode. The main thing we need to edit is the home page, as shown in Figure 2-9. The content comes from `src` ➤ `pages` ➤ `index.md`.

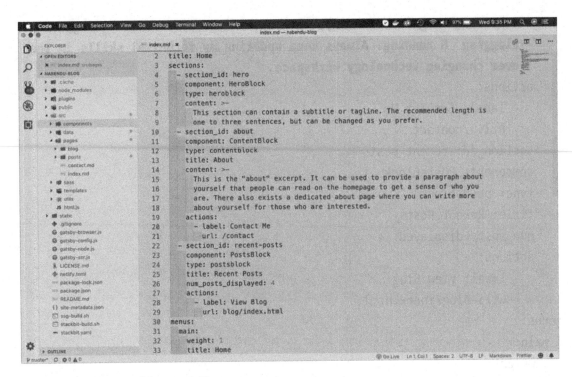

*Figure 2-9.  The index.md file*

We will now update the content (marked in bold) in index.md, as shown in Listing 2-1.

*Listing 2-1.*  The index.md File

```
---
title: Home
sections:
  - section_id: hero
    component: HeroBlock
    type: heroblock
    content: >-
      UI Developer | Tech Blogger | Team Lead
  - section_id: about
    component: ContentBlock
    type: contentblock
    title: About
    content: >-
```

61

```
      I live in Bengaluru (India), with my kid and wife. Love Coding,
      blogging  & running. Always keep updating my technical skills in the
      ever changing technology workspace.
      actions:
        - label: Contact Me
          url: /contact
  - section_id: recent-posts
    component: PostsBlock
    type: postsblock
    title: Recent Posts
    num_posts_displayed: 4
    actions:
      - label: View Blog
        url: blog/index.html
menus:
  main:
    weight: 1
    title: Home
template: home
---
```

Let's commit the changes and push it to our GitHub with the git push origin master command. It will also start updating the site in Netlify, as shown in Figure 2-10.

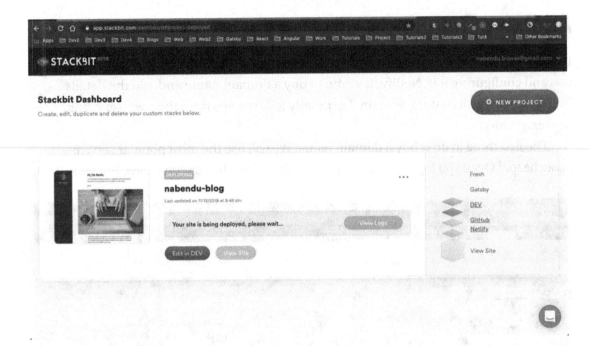

***Figure 2-10.*** *The site is updated*

And, after some time, the changes are pushed to production, as shown in Figure 2-11.

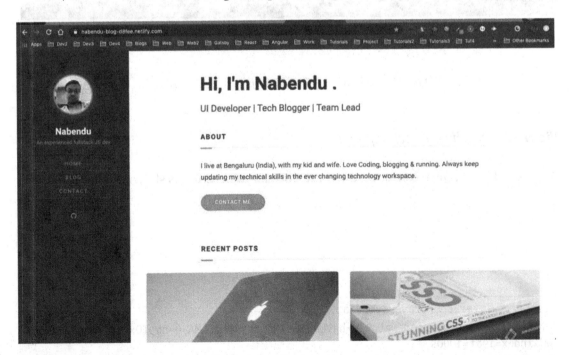

***Figure 2-11.*** *The site is updated*

# Adding a Domain

In this section, we go through the process of buying a domain name from namecheap.
com and configuring it in Netlify. It's time to buy a domain name and add the details
in Netlify. To add a custom domain, I generally follow steps from this awesome Brad
Traversy[9] video[10].

The first thing to do is buy a domain name. We will use the most popular service—
namecheap.[11] Once you log in to your account, you will see the screen shown in Figure 2-12.

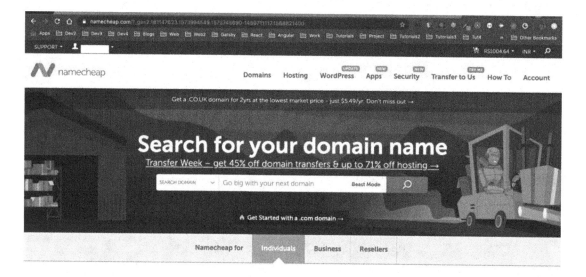

*Figure 2-12.* *The namecheap login*

I searched for my name and added the domain to my cart, as shown in Figure 2-13.

[9]https://twitter.com/traversymedia

[10]https://www.youtube.com/watch?v=bjVUqvcCnxM&list=PLuOLMA-n-nN9TOxtU11gNLaMZBXxCtv
WD&index=19&t=1000s

[11]http://www.namecheap.com

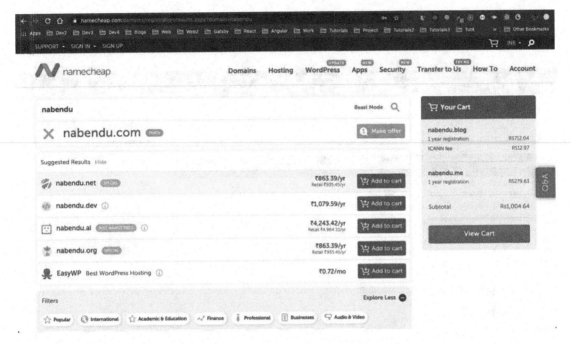

***Figure 2-13.***  *Buying domains*

Then click View Cart, which will show the next screen. See Figure 2-14.

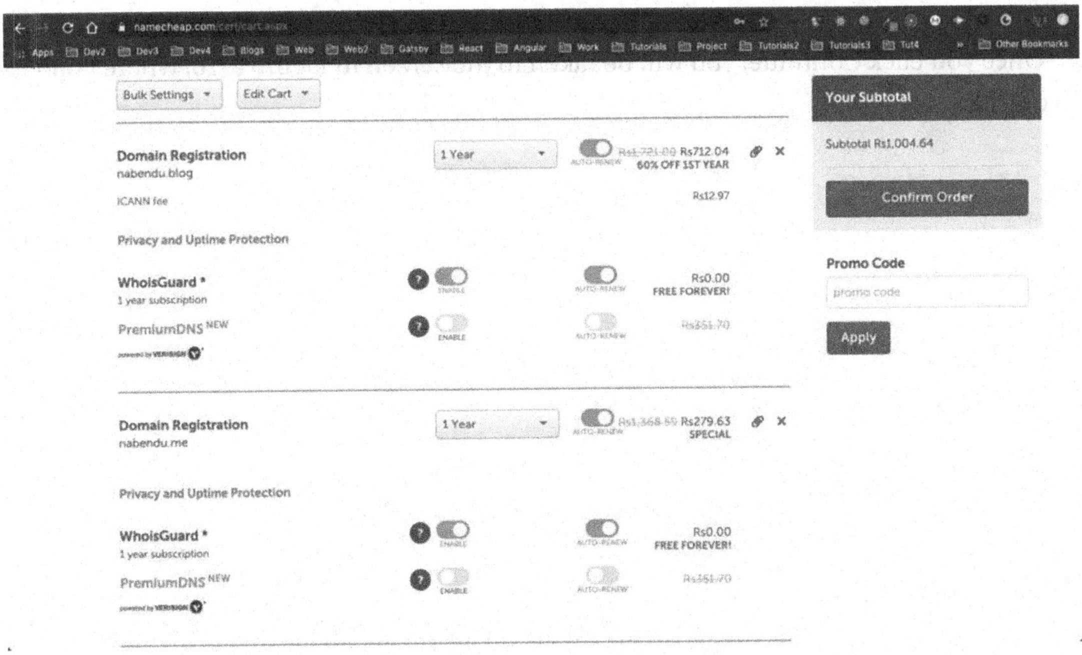

***Figure 2-14.***  *Buying a domain*

Once you click Confirm Order, you will be taken to the next screen, where you confirm your payment options, as shown in Figure 2-15.

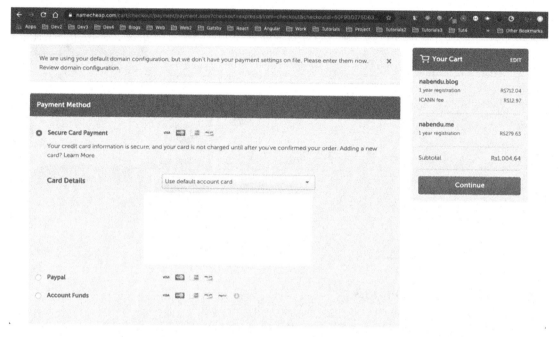

***Figure 2-15.***  *Payment options*

Once you click Continue, you will be taken to the screen in Figure 2-16, where you have to pay.

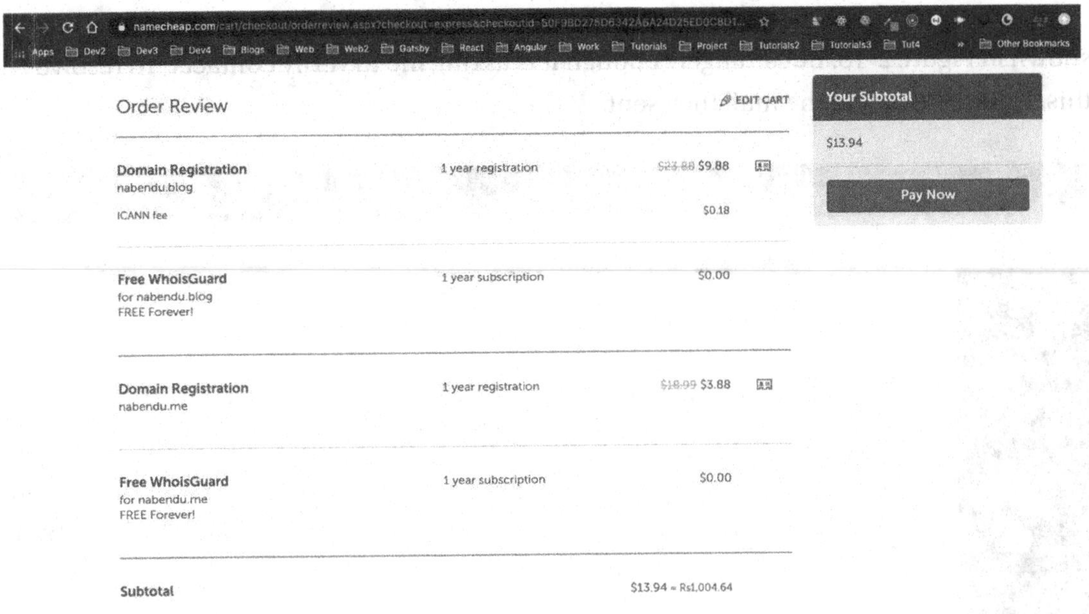

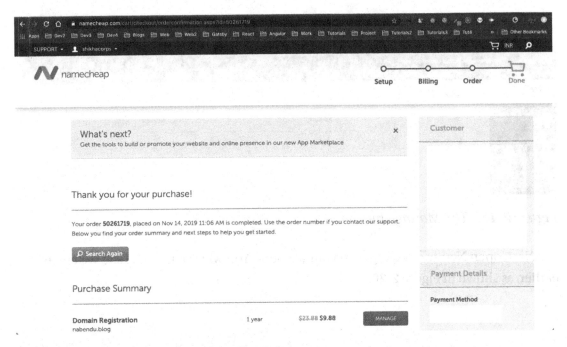

***Figure 2-16.*** *The Pay screen*

Once you click Pay Now, shown in Figure 2-17, the purchase will be completed.

***Figure 2-17.*** *The Purchase Completed screen*

After this, we have to click the Manage button. This will take us to our dashboard, as shown in Figure 2-18. But strangely enough it is asking me to verify contacts. To resolve this, I clicked a link in the mail they sent.

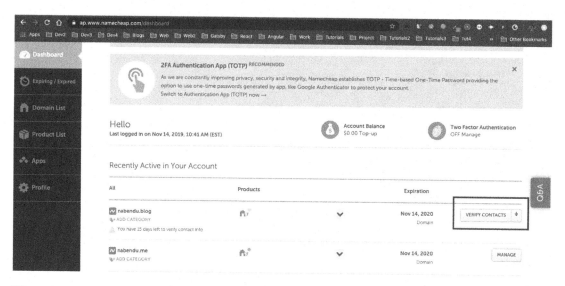

***Figure 2-18.*** *The error*

The error was resolved in an hour and I got a Manage button, as shown in Figure 2-19.

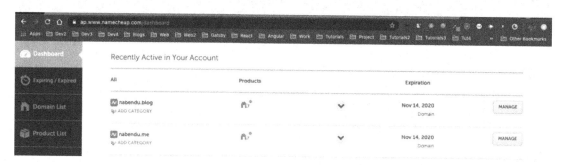

***Figure 2-19.*** *The Manage button*

Next, open Netlify[12] and log in to your account. You will see the blog site we created earlier, as shown in Figure 2-20.

---

[12]https://app.netlify.com/

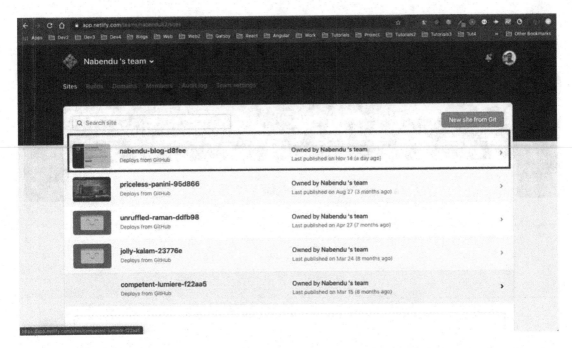

***Figure 2-20.***  *My blog*

In the next screen, click Set Up a Custom Domain, as shown in Figure 2-21.

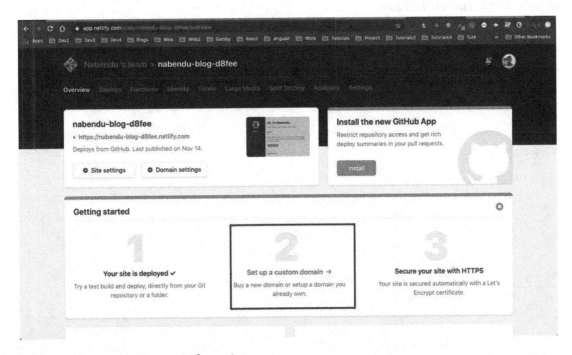

***Figure 2-21.***  *The Custom domain*

In the next screen, I will give the domain name (`nabendu.blog`), which I purchased from namecheap. Click the Verify button, as shown in Figure 2-22.

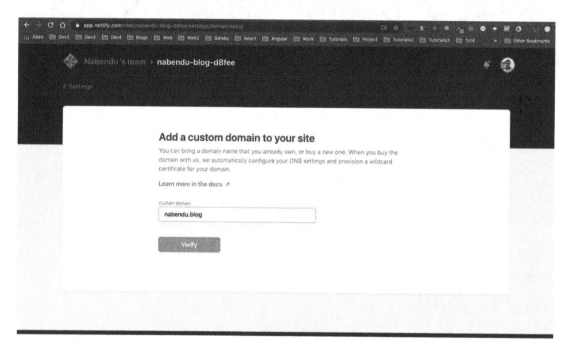

***Figure 2-22.*** *nabendu.blog*

Next, it will ask whether I am the owner, so I will click the Yes, Add Domain button, as shown in Figure 2-23.

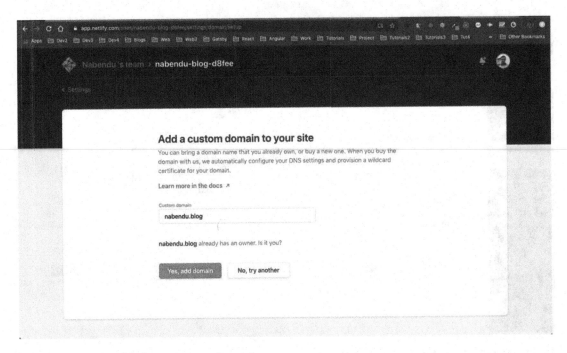

**Figure 2-23.** *Add the custom domain*

Now, it's time to go back to namecheap.com and click the Manage button in nabendu. blog on the dashboard, as shown in Figure 2-24.

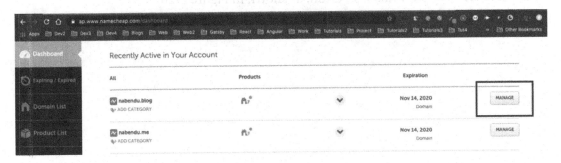

**Figure 2-24.** *The Manage button*

It will open the screen shown in Figure 2-25. Click the Advanced DNS tab.

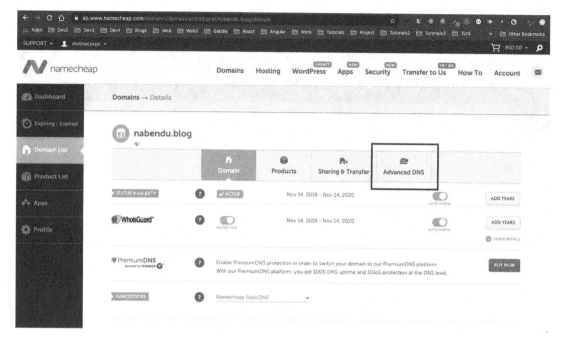

**Figure 2-25.** *The Advanced DNS tab*

We can use Netlify DNS to configure the DNS, but we will be using our service provider (namecheap) to do so. You can go through this[13] article for more details.

So, click the Add New Record button, as shown in Figure 2-26.

---

[13]https://docs.netlify.com/domains-https/custom-domains/configure-external-dns/
#configure-a-subdomain

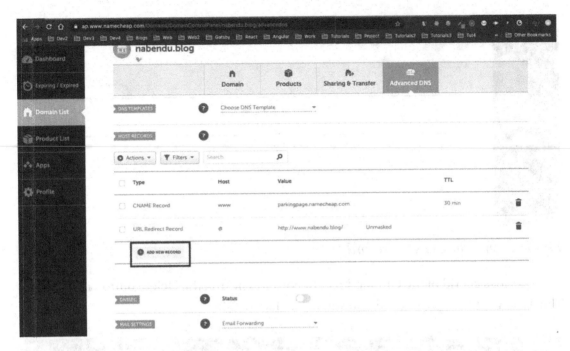

**Figure 2-26.** *Add new record*

According to Netlify docs, we need to add an A record and add their load balancer IP address, which is 104.198.14.52. Add the record and then click the small green tick mark, as shown in Figure 2-27.

**Figure 2-27.** *Add an A record*

Next, we will add a CNAME record. Since I already had one, I edited it. The value should be equal to the random domain name, which Netlify gave us, as shown in Figure 2-28.

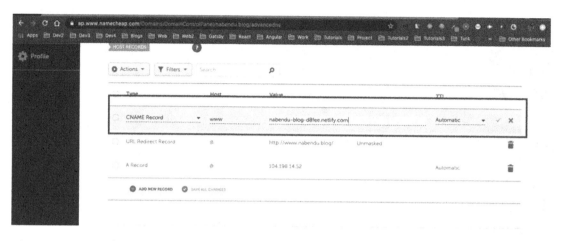

**Figure 2-28.** *The CNAME record*

Also, let's get rid of the URL Redirect Record by clicking the Delete button in its row. The Advanced DNS page should now look like Figure 2-29.

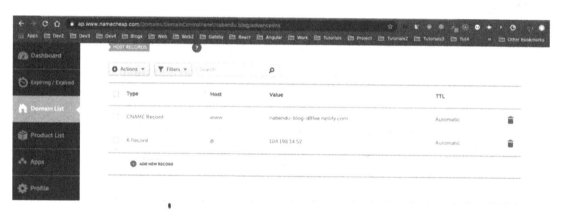

**Figure 2-29.** *Final advanced DNS page*

Now, go to your Netlify account and refresh the web page. You will see Figure 2-30 if everything is okay.

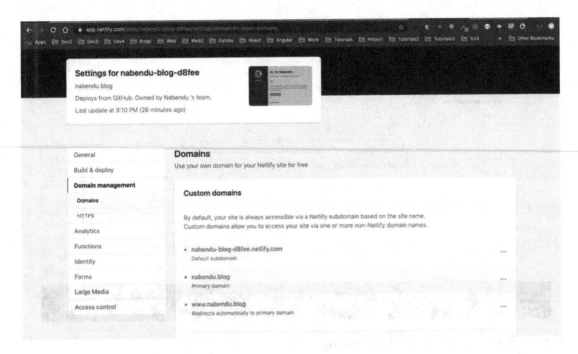

***Figure 2-30.*** *Everything is okay*

One of the very good features of Netlify is that it provides a secure HTTPS site. But it generally takes time. If you scroll down on the same page, it will show that it is waiting on DNS propagation, as shown in Figure 2-31.

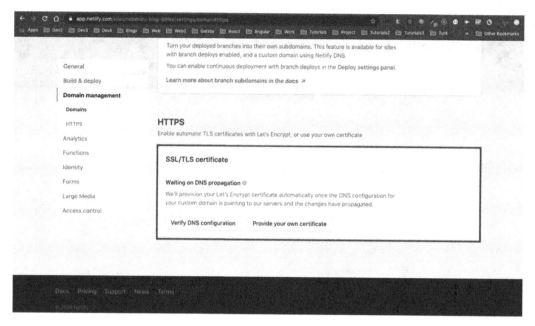

***Figure 2-31.*** *Waiting on DNS propagation*

It can take up to a day for DNS propagation. But we can view the HTTP version of our site, with the Not Secure warning in the title bar, as shown in Figure 2-32.

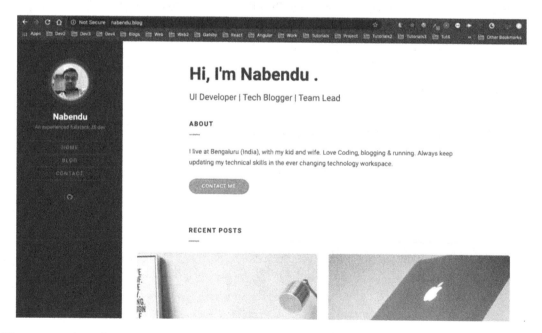

***Figure 2-32.*** *This site is not secure*

Netlify also provides a great contact form, which was given to us by Stackbit. We can check whether it is working by heading to the Contact page, as shown in Figure 2-33.

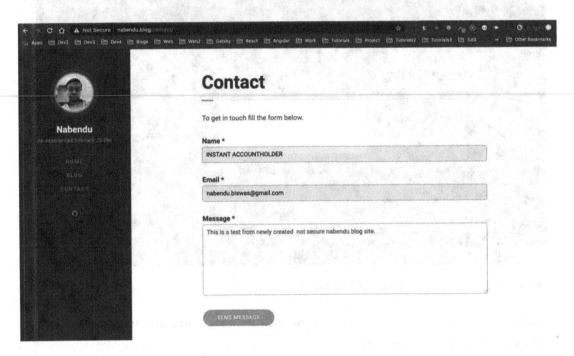

**Figure 2-33.** *Submitting a form*

If it is successful, we will get the screen shown in Figure 2-34.

***Figure 2-34.*** *Successful form submission*

Now, head over to Overview in Netlify and scroll down. You can see the newly sent message, as shown in Figure 2-35.

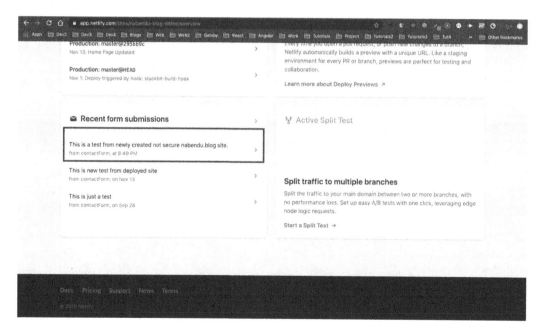

***Figure 2-35.*** *Contact form message*

I checked my HTTPS and it was activated in fewer than 30 minutes, as shown in Figure 2-36.

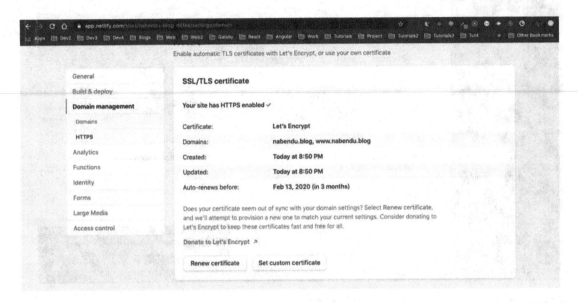

***Figure 2-36.***   *The HTTPS site*

Now, if we head over to https://nabendu.blog/,[14] we won't get any errors. Finally my blog site is live with HTTPS, as shown in Figure 2-37.

---

[14]https://nabendu.blog/

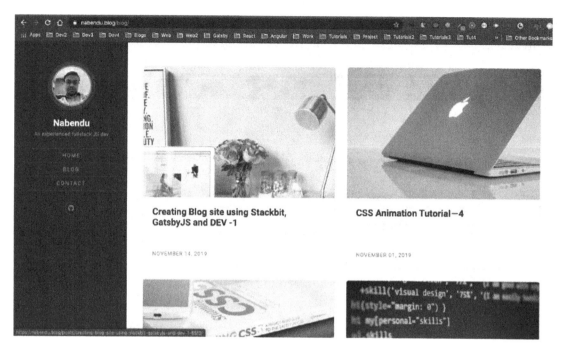

***Figure 2-37.***  *Secure blog site, with HTTPS*

# Adding Gatsby Plugins

In this section, we are going to add Gatsby plugins to our site, which are an easy way to add functionality to a Gatsby site. We are also going to add a plugin for Google analytics, for which you need a Google account.

We will start by adding Gatsby plugins to my newly created blog site[15]. I found a great article by Emeruche Cole[16] about this process.

So, let's head over to the terminal and run the command to get the latest data from Stackbit on our local machine. I got the following information from my `github repo`[17] for my blog site, which was initially created by Stackbit.

```
        npx @stackbit/stackbit-pull --stackbit-pull-api-
url=https://api.stackbit.com/pull/5d8d8fee6476dc00105e91ac
```

I will be adding two SEO plugins first.

---

[15]https://nabendu.blog/

[16]https://dev.to/cole_ruche/my-top-plugins-for-a-gatsbyjs-powered-blog-1oo1

[17]https://github.com/nabendu82/nabendu-blog

# gatsby-plugin-robots-txt

So, let's head over to the plugin page[18]. As the name suggests, it creates a robots.txt file for the Gatsby site. It's good for SEO as it tells Google bots on how to crawl your site.

We will follow the instructions and run an npm install in our directory, as shown here:

```
npm install --save gatsby-plugin-robots-txt
```

In the gatsby-config.js file, we need to add the code shown in Listing 2-2 to our plugin array.

*Listing 2-2.* gatsby-config.js

```
{
    resolve: `gatsby-plugin-robots-txt`,
    options: {
        host: 'https://nabendu.blog/',
        sitemap: 'https://nabendu.blog/sitemap.xml',
        policy: [{ userAgent: '*', allow: '/' }]
    }
}
```

# gatsby-plugin-sitemap

This plugin generates a sitemap for your site, which is very important for SEO purposes. As per the instructions on the plugin page[19], let's run npm install:

```
npm install --save gatsby-plugin-sitemap
```

Now, this plugin is easy to use. We need to add the plugin name to the gatsby-config.js file inside the plugins array:

```
`gatsby-plugin-sitemap`
```

---

[18]https://www.gatsbyjs.org/packages/
gatsby-plugin-robots-txt/?=gatsby-plugin-robots-txt
[19]https://www.gatsbyjs.org/packages/gatsby-plugin-sitemap/?=

We also need to have a `siteUrl` in our `siteMetaData`. But Stackbit creates a JSON for us. So, we need to add it there. We will also add some other useful keywords (see Listing 2-3) for SEO to the `site-metadata.json` file.

I found a helpful list at the Emeruche Cole GitHub link.[20]

***Listing 2-3.*** The site-metadata.json File

```
"title": "Nabendu's Blog",
"author": "Nabendu Biswas",
"siteUrl": "https://nabendu.blog/",
"description": "Blog posts started by Nabendu Biswas to share stuff I
learned in my Web development journey",
"keywords": [
    "Nabendu",
    "Biswas",
    "UI Lead",
    "GatsbyJs",
    "HTML",
    "CSS",
    "JavaScript",
    "ReactJs",
    "React developer",
    "Front-end Engineer"
]
```

Next, let's start our server to see if there are any errors. Start with `npm run develop`.

I have also checked `http://localhost:8000/`[21] and there were no errors. Next, let's add these changes to our production. With Netlify, it's simply a matter of pushing the changes to GitHub. So, I just committed my changes and pushed them to GitHub with `git push origin master`. When I head over to my Netlify dashboard, I see that it's building, as in Figure 2-38.

---

[20]https://github.com/kingingcole/myblog/blob/master/gatsby-config.js
[21]http://localhost:8000/

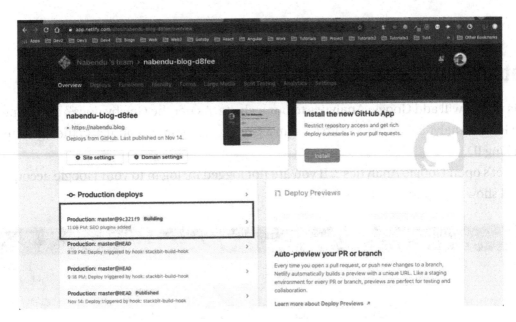

**Figure 2-38.** *Building*

It was published in less than five minutes. Now, when I head over to my site, my title change is there, as shown in Figure 2-39. Everything else is behind the scenes.

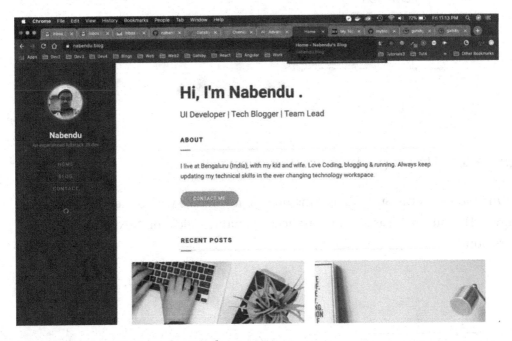

**Figure 2-39.** *The title has changed*

Next, we will add one of the most important plugins, one for analytics purposes.

# gatsby-plugin-google-analytics

This plugin will add Google Analytics to our website. As per the Gatsby docs[22] on setting up Google Analytics, we have to first set up a Google Analytics account and then get the tracking ID.

Let's open Google Analytics[23]. If you are not logged in, log in to your Google account. It will show the screen in Figure 2-40.

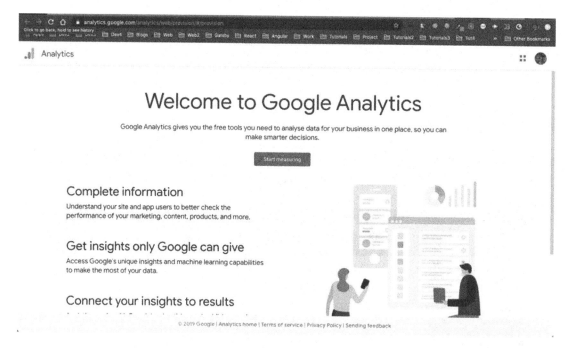

***Figure 2-40.***  *The Google Analytics Welcome page*

Once you click the Start Measuring button, it will take you to the page shown in Figure 2-41. You will be asked for your account name. Click the Next button when you're done.

---

[22]https://www.gatsbyjs.org/docs/adding-analytics/

[23]https://analytics.google.com/analytics/web/provision/#/provision

**Figure 2-41.** *Account name*

In the screen in Figure 2-42, select Web and then click Next.

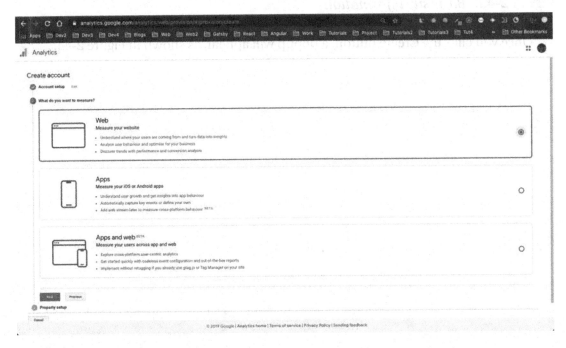

**Figure 2-42.** *Choose Web here*

In the screen in Figure 2-43, you have to provide some basic site information, including the site's URL.

***Figure 2-43.*** *Basic site information*

Once you click the Create button, a popup will appear, as shown in Figure 2-44.

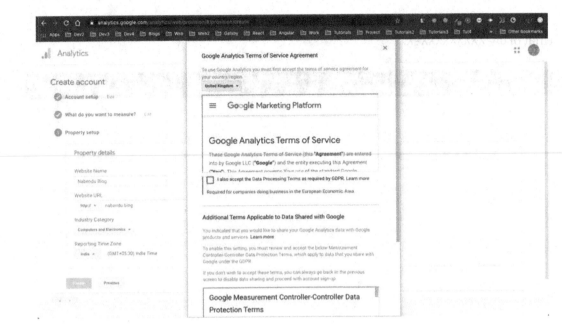

***Figure 2-44.*** *The popup asks you to accept the terms*

Here, you have to accept the terms and conditions. Click the Accept buttons, as shown in Figure 2-45.

***Figure 2-45.*** *You have to accept the terms*

The next screen, shown in Figure 2-46, will contain your tracking ID. It is in the format of UA-XXXXXXXXX-X.

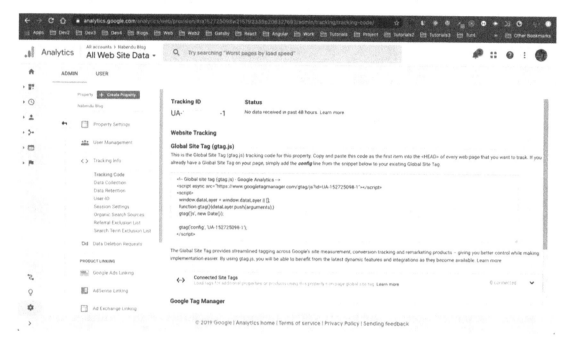

***Figure 2-46.***  *Tracking ID*

Now it's time to install the Gatsby Google Analytics plugin by executing npm install --save gatsby-plugin-google-analytics in the terminal.

Next, we need to add the plugin to the gatsby-config.js file (see Listing 2-4). You have to enter the Tracking ID you got from Google.

***Listing 2-4.***  gatsby-config.js

```
{
    resolve: `gatsby-plugin-google-analytics`,
    options: {
        trackingId: "UA-XXXXXXXXX-1",
    }
}
```

Next, let's start the DEV server to see if there are any issues. We need to restart the server by running the `npm run develop` command on the terminal. I also checked `http://localhost:8000/`[24] again and there were no errors. Next, let's add these changes to our production.

If you commit your changes and push them to GitHub, it will build the production site in Netlify again, as shown in Figure 2-47.

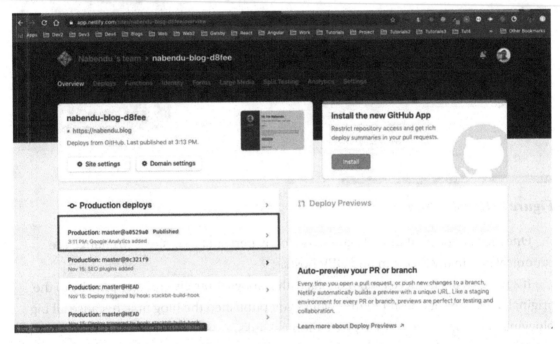

***Figure 2-47.*** *Changes have been published*

Once the site is published, go back to the Google Analytics page and click the Home tab. You will see your site data, as shown in Figure 2-48.

---

[24]`http://localhost:8000/`

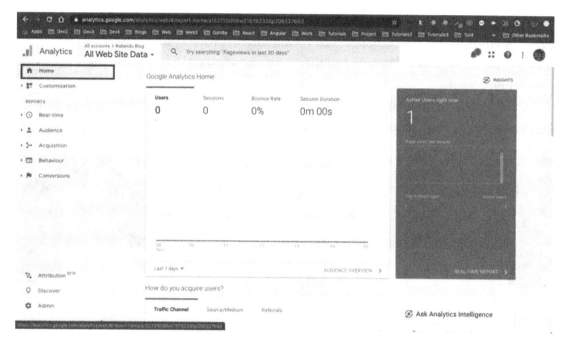

***Figure 2-48.*** *Site data*

One more important thing I want to do to my personal blog site is to change the canonical link in my Medium and DEV posts.

If a post occurs in more than one place, the Google bots give greater priority to the original post. Now, it doesn't matter where you published the blog first, because all big blogging platforms have ways to give canonical links.

My process is to create the blog in Medium first because that is what I have been doing for several years. After that, I use an awesome package called Medium Exporter[25] to change the post to a Markdown file.

After that, I had to paste the contents of the Markdown file to a new DEV post. Since Dev is also serving as my headless CMS for my site, due to the awesome service of Stackbit, it is published on my personal site.

I will show the process on one of my earlier blogs. First, we have to add a link to a Medium post. I opened one of my earlier Medium posts. Since I am logged in, I also get the Edit button. I first click the Settings icon and then choose the Edit Story option, as shown in Figure 2-49.

---

[25]https://medium.com/@macropus/export-your-medium-posts-to-markdown-b5ccc8cb0050

**Figure 2-49.** *Editing Medium*

After that, I click the three dots and then choose the Customize Canonical Link, as shown in Figure 2-50.

**Figure 2-50.** *More editing*

After that, I need to paste the original link into the Set Canonical URL: field. Here I gave the link from my blog site. After that, I click the Save button. See Figure 2-51.

**Figure 2-51.**  *Setting the canonical URL*

Next it's time to head over to dev.to and change the canonical link there also. When I head over to my same blog in DEV, I get the Edit button, as shown in Figure 2-52.

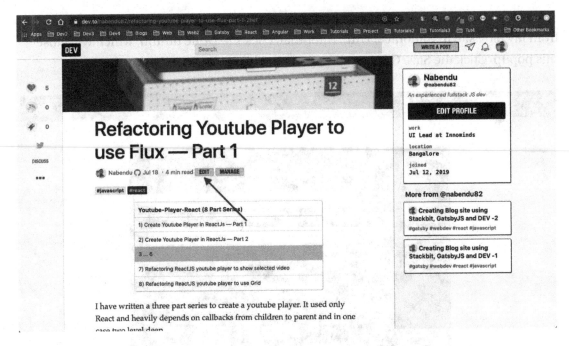

*Figure 2-52.* *DEV editing*

Next, I click the three dots, as shown in Figure 2-53.

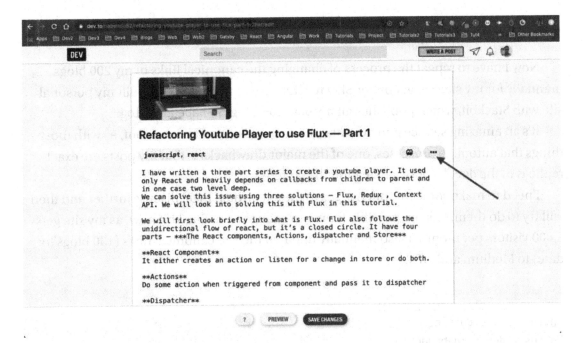

*Figure 2-53.* *Click the three dots*

It will open a popup, where we have to give the canonical link. I again give it the link from my blog site in Canonical URL. After that, click the Done button, which will close this popup. Click the Save Changes button next. This is shown in Figure 2-54.

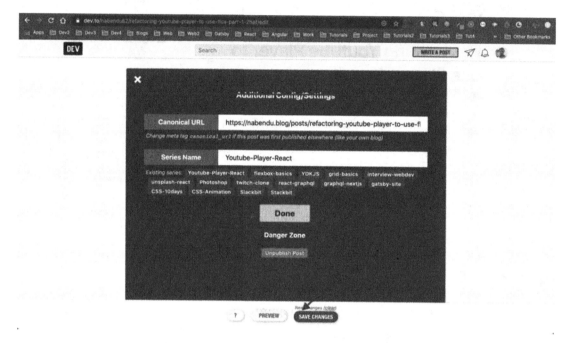

***Figure 2-54.*** *Canonical URL*

Now I have to repeat the process of changing the canonical links of my 200 blogs manually for my site[26] to get better SEO results. As you might know, I built my personal site with Stackbit, which publishes all my `dev.to`[27] blogs to `nabendu.blog`[28].

It's an amazing service and I created the site in less than an hour. But, as with most things that automate processes, one of the major drawbacks is that my posts are exact replicas of the `dev.to` posts and cannot be edited.

I need to make some minor changes to the site, which I will discuss further and then will try to do them. It is not possible for me to change from Stackbit now, as my site gets 1,000 visitors per month. I also manually updated the site canonical links (130 blogs to date) to Medium and DEV.

---

[26]https://nabendu.blog/
[27]https://dev.to/nabendu82
[28]https://nabendu.blog/

There are five things that I need to change on my blog:

- Add the disqus plugin to my blog, so that people can add comment and likes

- Add advertisement to the home page (not anywhere else, as I also don't like more ads)

- Add more social links to the home page

- Change my picture on the home page

- Change the favicon of the site

I was searching for a way to add the disqus plugin in the code, but I found a way to add social links to the home page.

# Adding Social Links

By default, we only have the GitHub social link on the home page. To add other social links, we need to add the code in Listing 2-5 to the social.json file.

*Listing 2-5.* The social.json File

```json
{
    "links": [
        {
            "type": "twitter",
            "title": "Twitter",
            "icon": "fa-twitter",
            "url": "https://twitter.com/nabendu82"
        },
        {
            "type": "github",
            "title": "GitHub",
            "icon": "fa-github",
            "url": "https://github.com/nabendu82"
        },
```

```
    {
        "type": "linkedin",
        "title": "Linkedin",
        "icon": "fa-linkedin",
        "url": "https://www.linkedin.com/in/nabendu-biswas-42aa4522/"
    },
    {

        "type": "instagram",
        "title": "Instagram",
        "icon": "fa-instagram",
        "url": "https://www.instagram.com/nabendu82/"
    }
  ]
}
```

In my local development server, the changes were not reflected, so I had to restart the gatsby develop. After that, the social links were updated, as shown in Figure 2-55.

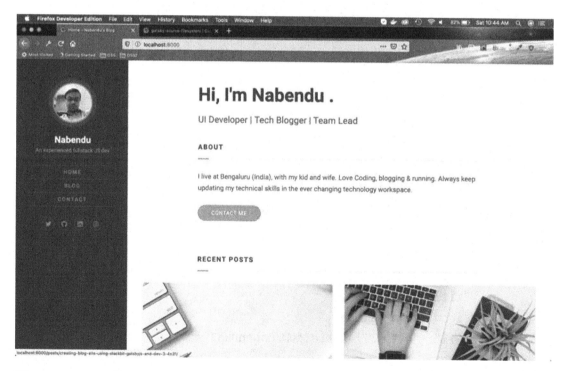

***Figure 2-55.*** *The social links*

# Adding the Disqus Plugin

After doing some research, I can install the Disqus plugin, as per the documentation[29] inside my project directory:

```
npm install -S gatsby-plugin-disqus
```

We need to register to disqus and get the website short name. You can get it from the screen shown in Figure 2-56.

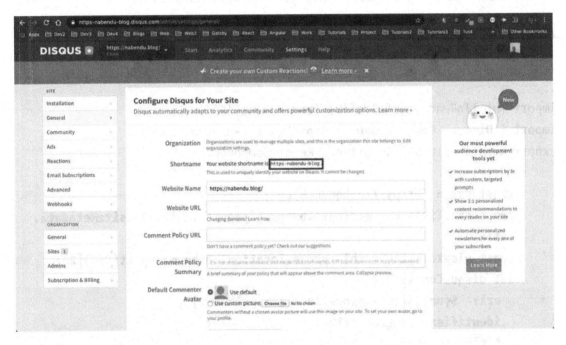

***Figure 2-56.***  *The short name*

Next, it's time to add the content in Listing 2-6 to the gatsby-config.js file.

***Listing 2-6.***  gatsby-config.js

```
    {
        resolve: `gatsby-plugin-disqus`,
```

---

[29]https://www.gatsbyjs.org/packages/gatsby-plugin-disqus/

```
    options: {
        shortname: `https-nabendu-blog`
    }
}
```

We need to add `disqus` to the `post.js` template. After some research and help from this GitHub[30] belonging to Cole Emeruche,[31]I was able to add `disqus`. We need to add the URL, the identifier, and the style to `disqusConfig`. To do this, we need a bit of JavaScript.

We need to add the bold code in `post.js`, as shown in Listing 2-7.

***Listing 2-7.*** The post.js File

```
. . .
. . .
import {htmlToReact, safePrefix} from '../utils';
import { Disqus, CommentCount } from "gatsby-plugin-disqus";
export default class Post extends React.Component {
    render() {
        const url = "https://nabendu.blog";
        const siteTitle = _.get(this.props, 'pageContext.site.siteMetadata.
        title');
        const blogIdentity = this.props.location.pathname.split("/")[2];
        let disqusConfig = {
          url: `${url}${this.props.location.pathname}`,
          identifier: blogIdentity,
          title: siteTitle,
        }
          return (
                        . . .
                          . . .
                  );
    }
}
```

---

[30]https://github.com/kingingcole/myblog
[31]https://coleruche.com/

It's time to add `CommentCount` and `Disqus` before and after your content, as shown in Listing 2-8.

***Listing 2-8.*** The post.js File

```
return (
    <Layout {...this.props}>
        <article className="post post-full">
        <CommentCount config={disqusConfig} placeholder={'...'} />
        ...
          ...
        </article>
        <Subscribe heading={true} />
        <Disqus config={disqusConfig} />
    </Layout>
);
```

The Comment section has started to appear in `localhost`, as shown in Figure 2-57.

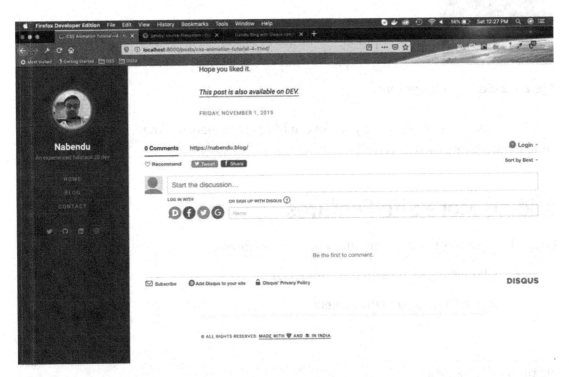

***Figure 2-57.*** *localhost disqus*

Next, it's time to push it to GitHub so it's automatically deployed to Netlify. After the deployment, it looks awesome and my site now has a Comment and Like section, as shown in Figure 2-58.

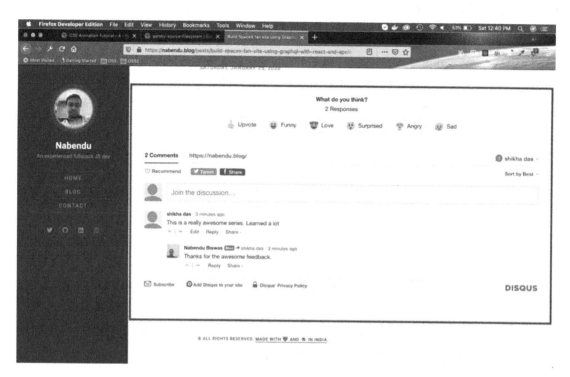

***Figure 2-58.*** *Just awesome*

Go ahead and start showing your love at `https://nabendu.blog/`.[32] You can find the code for this at my GitHub repo[33].

# Adding More Site Features

I have four features to add to my site. They are as follows:

- Change my picture on the home page

- Add a Google ad to the project

---

[32]`https://nabendu.blog/`
[33]`https://github.com/nabendu82/nabendu-blog`

- Integrate Mailchimp for subscriptions

- Change the favicon of the site

Let's start by changing my profile picture on the `sitemy` blog site. For this, we just need to change the `profile_img` in `site-metadata.json,` as shown in Figure 2-59. I saved my image on Cloudinary, but it can be saved on any platform on the web, which gives you access to a link.

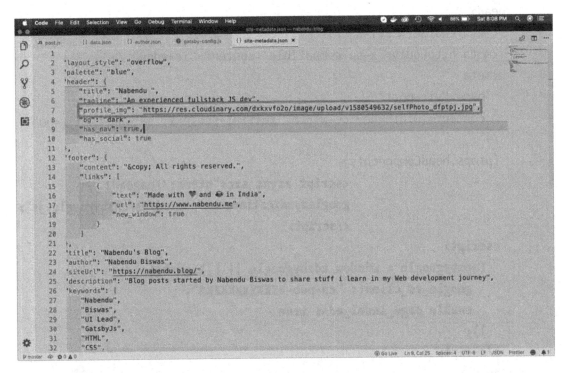

***Figure 2-59.*** *The metadata*

Adding Google AdSense to a GatsbyJS site is a bit tricky and I didn't find many articles on it. If you don't have an AdSense account activated, it's a different process.

First, copy the `html.js` file in the `src` folder, using `cp  .cache/default-html.js src/html.js` in the main directory.

Next, for AdSense activation, you need to add the script in Listing 2-9 inside the `<head>` tag. You need to use your own `google_ad_client`. The additions are shown in bold.

*Listing 2-9.* The Updated html.js File

```
import React from "react"
import PropTypes from "prop-types"

export default function HTML(props) {
  return (
    <html {...props.htmlAttributes}>
      <head>
        <meta charSet="utf-8" />
        <meta httpEquiv="x-ua-compatible" content="ie=edge" />
        <meta
          name="viewport"
          content="width=device-width, initial-scale=1, shrink-to-fit=no"
        />
        {props.headComponents}
                          <script async src="https://pagead2.
                          googlesyndication.com/pagead/js/adsbygoogle.js">
                          </script>
        <script>
          (adsbygoogle = window.adsbygoogle || []).push({
            google_ad_client: "ca-pub-8XXXXXXXXXXX",
            enable_page_level_ads: true
          });
        </script>
      </head>
      <body {...props.bodyAttributes}>
        {props.preBodyComponents}
        <noscript key="noscript" id="gatsby-noscript">
          This app works best with JavaScript enabled.
        </noscript>
        <div
          key={`body`}
          id="___gatsby"
          dangerouslySetInnerHTML={{ __html: props.body }}
        />
```

```
        {props.postBodyComponents}
      </body>
    </html>
  )
}

HTML.propTypes = {
  htmlAttributes: PropTypes.object,
  headComponents: PropTypes.array,
  bodyAttributes: PropTypes.object,
  preBodyComponents: PropTypes.array,
  body: PropTypes.string,
  postBodyComponents: PropTypes.array,
}
```

I deploy the site to Netlify and click a check box in Google AdSense to complete the process. It gives me the message shown in Figure 2-60, which means I need to wait a few days.

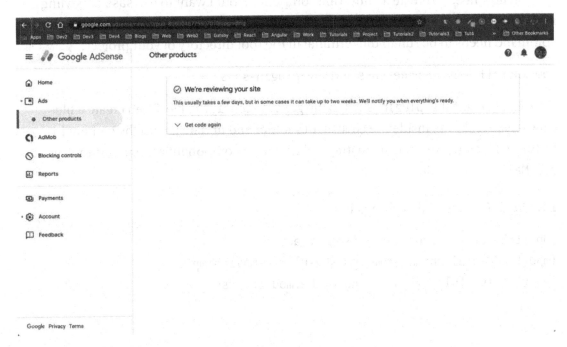

***Figure 2-60.*** *Waiting for Google AdSense approval*

Now it's time to add Mailchimp to the blog. I need to register for a Mailchimp account first. After that, I followed the instructions on this blog[34] to get my end point.

Then you need to install the Mailchimp plugin by running the following command. This command needs to be run in the terminal in the root directory of your project.

```
npm install --save gatsby-plugin-mailchimp
```

After that, you need to add the code in Listing 2-10 to the gatsby-config.js file.

***Listing 2-10.*** Code for the gatsby-config.js File

```
{
    resolve: "gatsby-plugin-mailchimp",
    options: {
        endpoint: "https://blog.us4.list-manage.com/subscribe/
        post?u=5c156d7649897240e9c994d38&id=67f40851e0",
    },
}
```

You now need to create a Subscribe component, but I want to use sass for styling in the project. So, I will first add a plugin for that by running the next command. This command needs to be run in the terminal in the root directory of your project.

```
npm install --save node-sass gatsby-plugin-sass
```

Next, add gatsby-plugin-sass to the gatsby-config.js file. Then create a file called subscribe.js inside the components folder and update it with the content in Listing 2-11. Here, we are just creating a class-based component and submitting it to the add Mailchimp function.

***Listing 2-11.*** The subscribe.js File

```
import React, { Component } from 'react';
import addToMailchimp from "gatsby-plugin-mailchimp";
import * as styles from './subscribe.module.scss';
```

---

[34]https://thetrevorharmon.com/blog/email-signup-forms-with-gatsby-and-mailchimp

```
class Subscribe extends Component  {
    state = {
        email: "",
        statusMsg: "",
        statusMsgColor: "green",
        subscribing: false,
    }

    handleSubmit = (e) => {
        e.preventDefault();
        this.setState({ statusMsg: "", subscribing: true });
        let { email } = this.state;
        addToMailchimp(email)
            .then(data => {
            data.result === "success"
                ? this.setState({
                    statusMsg: "Your subscription was successful!",
                    statusMsgColor: "green",
                    email: "",
                    subscribing: false,
                    })
                : this.setState({
                    statusMsg: "This email has already been subscribed.",
                    statusMsgColor: "red",
                    subscribing: false,
                    })
            })
            .catch(err => {
                this.setState({
                statusMsg: "An error occurred. Please re-try",
                statusMsgColor: "red",
                subscribing: false,
                })
            })
    };
```

```
    render() {
        let { statusMsg, subscribing } = this.state;
        let btnCTA = subscribing ? "Subscribing" : "Subscribe";
        return (
            <form onSubmit={this.handleSubmit} className={styles.
            EmailListForm}>
                <h2>Subscribe to receive updates on new posts!</h2>
                <div className={styles.Wrapper}>
                    <input
                        placeholder="Email address"
                        name="email"
                        type="text"
                        value={this.state.email}
                        onChange={e => this.setState({ email: e.target.
                        value })}
                    />
                    <button type="submit">{btnCTA}</button>
                    {statusMsg && (
                        <div className="col-12">
                            <p
                            className="text-left"
                            style={{ color: this.state.statusMsgColor }}
                            >
                            {statusMsg}
                            </p>
                        </div>
                    )}
                </div>
            </form>
        );
    }
};

export default Subscribe;
```

Next, create a `subscribe.module.scss` module in the same directory and add the content from Listing 2-12.

***Listing 2-12.*** subscribe.module.scss

```scss
.EmailListForm {
    display: flex;
    flex-direction: column;
    background: transparent;
    color: #2a2a2a;
    font-family: -apple-system, Helvetica, Arial, sans-serif;

    h2 {
        margin-top: 0;
        margin-bottom: 1rem;
    }

    .Wrapper {
        display: flex;
        flex-direction: column;
    }

    input {
        color: #2a2a2a;
        width: 100%;
        border: none;
    }

    input {
        padding: 1rem 1.5rem;
    }

    button {
        display: inline-block;
        border: none;
        background-image: none;
        background-color: #DD0505 !important;
        color: white;
        border-radius: 5px;
```

```
letter-spacing: 1px;
transition: all 0.1s linear;
margin-top:1%;

&:hover {
    cursor: pointer;
    background: darken(#DD0505, 15%) !important;
}
}
}
```

Next, we will add the Subscribe component to our post.js file, so that it is displayed after every post. It is marked in bold in Listing 2-13.

***Listing 2-13.*** The post.js File

```
...
...
import {Layout} from '../components/index';
import Subscribe from '../components/subscribe';
import {htmlToReact, safePrefix} from '../utils';
import { Disqus, CommentCount } from "gatsby-plugin-disqus";

export default class Post extends React.Component {
    render() {
            ...
            ...
    }
        return (
            <Layout {...this.props}>
                    ...
                    ...
                <Subscribe />
                <Disqus config={disqusConfig} />
            </Layout>
        );
    }
}
```

Once it's pushed to GitHub and deployed to Netlify, people can subscribe to my blog site, as shown in Figure 2-61.

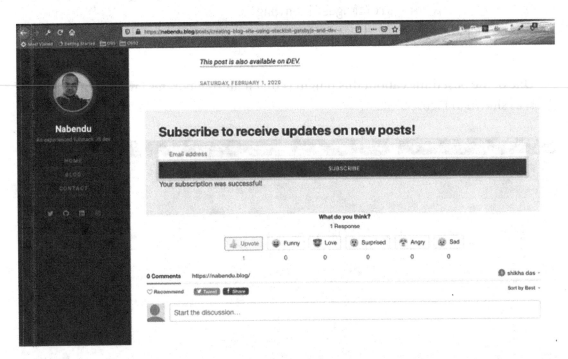

***Figure 2-61.*** *Subscription*

Now, we will add favicons to the site. For this, we need to use `gatsby-plugin-manifest`. Let's first install it by typing `npm install --save gatsby-plugin-manifest` in the root directory.

Then we need to add a favicon to any folder. I generated a 512x512 PNG image and created an `images` folder in `src` and placed it there. Also, I need to add the contents of Listing 2-14 to the `gatsby-config.js` file.

***Listing 2-14.*** The gatsby-config.js File

```
{
    resolve: `gatsby-plugin-manifest`,
    options: {
        name: `Nabendu Biswas`,
        short_name: `Nabendu`,
        start_url: `/`,
        background_color: `#ffffff`,
```

```
        theme_color: `#4ABCF8`,
        display: `standalone`,
        icon: `src/images/icon.png`,
    },
  }
```

One of the best things about this plugin is that it auto-generates favicons of other sizes, as shown in Figure 2-62.

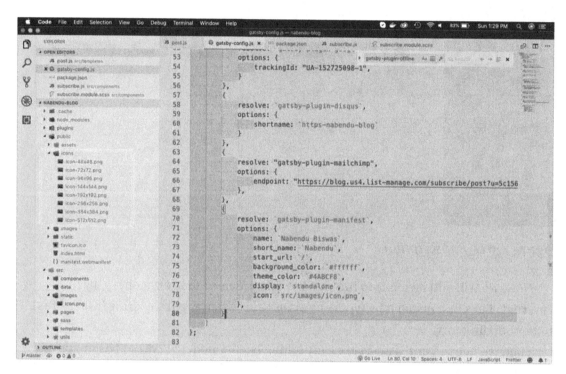

***Figure 2-62.*** *Other sizes of favicons*

The favicon is there, as in Figure 2-63 on my site (`https://nabendu.blog/`).[35]

---

[35]`https://nabendu.blog/`

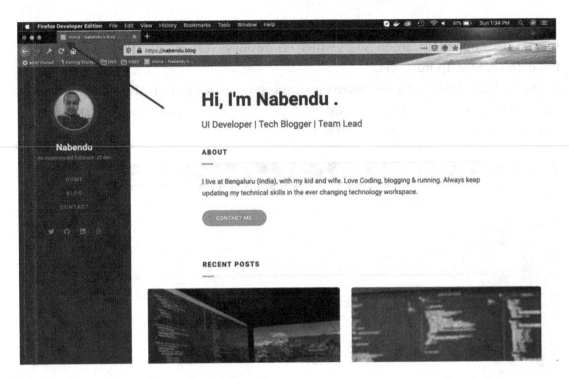

***Figure 2-63.*** *The favicon is displayed*

# Adding Advertisements

One of the main tasks remaining from the last post is to add advertisements to the site. I should tell you it's a great pain to add advertisements to a Gatsby site, as all the HTML files are generated on build. Most advertising networks provide you with JavaScript scripts to place in the head and body tags.

In the previous section, I applied for a Google AdSense account, but as my content is on three sites (even though I had canonical links to my primary domain `https://nabendu.blog/`[36] from DEV and Medium), it was rejected.

After searching the Internet, I found this[37] useful article with details of other popular ad networks.

---

[36]`https://nabendu.blog/`
[37]`https://www.adpushup.com/blog/the-best-ad-networks-for-publishers/`

I applied to Media.net, InfoLinks, and RevenueHits and got approval from all of them. I also applied to Carbon Ads[38], which is nowadays very popular with developers, but didn't get the approval yet.

I decided to add Media.net ads to my site, as they serve ads from the Yahoo network. Once you log in to the Media.net dashboard, you need to add a file called `Ads.txt` to your site root directory, as shown in Figure 2-64.

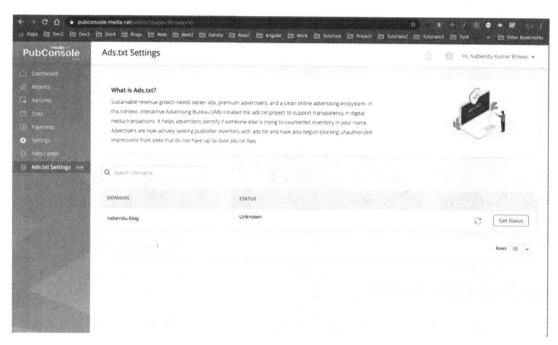

***Figure 2-64.*** *The Ads.txt file*

The Gatsby site must be placed inside the `static` folder, as shown in Figure 2-65.

---

[38]https://www.carbonads.net/

112

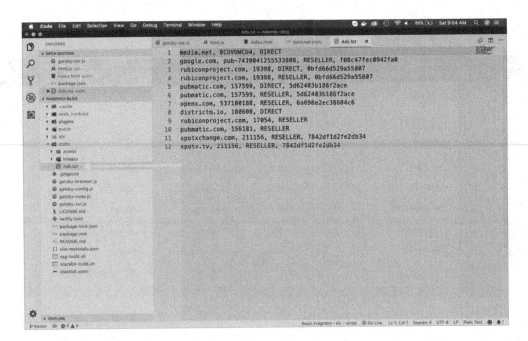

***Figure 2-65.*** *Static folder*

After deploying to Netlify, you can click the Refresh button and it will show the optimized domain, as shown in Figure 2-66.

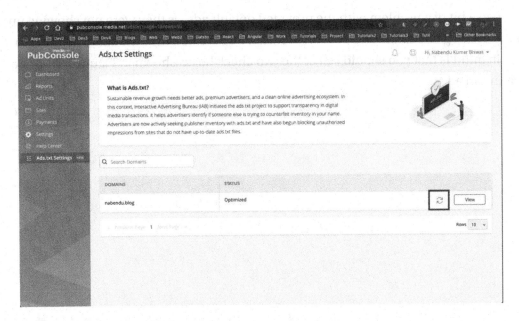

***Figure 2-66.*** *Optimized domain*

Go to the Ad Units tab to see all the ads, as shown in Figure 2-67.

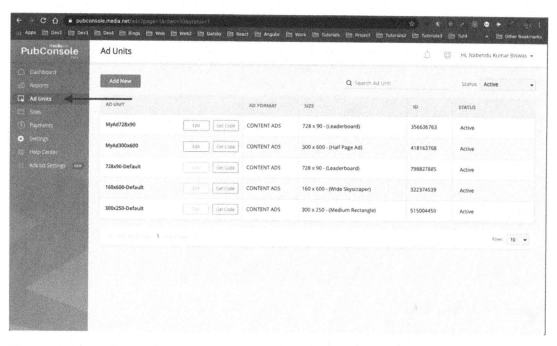

***Figure 2-67.*** *Ad units*

I had a bit of a problem with the provided default ads, as they were not showing up on the desktop due to the layout of my website. So I created my own ads. One thing to keep in mind is that you should select the two check boxes shown in Figure 2-68 while creating an ad.

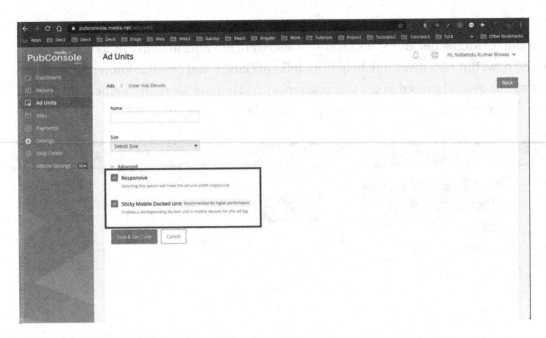

**Figure 2-68.** *Responsive ads*

Now, when you go inside any ad unit, you will get two scripts to be placed in the head and body tags of your website, as shown in Figure 2-69.

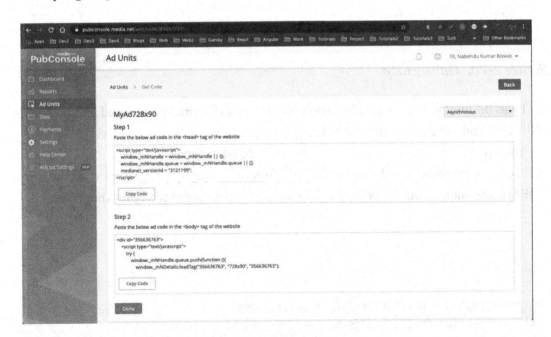

**Figure 2-69.** *Scripts for the head and body tags*

I was not able to figure out where to put these scripts in my Gatsby site. The tech support of Media.net and Stack Overflow also were not able to help me, as Gatsby is quite new. But I got awesome help from folks at Gatsby and came to know about their *spectrum chat*[39]. I posted in the General forum and Jeremy Albright[40] helped me through the complete process. Thanks, Jeremy, for your help (see Figure 2-70).

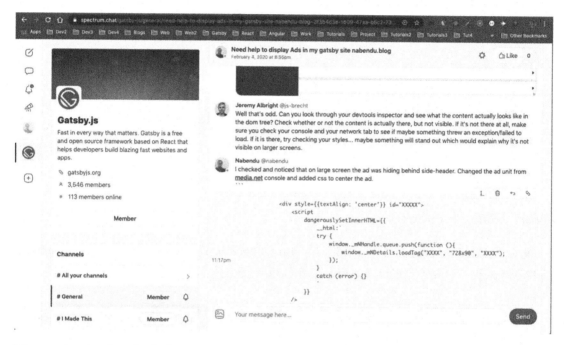

***Figure 2-70.*** *Gatsby help*

I was pointed to a great article[41] about how to insert scripts in the head and body tags of the site. You need to update the `gatsby-ssr.js` file in the root directory.

You must have `setHeadComponents`, `setPostBodyComponents`, and `setPreBodyComponents` in the `onRenderBody` function. The head tag script will come in `setHeadComponents`, but it needs to be updated to have `dangerouslySetInnerHTML`.

---

[39]https://spectrum.chat/gatsby-js/general?tab=posts

[40]https://spectrum.chat/users/js-brecht

[41]https://uxworks.online/how-to-add-a-script-in-head-or-body-tag-in-your-gatsby-website/

Similarly, the body tag script will come in setPreBodyComponents with dangerouslySetInnerHTML. Also, notice that I put an inline style={{textAlign: 'center'}} to center the ad. I did this because my ads were not properly lining up on the desktop. The updated gatsby-ssr.js file is shown in Listing 2-15.

***Listing 2-15.*** The Updated gatsby-ssr.js File

```
const React = require("react");
const safePrefix = require("./src/utils/safePrefix").default;

exports.onRenderBody = function({ setHeadComponents, setPostBodyComponents,
setPreBodyComponents }) {

    setHeadComponents([
        <script
        dangerouslySetInnerHTML={{
            __html:`
            window._mNHandle = window._mNHandle || {};
            window._mNHandle.queue = window._mNHandle.queue || [];
            medianet_versionId = "3121199";

            `
        }}
    />,
    <script src="//contextual.media.net/dmedianet.js?cid=8CUVUWCU4"
    async="async" />
    ]);

    setPreBodyComponents([
            <div style={{maxWidth: '54vw', margin: '0 auto'}} id="356636763">
                <script
                    dangerouslySetInnerHTML={{
                        __html:`
                        try {
                            window._mNHandle.queue.push(function (){
                                window._mNDetails.loadTag("356636763",
                                "728x90", "356636763");
                            });
                        }
```

```
                           catch (error) {}
                           `

                    }}
              />
          </div>
   ]);

   setPostBodyComponents([
       <React.Fragment>
           <script src={safePrefix('assets/js/plugins.js')}/>
           <script src={safePrefix('assets/js/main.js')}/>
           <div style={{maxWidth: '54vw', margin: '0 auto'}}
           id="104240845">
               <script
                   dangerouslySetInnerHTML={{
                       __html:`
                       try {
                           window._mNHandle.queue.push(function (){
                               window._mNDetails.loadTag("104240845",
                               "300x250", "104240845");
                           });
                       }
                       catch (error) {}
                       `

                   }}
              />
          </div>
          <div id="172542266">
              <script
                  dangerouslySetInnerHTML={{
                      __html:`
                      try {
                          window._mNHandle.queue.push(function (){
                              window._mNDetails.loadTag("172542266",
                              "320x50", "172542266");
                          });
```

```
                    }
                    catch (error) {}
                    `

                }}
            />
        </div>
    </React.Fragment>
  ]);

};
```

Commit the changes and deploy in Netlify. You will get ads shown in all pages and blogs before it, as shown in Figure 2-71.

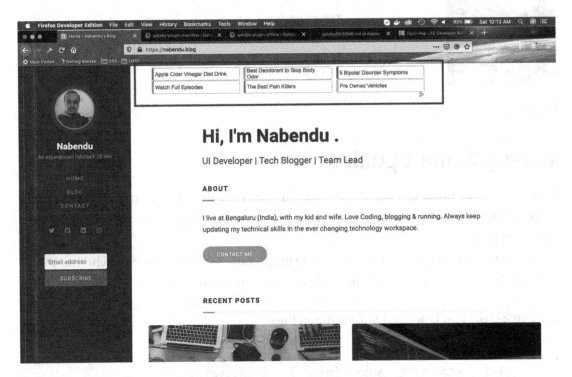

***Figure 2-71.***  *Ads*

You will get ads shown in all pages and blogs after it, as shown in Figure 2-72.

***Figure 2-72.*** *After ads*

# Making Minor Updates

I made one more update to my site, as you might have noticed in Figure 2-72. I added a subscription component to my sidebar. Earlier, my subscription component was shown after each blog.

In the subscribe.js file, I am expecting props now, which will decide whether to show the headings. Update the line marked in bold in Listing 2-16.

***Listing 2-16.*** The Updated subscribe.js File

```
render() {
    let { statusMsg, subscribing } = this.state;
    let btnCTA = subscribing ? "Subscribing" : "Subscribe";
    return (
        <form onSubmit={this.handleSubmit} className={styles.
        EmailListForm}>
            {this.props.heading && <h2>Subscribe to receive updates on
            new posts!</h2>}
```

```
        <div className={styles.Wrapper}>
                ...
                ...
        </div>
    </form>
);
}
```

One of the other changes I made was to make the background transparent in subscribe.module.scss. This change is marked in bold in Listing 2-17.

***Listing 2-17.*** The Updated subscribe.module.scss File

```scss
.EmailListForm {
    display: flex;
    flex-direction: column;
    background: transparent;
    color: #2a2a2a;
    font-family: -apple-system, Helvetica, Arial, sans-serif;
    ...
    ...
    ...
}
```

It's time to update it, first in post.js, and pass the new props as true. These changes are marked in bold in Listing 2-18.

***Listing 2-18.*** The Updated post.js File

```js
        return (
            <Layout {...this.props}>
                    ...
                    ...
                <Subscribe heading={true} />
                <Disqus config={disqusConfig} />
            </Layout>
        );
```

This will now show the updated Subscribe component without any background color after every post, as shown in Figure 2-73.

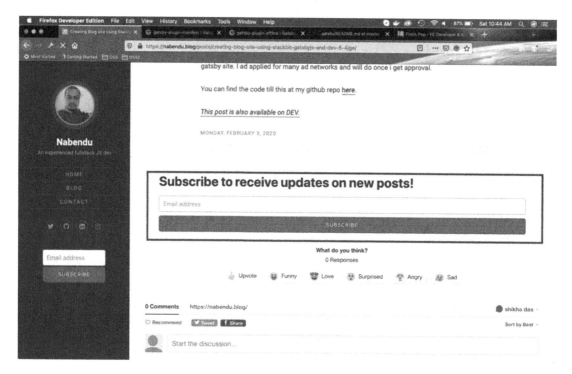

***Figure 2-73.*** *The updated Subscribe button*

To show the Subscribe component in the sidebar, I updated the `Social.js` file. I included it in the file, followed by adding a React fragment, and added it by passing the props heading as `false`. It is marked in bold in Listing 2-19.

***Listing 2-19.*** Social.js

```
import React from 'react';
import _ from 'lodash';
import {Link} from '../utils';
import Subscribe from './subscribe';
import Advert from './Advert';
```

```
export default class Social extends React.Component {
    render() {
        return (

            <div className="social-links">
            ...

            ...
            </div>
            <Advert />
            <Subscribe heading={false} />

        );
    }
}
```

It is showing the mini-subscribe component in the sidebar. Subscribe to my weekly newsletter, which contains the updates on my posts. You can find this code at my GitHub repo.[42]

# Summary

This completes Chapter 2 and the blog site with Stackbit project. You can use this chapter to create your own personal blog site with your dev.to posts. We covered the following topics in this chapter:

- Creating a Gatsby blog site from your dev.to posts using Stackbit

- Buying a domain from namecheap and configuring it

- Adding Gatsby plugins to the site, which add easy feature integration to the site

- Adding advertisements to the site using the Media.net ad network

In the next chapter, we are going to learn how to create a tourism site with a backend system that uses Contentful, an awesome CMS.

---

[42]https://github.com/nabendu82/nabendu-blog

# CHAPTER 3

# Creating a Tourism Site with Contentful: Part One

After creating two sites with GatsbyJS in the past two chapters, it's time to create a site about the World Heritage place in India, known as *Hampi*. We will be using a CMS called Contentful in the project to display the data stored in it. We will also store the blogs in Contentful, which will be used in the site.

## The Setup

Let's head over to a terminal and create a new Gatsby project called gatsbyTourism, using the hello-world starter kit. The command is shown in Listing 3-1.

*Listing 3-1.* The npm install Command

```
gatsby new gatsbyTourism https://github.com/gatsbyjs/gatsby-starter-hello-world
```

Next, we will change to the directory and run gatsby develop (see Listing 3-2) to start our project on the localhost.

*Listing 3-2.* Change the Directory

```
cd gatsbyTourism
gatsby develop
```

It will start our basic hello-world starter, as shown in Figure 3-1, which will just show Hello World! on http://localhost:8000/[1]

---

[1]http://localhost:8000/

© Nabendu Biswas 2021

N. Biswas, *Foundation Gatsby Projects*, https://doi.org/10.1007/978-1-4842-6558-1_3

***Figure 3-1.*** *Hello World*

We will open our code in VSCode. Any page we create inside the `pages` folder will become an endpoint in the browser. We don't have to implement anything like `react-router` here. We will create four pages required for our project—Blog, Contact, Places, and 404.

We can create any type of React component, but we will make functional components as of now, for consistency. The `index.js` and `404.js` files are special pages and are displayed in home and error. We will create the `404.js` file with the content shown in Listing 3-3.

***Listing 3-3.*** The 404.js File

```
import React from "react"

export default function error() {
return (
      <div>
          Error Page
      </div>
   )
}
```

If you move to a nonexistent page, you will see Figure 3-2.

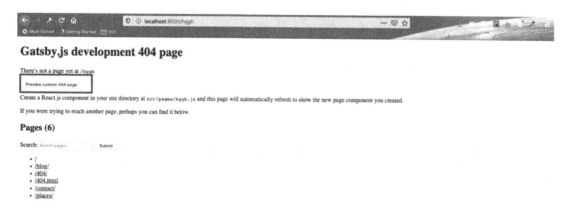

***Figure 3-2.*** *The preview page*

Upon clicking the Preview Custom 404 page, we will get the error page shown in Figure 3-3.

*Figure 3-3.* *The error page*

We will create the blog.js page next, with the contents in Listing 3-4.

*Listing 3-4.* The blog.js Page

```
import React from "react"

export default function blog() {
return (
        <div>
            Blog Page
        </div>
    )
}
```

Now, on moving to http://localhost:8000/blog,[2] we will see our blog page, as shown in Figure 3-4.

*Figure 3-4.* *The blog page*

We will create the contact.js and places.js pages in a similar manner. The contents are shown in Listing 3-5 and Listing 3-6, respectively.

---

[2]http://localhost:8000/blog

***Listing 3-5.*** The contact.js Page

```
import React from "react"

export default function contact() {
return (
        <div>
            Contact Page
        </div>
    )
}
```

***Listing 3-6.*** The places.js Page

```
import React from "react"

export default function places() {
return (
        <div>
            Places Page
        </div>
    )
}
```

Now, let's add navbar and footer components. We will make them inside the components folder, which will be inside the src folder. Place the contents of Listing 3-7 in the Navbar.js file.

***Listing 3-7.*** The Navbar.js File

```
import React from "react"

export default function Navbar() {
return (
        <div>
            Navbar Component
        </div>
    )
}
```

Likewise, place the contents of Listing 3-8 in the `Footer.js` file.

***Listing 3-8.*** The Footer.js File

```
import React from "react"

export default function Footer() {
return (
        <div>
            Footer Component
        </div>
    )
}
```

The most common React way to show these two components on any page is to import them and show it. We will change the `index.js` file with the content in Listing 3-9.

***Listing 3-9.*** The index.js File

```
import React from "react"
import Navbar from "../components/Navbar"
import Footer from "../components/Footer"

export default () => (

<Navbar />
    Hello World!
<Footer />

)
```

Figure 3-5 shows the component that will appear.

***Figure 3-5.*** *Showing the component*

We could do this for every page, but Gatsby provides an easier solution. We will use a Layout component and include the navbar and the footer components there. We will also pass the children props to the Layout component. It will be obvious in a minute why we use this, after we use the Layout component in our pages.

So, create a Layout.js file inside the components folder and place Listing 3-10's contents in that file.

***Listing 3-10.*** The Layout.js File

```
import React from 'react'
import Navbar from './Navbar'
import Footer from './Footer'

const Layout = ({children}) => {
    return (

        <Navbar />
                {children}
          <Footer />

    )
}

export default Layout;
```

Next, let's use this in the index.js file. As you might have noticed, the Layout component wraps all the other things, which is only Hello World! now. These are the children, which is the props passed to the Layout component. Update the index.js file with the contents in Listing 3-11.

***Listing 3-11.*** The index.js File

```
import React from "react"
import Layout from "../components/Layout"

export default () => (
<Layout>
      Hello World!
</Layout>
)
```

The home page is still the same, as shown in Figure 3-6.

**Navbar Component**

Hello World!

**Footer component**

***Figure 3-6.*** *The home page*

We can use the reusable Layout component in all our other pages and they will show the navbar and footer components. Update blog.js with the contents in Listing 3-12.

***Listing 3-12.*** The blog.js File

```
import React from "react"
import Layout from "../components/Layout"

export default function blog() {
return (
        <Layout>
            Blog Page
        </Layout>
    )
}
```

Update places.js with the contents in Listing 3-13.

***Listing 3-13.*** The places.js File

```
import React from "react"
import Layout from "../components/Layout"

export default function places() {
return (
        <Layout>
            Places Page
        </Layout>
    )
}
```

Update contact.js with the contents in Listing 3-14.

***Listing 3-14.*** The contact.js File

```
import React from "react"
import Layout from "../components/Layout"

export default function contact() {
return (
      <Layout>
          Contact Page
      </Layout>
   )
}
```

Update 404.js with the contents in Listing 3-15.

***Listing 3-15.*** The 404.js File

```
import React from "react"
import Layout from "../components/Layout"

export default function error() {
return (
      <Layout>
          Error Page
      </Layout>
   )
}
```

If you use any other path, you will see navbar and footer present there as well, as shown in Figure 3-7.

***Figure 3-7.*** *The blog components*

I hope you learned something new. You can find the code at this[3] link. We don't go through the CSS in this series, as it's a Gatsby series.

The global CSS is in the `layout.css` file, in the `components` directory. You can get the contents from my GitHub[4].

Place an `images` folder inside the `src` folder. The contents are on my GitHub as well.

We also need to import the `layout.css` file in `Layout.js`, which is marked in bold in Listing 3-16.

*Listing 3-16.* The Layout.js File

```
import React from 'react'
import Navbar from './Navbar'
import Footer from './Footer'
import './layout.css'

const Layout = ({children}) => {
    return (

        <Navbar />
            {children}
        <Footer />

    )
}

export default Layout;
```

This will show the home page at `http://localhost:8000/`[5] with the new fonts, as shown in Figure 3-8.

*Figure 3-8.* *The home page with new fonts*

---

[3]https://github.com/nabendu82/gatsbyTourism
[4]https://github.com/nabendu82/gatsbyTourism
[5]http://localhost:8000/

We will now install a package called react-icons, which will help us show nice icons in the project. Go ahead and exit gatsby develop and then npm install on the package, in your project directory, with the command shown in Listing 3-17.

***Listing 3-17.*** The npm install Command

```
npm install --save react-icons
-
```

Make sure to run your gatsby develop again. Next, we will create a folder of constants inside src and create two files (links.js and social-icons.js) inside that folder.

The contents of links.js are shown in Listing 3-18. We will use this code at various places in this project to navigate to different links.

***Listing 3-18.*** The links.js File

```
export default [
  {
    path: "/",
    text: "home",
  },
  {
    path: "/places",
    text: "places",
  },
  {
    path: "/blog",
    text: "blog",
  },
  {
    path: "/contact",
    text: "contact",
  }
]
```

The contents of social-icons.js are in Listing 3-19. It contains our icons from react-icons, which we will show at various places in this project.

***Listing 3-19.***  The social-icons.js File

```
import React from "react"
import { FaFacebook, FaTwitterSquare, FaInstagram } from "react-icons/fa"

export default [
  {
    icon: <FaFacebook />,
    url: "https://facebook.com/nabendu.biswas.77",
  },
  {
    icon: <FaTwitterSquare />,
    url: "https://twitter.com/nabendu82",
  },
  {
    icon: <FaInstagram />,
    url: "https://www.instagram.com/nabendu82/",
  },
]
```

Next, we will create a `css` folder inside our `src` folder. Place the `navbar.module.css` file inside it. You can get the contents from Listing 3-20.

***Listing 3-20.***  The navbar.module.css File

```
.nav-header {
  display: flex;
  justify-content: space-between;
  align-items: center;
  padding: 1rem 1.25rem;
}
.brand-logo {
  width: 170px;
  height: 40px;
}
```

```css
.logo-btn {
  background: transparent;
  border: none;
  outline: none;
}
.logo-btn:hover {
  cursor: pointer;
}
.logo-icon {
  color: var(--primaryColor);
  font-size: 1.5rem;
}

.nav-links {
  list-style-type: none;
  transition: var(--mainTransition);
  height: 0;
  overflow: hidden;
}
.show-nav {
  height: 268px;
}
.nav-links a {
  display: block;
  padding: 1rem 1.25rem;
  text-decoration: none;
  text-transform: capitalize;
  color: var(--mainBlack);
  transition: var(--mainTransition);
  font-weight: bold;
  letter-spacing: var(--mainSpacing);
}
.nav-links a:hover {
  color: var(--primaryColor);
}
```

```css
.nav-social-links {
  display: none;
}
@media screen and (min-width: 576px) {
  .navbar {
    padding: 0 2rem;
  }
}

@media screen and (min-width: 992px) {
  .logo-btn {
    display: none;
  }
  .nav-center {
    max-width: 1170px;
    margin: 0 auto;
    display: flex;
    justify-content: space-between;
    align-items: center;
  }
  .nav-links {
    height: auto;
    display: flex;
  }
  .nav-social-links {
    display: flex;
    line-height: 0;
  }
  .nav-social-links a {
    color: var(--primaryColor);
    margin: 0 0.5rem;
    font-size: 1.2rem;
    transition: var(--mainTransition);
  }
```

```
.nav-social-links a:hover {
  color: var(--mainBlack);
  transform: translateY(-5px);
  }
}
```

# Navbar and Footer

Let's start creating the navbar component. Go ahead and update your Navbar.js file with Listing 3-21.

*Listing 3-21.* The Updated Navbar.js File

```
import React, { useState } from "react"
import { Link } from "gatsby"
import styles from "../css/navbar.module.css"
import { FaAlignRight } from "react-icons/fa"
import links from "../constants/links"
import socialIcons from "../constants/social-icons"
import logo from "../images/logo.png"
const Navbar = () => {
    const [isOpen, setNav] = useState(false);
    const toggleNav = () => {
        setNav(isOpen => !isOpen)
    }

    return (
        <nav className={styles.navbar}>
            <div className={styles.navCenter}>
                <div className={styles.navHeader}>
                    <img src={logo} className={styles.brandLogo}
                    alt="backroads logo" />
                    <button type="button" className={styles.logoBtn}
                    onClick={toggleNav}>
                        <FaAlignRight className={styles.logoIcon} />
                    </button>
```

```
        </div>
        <ul className={isOpen ? `${styles.navLinks} ${styles.showNav}` :
        `${styles.navLinks}`}>
            {links.map((item, index) => {
                return (
                    <li key={index}>
                        <Link  to={item.path}>{item.text}</Link>
                    </li>
                )
            })}
        </ul>
        <div className={styles.navSocialLinks}>
            {socialIcons.map((item, index) => {
                return (
                    <a key={index} href={item.url} target="_blank"
                    rel="noopener noreferrer">
                        {item.icon}
                    </a>
                )
            })}
        </div>
        </div>
    </nav>
    )
}

export default Navbar
```

Here, we are using the useState hook to toggle our links on a smaller screen. You can learn more about hooks from this post: "Understanding React Hooks by Building a Simple App"[6]. First we show a react-icon FaAlignRight on a smaller screen. When the user clicks the button, we call the toggleNav function, which will set isOpen to true. When isOpen is true we will be loading different CSS classes, which will basically open a drawer to show the links on a smaller screen, as shown in Figure 3-9.

---

[6]https://dev.to/nabendu82/understanding-react-hooks-by-building-a-simple-app-4i6d

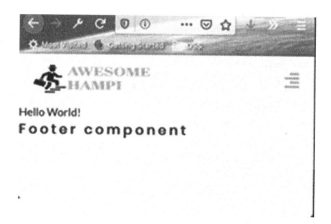

***Figure 3-9.*** *The smaller screen*

On a desktop, we get the whole menu and the `react-icon` will be hidden, as shown in Figure 3-10.

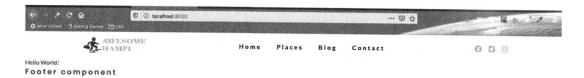

***Figure 3-10.*** *Navbar on a desktop*

We will create a footer first. Inside the `css` folder, add an `footer.module.css` file. You can get the contents from Listing 3-22.

***Listing 3-22.*** The footer.module.css File

```
.footer {
  margin-top: auto;
  background: var(--mainBlack);
  padding: 2rem;
  text-align: center;
  color: var(--mainWhite);
}
.links a {
  display: inline-block;
  text-decoration: none;
```

```
  text-transform: uppercase;
  color: var(--mainWhite);
  margin: 0.5rem 1rem;
  letter-spacing: var(--mainSpacing);
  transition: var(--mainTransition);
  font-weight: bold;
}
.links a:hover {
  color: var(--primaryColor);
}
.icons a {
  display: inline-block;
  margin: 1rem;
  font-size: 1.3rem;
  color: var(--mainWhite);
  transition: var(--mainTransition);
}
.icons a:hover {
  color: var(--primaryColor);
}
.copyright {
  text-transform: capitalize;
  letter-spacing: var(--mainSpacing);
  line-height: 2;
}
```

Next, we will update our Footer.js component to use this CSS. We are just mapping through our links and social icons from the constant files and displaying them. We also have a copyright section. The contents are shown in Listing 3-23.

**Listing 3-23.** The Footer.js File

```
import React from "react"
import styles from "../css/footer.module.css"
import links from "../constants/links"
import socialIcons from "../constants/social-icons"
import { Link } from "gatsby"
```

```
const Footer = () => {
return (
    <footer className={styles.footer}>
        <div className={styles.links}>
        {links.map((item, index) => {
            return (
            <Link key={index} to={item.path}>
                {item.text}
            </Link>
            )
        })}
        </div>
        <div className={styles.icons}>
        {socialIcons.map((item, index) => {
            return (
    <a key={index} href={item.url} target="_blank" rel="noopener
    noreferrer">{item.icon}</a>
            )
        })}
        </div>
        <div className={styles.copyright}>
            copyright &copy; Amazing Hampi {new Date().getFullYear()} all
            rights reserved
        </div>
    </footer>
)
}

export default Footer;
```

It will show our footer in desktop view, as shown in Figure 3-11.

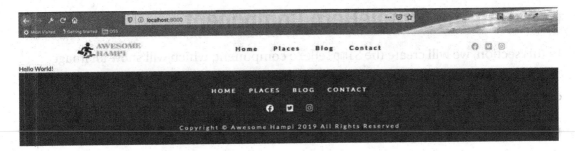

***Figure 3-11.*** *Footer on a desktop*

The footer is very responsive in the mobile view, as shown in Figure 3-12.

***Figure 3-12.*** *Footer in mobile view*

# Creating the SimpleHero Component

In this section, we will create the `SimpleHero` component, which will show an image covering the whole home page. Create a new file called `SimpleHero.js` inside the `components` directory. The contents are shown in Listing 3-24.

***Listing 3-24.*** The SimpleHero.js File

```
import React from "react"

const SimpleHero = ({ children }) => {
  return <header className="defaultHero">{children}</header>
}

export default SimpleHero
```

One of the main things to check in the `SimpleHero` component is the `defaultHero` class. It comes from the `layout.css` file. Here, we are using `min-height` to display it in the whole page, minus the header. We are also using `linear-gradient` here. Then we are using `display: flex`, which will display the center text. You need to add the Listing 3-25 contents to the `layout.css` file.

***Listing 3-25.*** The layout.css File

```
.defaultHero {
  min-height: calc(100vh - 62px);
  background: linear-gradient(rgba(63, 208, 212, 0.7), rgba(0, 0, 0, 0.7)),
    url("../images/defaultBcg.jpeg") center/cover no-repeat;
  display: flex;
  justify-content: center;
  align-items: center;
}
```

We will then update the `index.js` page to show this component, using the code in Listing 3-26.

*Listing 3-26.* The Updated index.js File

```
import React from "react"
import Layout from "../components/Layout"
import SimpleHero from "../components/SimpleHero"

export default () => (
    <Layout>
        <SimpleHero />
    </Layout>
)
```

This file will show the huge image on the home page, as you can see in Figure 3-13.

*Figure 3-13.  Huge image on the home page*

After this, we will create a banner that will contain a large heading, then a paragraph and a large button to take us to the Places page. Go ahead and create `banner.module. css` inside the `css` folder and the code in Listing 3-27 to it.

***Listing 3-27.*** The banner.module.css File

```css
.banner {
  text-align: center;
  letter-spacing: var(--mainSpacing);
  color: var(--mainWhite);
}
.banner h1 {
  font-size: 3.3rem;
  text-transform: uppercase;
  margin-bottom: 2rem;
  padding: 0 1rem;
  letter-spacing: 6px;
}
.banner p {
  width: 85%;
  margin: 0 auto;
  margin-bottom: 2rem;
}
@media screen and (min-width: 768px) {
  .banner h1 {
    font-size: 4.5rem;
  }
  .banner p {
    width: 70%;
  }
}
```

Next, we will create Banner.js inside the components folder and it will contain the code in Listing 3-28. We can pass the title, info, and children props to it.

***Listing 3-28.*** The Banner.js File

```js
import React from "react"
import styles from "../css/banner.module.css"
const Banner = ({ title, info, children }) => {
  return (
```

```
    <div className={styles.banner}>
      <h1>{title}</h1>
      <p>{info}</p>
      {children}
    </div>
  )
}

export default Banner
```

Now, we will add the banner component to the index.js file and pass the required props (title and info). Also, we are passing a Link as children. The updated code is marked in bold in Listing 3-29.

***Listing 3-29.*** The index.js File

```
import React from "react"
import Layout from "../components/Layout"
import SimpleHero from "../components/SimpleHero"
import Banner from "../components/Banner"
import { Link } from "gatsby"

export default () => (
    <Layout>
        <SimpleHero>
            <Banner  title="Amazing Hampi"  info="Come and Explore Hampi,
            the city of ruins, which is a UNESCO World Heritage Site.">
                <Link to="/places" className="btn-white">explore places
                </Link>
            </Banner>
        </SimpleHero>
    </Layout>
)
```

This will show our Banner text inside the large image, as shown in Figure 3-14.

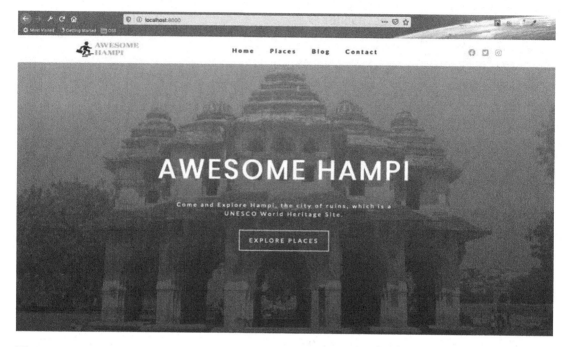

***Figure 3-14.*** *Banner text*

Next, we update our Error component. Go ahead and create error.module.css inside the css folder and add the code in Listing 3-30 to it.

***Listing 3-30.*** The error.module.css File

```css
.error {
  background: var(--primaryColor);
  min-height: calc(100vh - 62px);
  display: flex;
  justify-content: center;
  align-items: center;
}
```

Next, update the 404.js page with the code in Listing 3-31. As you might have noticed, we are reusing the Banner component.

***Listing 3-31.*** The 404.js File

```js
import React from "react"
import Layout from "../components/Layout"
```

```
import styles from "../css/error.module.css"
import { Link } from "gatsby"
import Banner from "../components/Banner"

export default function error() {
return (
    <Layout>
        <header className={styles.error}>
        <Banner title="oops it's a dead end">
            <Link to="/" className="btn-white">
                back to home page
            </Link>
        </Banner>
        </header>
    </Layout>
     )
}
```

When we go to any nonexistent page, the text in Figure 3-15 will be displayed.

*Figure 3-15.* *The dead end page*

We will use `styled-components` in this post to style our project. Install the `gatsby-plugin-styled-components` plugin in the project.

As per the official document,[7] we need to install these packages first, with the command in Listing 3-32.

***Listing 3-32.*** The npm install Command

```
npm install --save gatsby-plugin-styled-components styled-components babel-
plugin-styled-components
1
```

Head over to your project root directory and stop the `gatsby develop` and then run `npm install`.

Then head over to the `gatsby-config.js` file in the root directory and add the plugin in Listing 3-33.

***Listing 3-33.*** The gatsby-config.js File

```
module.exports = {
        plugins: [`gatsby-plugin-styled-components`]
}
```

Next, head over to your terminal and run the `gatsby develop` again.

# About Section

Next, we will create the About Hampi section in the home page. Add the `about.module.css` file to the `css` folder. You can get the content from Listing 3-34.

***Listing 3-34.*** The about.module.css File

```
.about {
  padding: 4rem 0;
}
.about-center {
  width: 80vw;
```

---

[7]https://www.gatsbyjs.org/packages/gatsby-plugin-styled-components/

```css
  margin: 0 auto;
}
.about-img {
  margin: 3rem 0;
}
.about-info {
  margin-top: 3rem;
}
.about-img {
  position: relative;
}

.about-img img {
  width: 100%;
  display: block;
  box-shadow: var(--lightShadow);
}
.about-img div {
  box-shadow: var(--lightShadow);
}
.about-info h4 {
  font-size: 1.9rem;
  text-transform: uppercase;
}

@media screen and (min-width: 768px) {
  .about-center {
    display: grid;
    grid-template-columns: 1fr 1fr;
    grid-column-gap: 3rem;
    align-items: center;
    margin-top: 3rem;
  }

  .about-img,
  .about-info {
```

```
      margin: 0;
    }
    .about-img img {
      max-height: 500px;
    }
    .img-container {
      max-height: 500px;
    }
    .about-info p {
      width: 80%;
    }
}
@media screen and (min-width: 992px) {
    .img-container::before {
      content: "";
      position: absolute;
      width: 100%;
      height: 100%;
      border: 3px solid var(--primaryColor);
      box-sizing: border-box;
      top: -16px;
      left: -16px;
      z-index: -1;
    }
}

@media screen and (min-width: 1200px) {
    .about-center {
      width: 95vw;
      max-width: 1170px;
    }
}
```

Next, we will create the About section inside the `components` folder. We will create another folder, called `Home`, inside it and the `About.js` file inside it. The contents are shown in Listing 3-35.

***Listing 3-35.*** The About.js File

```
import React from "react"
import Title from "../Title"

const About = () => {
    return (
        <div>
            About Component
            <Title title="about" subtitle="hampi" />
        </div>
    )
}

export default About
```

We will have a general-purpose Title component inside About, in which we are using styled-components. We are styling the two words differently, which we had passed as props from the About component. Create a file called `Title.js` inside the `components` folder and put the code in Listing 3-36 into it.

***Listing 3-36.*** The Title.js File

```
import React from "react"
import styled from "styled-components"
const Title = ({ title, subtitle }) => {
  return (
    <TitleWrapper>
      <h4>
        <span className="title">{title}</span>
        <span>{subtitle}</span>
      </h4>
    </TitleWrapper>
  )
}

const TitleWrapper = styled.div`
  text-transform: uppercase;
  font-size: 2.3rem;
```

```
    margin-bottom: 2rem;
    h4 {
      text-align: center;
      letter-spacing: 7px;
      color: var(--primaryColor);
    }
    .title {
      color: var(--mainBlack);
    }
    span {
      display: block;
    }
    @media (min-width: 576px) {
      span {
        display: inline-block;
        margin: 0 0.35rem;
      }
    }
  }
`

export default Title
```

Now, let's show the About component in `index.js`. The updated code is marked in bold in Listing 3-37.

***Listing 3-37.*** The index.js File

```
import React from "react"
import Layout from "../components/Layout"
import SimpleHero from "../components/SimpleHero"
import Banner from "../components/Banner"
import About from "../components/Home/About"
import { Link } from "gatsby"

export default () => (
    <Layout>
        <SimpleHero>
            <Banner
```

```
            title="Amazing Hampi"
            info="Come and Explore Hampi, the city of ruins, which is a
            UNESCO World Heritage Site."
        >
            <Link to="/places" className="btn-white">explore places
            </Link>
        </Banner>
    </SimpleHero>
    <About />
</Layout>
)
```

It will show the About component, which contains the Title component in our home page, as shown in Figure 3-16.

***Figure 3-16.*** *Showing the title only*

Next, we will complete our About component, in which we will show an image, a subtitle, two paragraphs, and a button. Update the About.js file with Listing 3-38.

***Listing 3-38.*** The About.js File

```
import React from "react"
import Title from "../Title"
import styles from "../../css/about.module.css"
import img from "../../images/defaultBcg.jpeg"

const About = () => {
  return (
    <section className={styles.about}>
      <Title title="about" subtitle="hampi" />
      <div className={styles.aboutCenter}>
        <article className={styles.aboutImg}>
          <div className={styles.imgContainer}>
            <img src={img} alt="about company" />
          </div>
        </article>
        <article className={styles.aboutInfo}>
          <h4>The abode of bygone ruins</h4>
          <p>
          Hampi, the city of ruins, is a UNESCO World Heritage Site.
          Situated in the shadowed depth of hills and valleys in the state
          of Karnataka, this place is a historical delight for travellers.
          </p>
          <p>
          Surrounded by 500 ancient monuments, beautiful temples, bustling
          street markets, bastions, treasury building and captivating
          remains of Vijayanagar Empire, Hampi is a backpacker's delight.
          </p>
          <a href="https://en.wikipedia.org/wiki/Hampi" className="btn-
          primary" target="_blank" rel="noopener noreferrer">
            read more
          </a>
        </article>
```

```
    </div>
  </section>
)
}

export default About
```

It will show our beautiful About Hampi section, as shown in Figure 3-17.

**Figure 3-17.** *The About Hampi section*

# Creating a Hot Tips Section

Next, we will create the Hot Tips section in the home page. Add the `tips.module.css` file to the `css` folder. The contents are shown in Listing 3-39.

**Listing 3-39.** The tips.module.css File

```
.tips {
  background: var(--mainGrey);
  padding: 4rem 0;
}
```

```css
.center {
  width: 80vw;
  margin: 0 auto;
  display: grid;
  grid-template-columns: repeat(auto-fit, minmax(250px, 1fr));
  grid-column-gap: 2rem;
}
.tip {
  margin: 2rem 0;
  text-align: center;
}
.tip span {
  background: var(--primaryColor);
  padding: 0.5rem;
  display: inline-block;
  font-size: 2rem;
  margin-bottom: 1.5rem;
}
.tip h4 {
  text-transform: uppercase;
}
```

Then add `tips.js` inside the `constants` folder and add the content from Listing 3-40.

***Listing 3-40.*** The tips.js File

```javascript
import React from "react"
import { FaWallet, FaCamera, FaSocks } from "react-icons/fa"

export default [
  {
    icon: <FaWallet />,
    title: "saving money",
    text: "Travel by train from Bangalore, instead of taxi or bus.",
  },
  {
    icon: <FaCamera />,
```

```
    title: "top attractions",
    text: "Top attractions are Vittala Temple, Virupaksha Temple,
    Achyutaraya Temple.",
  },
  {
    icon: <FaSocks />,
    title: "amazing comfort",
    text: "Stay in Oyo rooms, instead of Airbnb or some travel site.",
  },
]
```

Now, we will add a `Tips.js` file inside the `components->`Home folder. As you can see, we are reusing the Title component here. Also, we are mapping through the `tips` constant to display all its items. The contents are shown in Listing 3-41.

***Listing 3-41.*** The Tips.js File

```
import React from "react"
import Title from "../Title"
import styles from "../../css/tips.module.css"
import tips from "../../constants/tips"

const Tips = () => {
  return (
    <section className={styles.tips}>
      <Title title="hot" subtitle="tips" />
      <div className={styles.center}>
        {tips.map((item, index) => {
          return (
            <article key={index} className={styles.tip}>
              <span>{item.icon}</span>
              <h4>{item.title}</h4>
              <p>{item.text}</p>
            </article>
          )
        })}
      </div>
```

```
    </section>
  )
}

export default Tips
```

Let's show the `Tips` component in the `index.js` file. The updated code is marked in bold in Listing 3-42.

***Listing 3-42.*** The index.js File

```
import React from "react"
import Layout from "../components/Layout"
import SimpleHero from "../components/SimpleHero"
import Banner from "../components/Banner"
import About from "../components/Home/About"
import Tips from "../components/Home/Tips"
import { Link } from "gatsby"

export default () => (
    <Layout>
        <SimpleHero>
            <Banner
                title="Amazing Hampi"
                info="Come and Explore Hampi, the city of ruins, which is a
                UNESCO World Heritage Site."
            >
                <Link to="/places" className="btn-white">explore places
                </Link>
            </Banner>
        </SimpleHero>
        <About />
        <Tips />
    </Layout>
)
```

This will show the Hot Tips section on the home page, as shown in Figure 3-18.

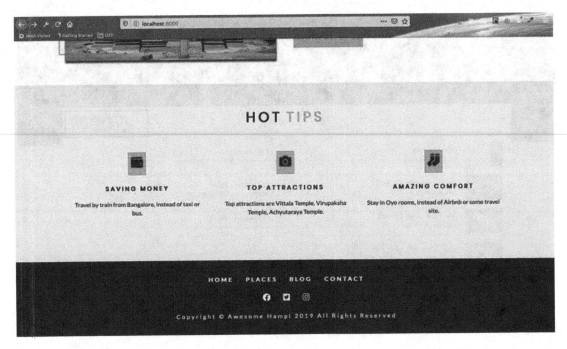

***Figure 3-18.*** *The Hot Tips section*

# Creating a Deployment Site

In this section, we will learn how to do continuous deployment using Netlify. It is a great service to host your Gatsby project. Since this project is already on GitHub,[8] I simply have to log in to my Netlify and link it to host the site.

Log in to your Netlify[9] account or create one. Since I already have a Netlify account and have many sites hosted on it, my login screen is shown in Figure 3-19. Click the New Site from Git button, shown in Figure 3-19.

---

[8]https://github.com/nabendu82/gatsbyTourism
[9]https://www.netlify.com/

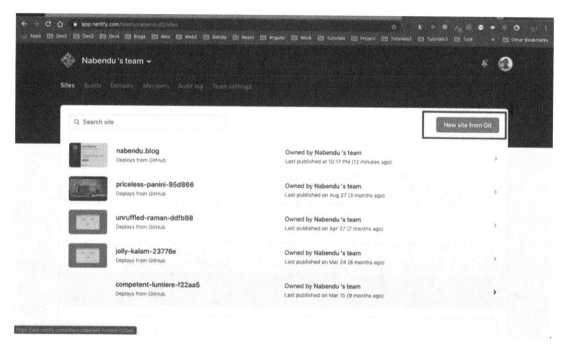

***Figure 3-19.*** *Netlify*

Since, my project is hosted on Github, I will click the same. It is shown in Figure 3-20.

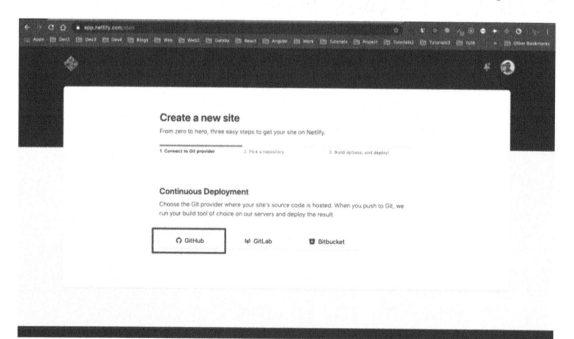

***Figure 3-20.*** *The GitHub site*

It will open a popup window and ask you to authorize with your GitHub credentials for the first time. Since I was already authorized, it took me directly to this screen, which shows all my GitHub repos, shown in Figure 3-21.

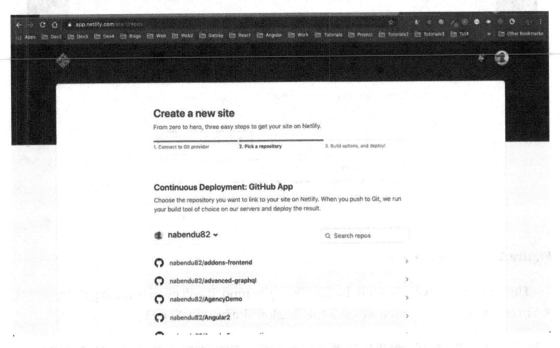

*Figure 3-21. GitHub repos*

I have many repos so I have to search for the repo and then click it, as shown in Figure 3-22.

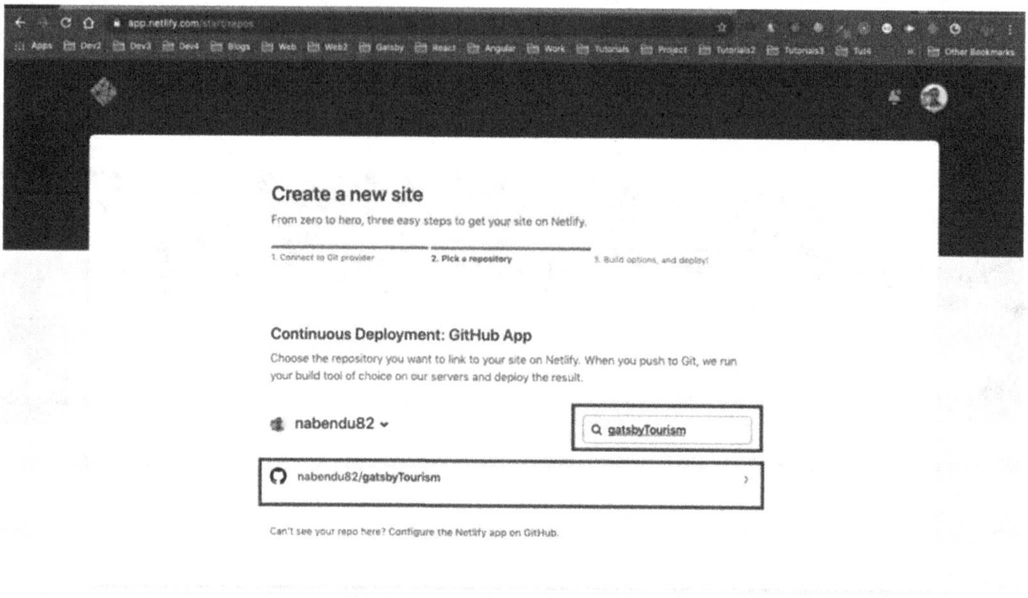

***Figure 3-22.*** *Tourism repo*

The next screen will show all the details of the repo. It will even run the `gatsby build` command for us, once we click the Deploy Site button. See Figure 3-23.

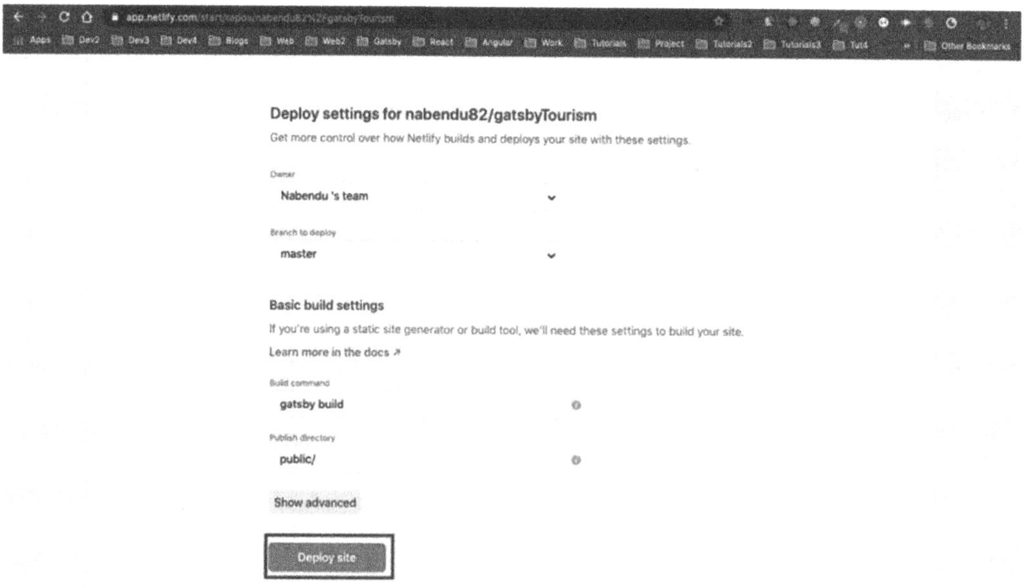

***Figure 3-23.*** *The gatsby build command*

The next page will show the random site name in which Netlify is deploying. We can click the Site Settings button to change the site name to a more suitable name, as shown in Figure 3-24.

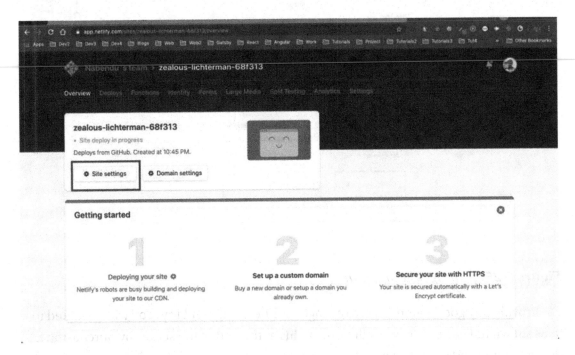

**Figure 3-24.** *Random site*

Click the Change Site Name button, as shown in Figure 3-25.

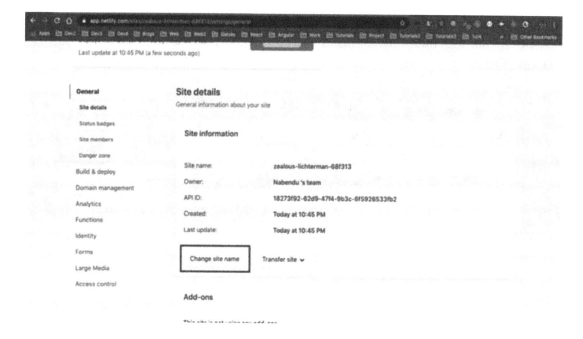

***Figure 3-25.*** *Change the site name*

Provide any good name. I use `amazinghampi` here, but `netlify.com` will be added to it, as shown in Figure 3-26. We will remove this at the end of the series, by purchasing a domain name and changing it.

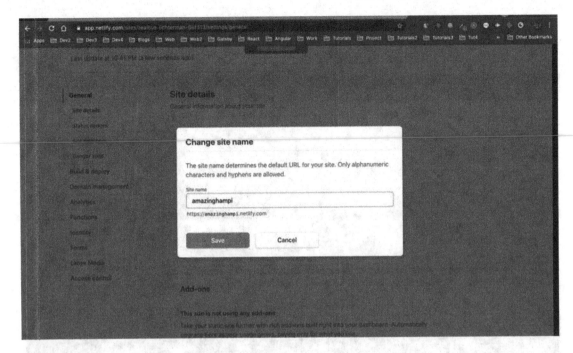

**Figure 3-26.** *Save the site with a new name*

Once you click the Save button, the site will be deployed, as shown in Figure 3-27.

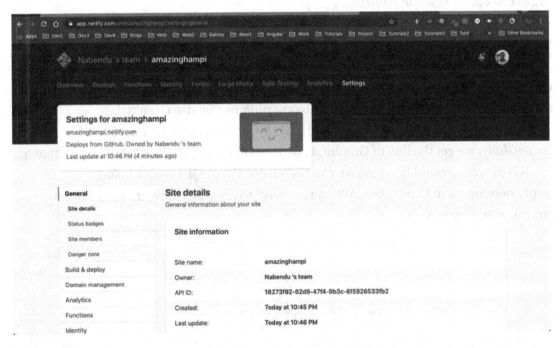

**Figure 3-27.** *The site has been deployed*

Click the deployed site. It is now on the Internet, as shown in Figure 3-28. Now, whenever you push some new code in GitHub, Netlify will directly update the site.

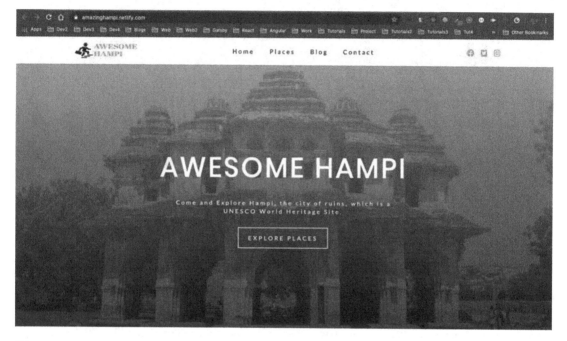

***Figure 3-28.*** *Awesome Hampi*

# Image Optimization

Up to this moment, we used React to do things in Gatsby. But the real power of Gatsby comes from GraphQL and with using different plugins that use GraphQL.

When we run any Gatsby project with `gatsby develop` and, when it compiles successfully, we get the link of GraphiQL, which is `http://localhost:8000/___graphql`.

It is the playground in which we can test all our GraphQL queries before implementing them in our code. We can open it[10] in the web browser and it will be shown, as in Figure 3-29.

---

[10]`http://localhost:8000/graphql`

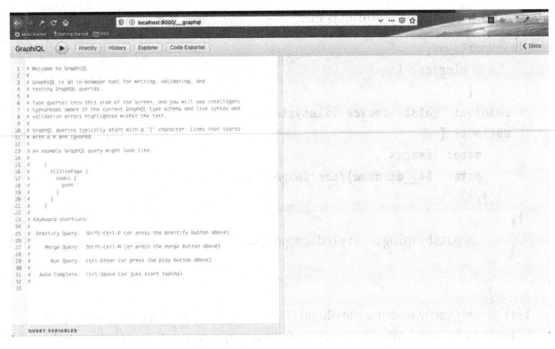

***Figure 3-29.***  *Open it in the browser*

Here, we will test our GraphQL queries before using them by StaticQuery or PageQuery in the Gatsby code. We will be using image optimization in our project through GraphQL, as that is one of the main reasons that sites load slowly.

But before we do that, we need to install some plugins and do some configurations.

We need to install gatsby-source-filesystem first. This plugin is for using data in your Gatsby application from a local filesystem. In our case, this will be images. The docs can be found here[11]. As per the docs, we need to npm install the plugin in our project directory.

Head over to the project directory and stop any gatsby develop, if any is running. Run the command in Listing 3-43 to install the plugin.

***Listing 3-43.***  The npm install Command

```
npm install --save gatsby-source-filesystem
```

Next, we will update our gatsby-config.js file to use this plugin to get our images folder path. The updated code is marked in bold in Listing 3-44.

---

[11]https://www.gatsbyjs.org/packages/gatsby-source-filesystem/

***Listing 3-44.*** The gatsby-config.js File

```
module.exports = {
            plugins: [
          {
    resolve: `gatsby-source-filesystem`,
    options: {
        name: `images`,
        path: `${__dirname}/src/images/`,
       },
    },
            `gatsby-plugin-styled-components`
              ]
}
```

Let's quickly verify whether the plugin is working properly. Head over to GraphiQL and refresh the browser. After that, run the following query. It will give us the number of files in the images folder. We have six files in the images folder, so it will give the output as 6, as shown in Figure 3-30.

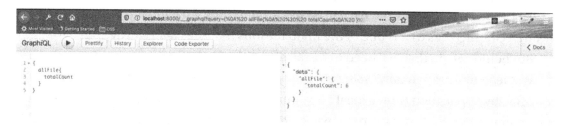

***Figure 3-30.*** *GraphiQL*

The gatsby-source-filesystem file also provides us with another query called file, which provides the details of any file present in the images folder, as shown in Figure 3-31.

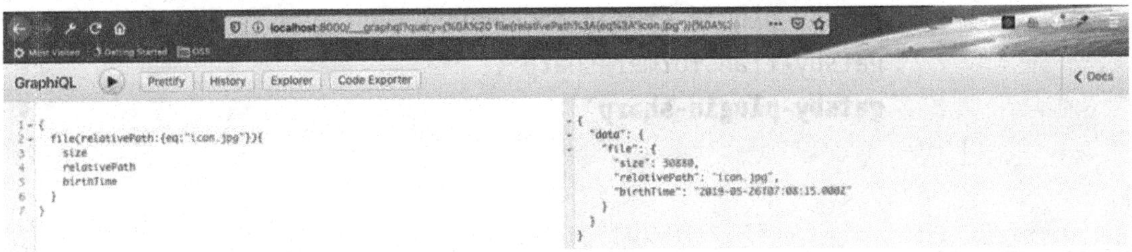

*Figure 3-31.*  *The file query*

Next, we will install the `gatsby-image`[12] plugin. This is the plugin that we will use in our project to speed up image loading.

As per the docs[13], we have to do two `npm  installs`. The command is shown in Listing 3-45.

*Listing 3-45.*  The npm install Command

```
npm install --save gatsby-image
npm install --save gatsby-transformer-sharp gatsby-plugin-sharp
```

After the installs are complete, update the **gatsby-config.js** file. The updated code is marked in bold in Listing 3-46.

*Listing 3-46.*  The gatsby-config.js File

```
module.exports = {
        plugins: [
        {
    resolve: `gatsby-source-filesystem`,
    options: {
      name: `images`,
      path: `${__dirname}/src/images/`,
    },
  },
```

---

[12]https://www.gatsbyjs.org/packages/gatsby-image/

[13]https://www.gatsbyjs.org/packages/gatsby-image/

```
            `gatsby-plugin-styled-components`,
            `gatsby-transformer-sharp`,
            `gatsby-plugin-sharp`
        ]
}
```

Next, start the project by running gatsby develop. As per the documentation, we need to use the gatsby-image plugin shown in Figure 3-32. We can have two types of images—fixed or fluid.

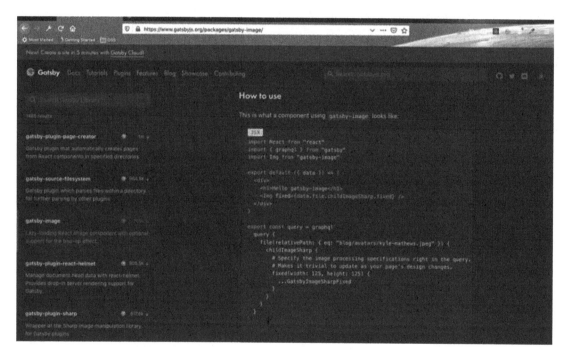

***Figure 3-32.***  *How to use the component*

We can use the fragments, shown in Figure 3-33, in place of GatsbyImageSharpFixed.

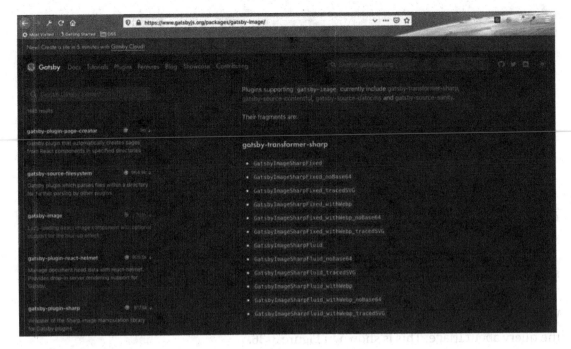

***Figure 3-33.*** *These fragments can be used*

We will use this later in our project. For now, we can check the query on the GraphiQL, as shown in Figure 3-34.

***Figure 3-34.*** *GraphiQL*

Let's also check for the fluid one. We can check this from the same `file` code, but we need to give aliases, as the name is the same. This is shown in Figure 3-35.

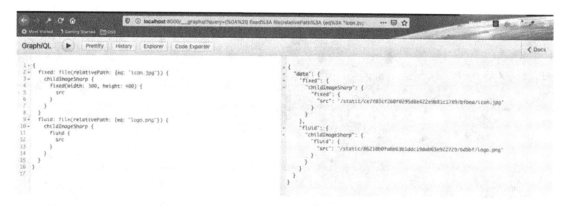

***Figure 3-35.*** *fixed and fluid*

As you can see in Figure 3-35, you cannot use the fragments in GraphiQL and use `src`. This is a limitation as of now, but we can use them without any error in our code.

It's time to use `gatsby-image` in the About component, which is on the home page. We will again create our GraphQL query in GraphiQL. Notice that we have also named the query `aboutImage`. This is shown in Figure 3-36.

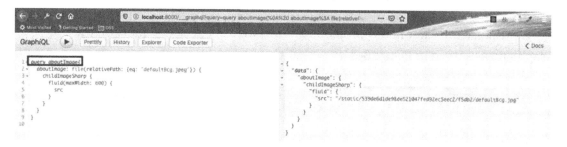

***Figure 3-36.*** *The aboutImage query*

Next, we will move to About component and paste our query from GraphiQL, to a `getAbout` variable. Also, notice that we replaced `src` with a fluid fragment `GatsbyImageSharpFluid_-tracedSVG`.

I did some required `imports` at the top of the file and commented out the earlier `import`, which was used to display the image. After that, we are destructuring `aboutImage` and using `useStaticQuery`, which is a hook provided by Gatsby.

Finally, we use `Img` from `gatsby-image` to display the image. The updates are marked in bold in Listing 3-47.

***Listing 3-47.*** The About.js File

```
import React from "react"
import Title from "../Title"
import styles from "../../css/about.module.css"
//import img from "../../images/defaultBcg.jpeg"
import { useStaticQuery, graphql } from 'gatsby'
import Img from 'gatsby-image'

const getAbout = graphql`
query aboutImage{
  aboutImage: file(relativePath: {eq: "defaultBcg.jpeg"}) {
    childImageSharp {
      fluid(maxWidth: 600) {
        ...GatsbyImageSharpFluid_tracedSVG
      }
    }
  }
}
`;

const About = () => {
  const { aboutImage } = useStaticQuery(getAbout);
  return (
    <section className={styles.about}>
      <Title title="about" subtitle="hampi" />
      <div className={styles.aboutCenter}>
        <article className={styles.aboutImg}>
          <div className={styles.imgContainer}>
            {/* <img src={img} alt="about company" /> */}
            <Img fluid={aboutImage.childImageSharp.fluid} alt="landscape" />
          </div>
        </article>
        <article className={styles.aboutInfo}>
          ...
          ...
```

```
      </article>
    </div>
  </section>
)
}
```

```
export default About
```

When you see the output on your browser, you can see the About component displaying the same image, as shown in Figure 3-37. But what you see is an optimized image, which loads very quickly on all screens with even with slow Internet speeds.

**ABOUT** HAMPI

**THE ABODE OF BYGONE RUINS**

Hampi, the city of ruins, is a UNESCO World Heritage Site.Situated in the shadowed depth of hills and valleys in the state of Karnataka, this place is a historical delight for travellers.

Surrounded by 500 ancient monuments, beautiful temples, bustling street markets, bastions, treasury building and captivating remains of Vijayanagar Empire, Hampi is a backpacker's delight.

READ MORE

***Figure 3-37.*** *The new image*

# Background Image Optimization

In this section, we will start optimizing the background images on the site. Right now we have only one big background image on the home page. For this, we will use the gatsby-background-image plugin. The doc is here[14].

Stop the gatsby develop and npm install the plugin by running npm install --save gatsby-background-image from the terminal. Next, start the development server using gatsby develop. After that, head over to your code editor and create a new file called StyledHero.js inside it.

---

[14]https://www.gatsbyjs.org/packages/gatsby-background-image/

Put the contents in Listing 3-48 in the StyledHero.js file. We are making StyledHero.js a general-purpose component, which can be used in all pages for the large image. All of the code for the component is taken from the docs[15] of the gatsby-background-image plugin.

***Listing 3-48.*** The StyledHero.js File

```
import React from 'react'
import styled from 'styled-components'
import BackgroundImage from 'gatsby-background-image'

const StyledHero = ({ img, className, children, home }) => {
    return (
        <BackgroundImage className={className} fluid={img} home={home}>
            {children}
        </BackgroundImage>
    )
}

export default styled(StyledHero)`
    min-height:${props => props.home ? 'calc(100vh - 62px)': '50vh'};
    background:${props => props.home ? 'linear-gradient(rgba(63, 208,
    212, 0.7), rgba(0, 0, 0, 0.7))': 'none'};
    background-position: center;
    background-size: cover;
    opacity: 1 !important;
    display: flex;
    justify-content: center;
    align-items: center;
`
```

We are using one additional props in our component, which is home. Our home page will also contain a linear gradient and the size of the image will cover the entire page.

Now let's render StyledHero on the home page. Move over to index.js and replace SimpleHero with StyledHero, as marked in bold in Listing 3-49.

---

[15]https://www.gatsbyjs.org/packages/gatsby-background-image/

***Listing 3-49.*** The index.js File

```
import React from "react"
import Layout from "../components/Layout"
import StyledHero from "../components/StyledHero"
import Banner from "../components/Banner"
import About from "../components/Home/About"
import Tips from "../components/Home/Tips"
import { Link } from "gatsby"

export default () => (
    <Layout>
        <StyledHero>
            <Banner
                title="Amazing Hampi"
                info="Come and Explore Hampi, the city of ruins, which is a
                UNESCO World Heritage Site."
            >
                <Link to="/places" className="btn-white">explore places
                </Link>
            </Banner>
        </StyledHero>
        <About />
        <Tips />
    </Layout>
)
```

Next, we will create a query to display the images in GraphiQL, as shown in Figure 3-38.

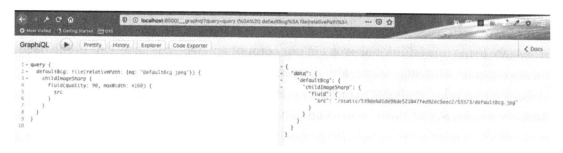

***Figure 3-38.*** *GraphiQL*

Earlier we used StaticQuery, but we will be using PageQuery because index.js is a page. Here, we are using the query we created in our GraphiQL and then passing it as props to our StyledHero component. The updated code is marked in bold in Listing 3-50.

*Listing 3-50.* The index.js File

```
import React from "react"
import Layout from "../components/Layout"
import StyledHero from "../components/StyledHero"
import Banner from "../components/Banner"
import About from "../components/Home/About"
import Tips from "../components/Home/Tips"
import { Link } from "gatsby"
import { graphql } from 'gatsby'

export const query = graphql`
query {
    defaultBcg: file(relativePath: {eq: "defaultBcg.jpeg"}) {
        childImageSharp {
            fluid(quality: 90, maxWidth: 4160) {
                ...GatsbyImageSharpFluid_withWebp
            }
        }
    }
}
`;

export default ({ data }) => (
    <Layout>
        <StyledHero home="true" img={data.defaultBcg.childImageSharp.fluid}>
            <Banner
                title="Amazing Hampi"
                info="Come and Explore Hampi, the city of ruins, which is a
                UNESCO World Heritage Site."
            >
```

```
        <Link to="/places" className="btn-white">explore places
        </Link>
      </Banner>
    </StyledHero>
    <About />
    <Tips />
  </Layout>
)
```

Now, when we check the browser, we can see the optimized background image, as shown in Figure 3-39.

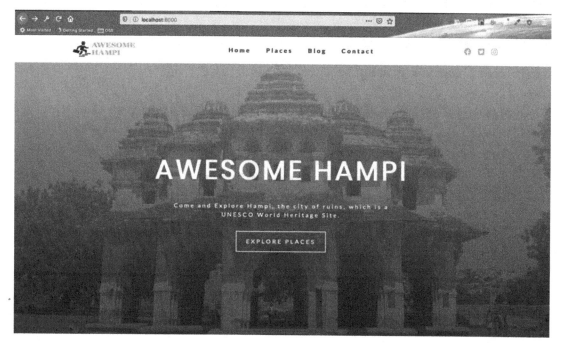

***Figure 3-39.***  *The optimized background*

Next, we will add background images to all the pages. First, we will add the places.js file. Everything will be similar to index.js, except that we are not passing the home prop in StyledHero. The updated code is marked in bold in Listing 3-51.

***Listing 3-51.*** The places.js File

```
import React from 'react'
import Layout from "../components/Layout"
import StyledHero from "../components/StyledHero"
import { graphql } from 'gatsby'

export const query = graphql`
query {
    defaultBcg: file(relativePath: {eq: "defaultBcg.jpeg"}) {
        childImageSharp {
            fluid(quality: 90, maxWidth: 4160) {
                ...GatsbyImageSharpFluid_withWebp
            }
        }
    }
}
`;

export default function places({ data }) {
    return (
        <Layout>
                <StyledHero img={data.defaultBcg.childImageSharp.fluid}>
                        Places page
                    </StyledHero>
                </Layout>
        )
}
```

By not passing the home prop, we get a smaller image with no linear gradient, as shown in Figure 3-40.

***Figure 3-40.*** *The Places page*

Next, we will update the contact.js page. Here we are using a different image. The updated code is marked in bold in Listing 3-52.

***Listing 3-52.*** The contact.js Page

```
import React from 'react'
import Layout from "../components/Layout"
import StyledHero from "../components/StyledHero"
import { graphql } from 'gatsby'

export const query = graphql`
query {
    connectBcg: file(relativePath: {eq: "connectBcg.jpeg"}) {
        childImageSharp {
            fluid(quality: 90, maxWidth: 4160) {
                ...GatsbyImageSharpFluid_withWebp
            }
        }
    }
}
`;
```

```
export default function contact({ data }) {
    return (
        <Layout>
            <StyledHero img={data.connectBcg.childImageSharp.fluid}>
                Contact Page
            </StyledHero>
        </Layout>
    )
}
```

It will result in a change to the Contact page in the browser, as shown in Figure 3-41.

***Figure 3-41.*** *The updated Contact page*

Next, we will update the blog.js file. We are using a different image here too. The updated code is marked in bold in Listing 3-53.

***Listing 3-53.*** The blog.js File

```
import React from 'react'
import Layout from "../components/Layout"
import StyledHero from "../components/StyledHero"
import { graphql } from 'gatsby'
```

```
export const query = graphql`
query {
    blogBcg: file(relativePath: {eq: "blogBcg.jpeg"}) {
        childImageSharp {
            fluid(quality: 90, maxWidth: 4160) {
                ...GatsbyImageSharpFluid_withWebp
            }
        }
    }
}
`;

export default function blog({ data }) {
    return (
        <Layout>
            <StyledHero img={data.blogBcg.childImageSharp.fluid}>
                Blog Page
            </StyledHero>
        </Layout>
    )
}
```

The blog page is shown in Figure 3-42.

***Figure 3-42.*** *The blog page*

You can find the code for this page at this[16] link. Since I pushed my code to GitHub, it also did an automatic deployment to Netlify. You can also find the updated site on `https://amazinghampi.netlify.com/`.[17]

# Creating a Page Transition

We will start with our page transition, which will occur when we navigate to a different page. We will be again using an awesome Gatsby plugin, called `gatsby-plugin-transition-link`. The doc link can be found here[18].

Now, as per the docs, we need to `npm install` the plugin first. So, head over to your terminal and close `gatsby develop` if it is running. After that, install the plugin through the terminal by running `npm i gatsby-plugin-transition-link`.

Then open `gatsby-config.js` and add the plugin. It is marked in bold in Listing 3-54.

*Listing 3-54.* The gatsby-config.js File

```
module.exports = {
        plugins: [
        {
    resolve: `gatsby-source-filesystem`,
    options: {
      name: `images`,
      path: `${__dirname}/src/images/`,
    },
  },
        `gatsby-plugin-styled-components`,
        `gatsby-transformer-sharp`,
        `gatsby-plugin-sharp`,
        `gatsby-plugin-transition-link`
        ]
}
```

---

[16]`https://github.com/nabendu82/gatsbyTourism`
[17]`https://amazinghampi.netlify.com/`
[18]`https://transitionlink.tylerbarnes.ca/docs/`

We also need to install one more package to start using the transition link. This package will be used for AniLink, which is a part of the transition link. We need to run npm i gsap from the terminal.

Then start the development server by running gatsby develop. After that, we will start replacing our Link with AniLink. Head over to Navbar.js and update it. Notice that we are using a prop paintDrip and a hex code. These are used to customize the transition. We can use other props as well, as per their docs[19]. The updated code is marked in bold in Listing 3-55.

***Listing 3-55.*** The Navbar.js File

```
import React, { useState } from "react"
//import { Link } from "gatsby"
import AniLink from "gatsby-plugin-transition-link/AniLink"
import styles from "../css/navbar.module.css"
import { FaAlignRight } from "react-icons/fa"
...

...


    return (
        <nav className={styles.navbar}>
            <div className={styles.navCenter}>
                <div className={styles.navHeader}>
                            ...

                            ...

                </div>
                <ul className={isOpen ? `${styles.navLinks} ${styles.
                showNav}` : `${styles.navLinks}`}>
                    {links.map((item, index) => {
                        return (
                            <li key={index}>
                                <AniLink paintDrip hex="#AEECEE" to={item.
                                path}>{item.text}</AniLink>
                            </li>
                        )
```

---

[19]https://transitionlink.tylerbarnes.ca/docs/anilink/

```
                })}
            </ul>
            <div className={styles.navSocialLinks}>
                        ...
                        ...
            </div>
        </div>
      </nav>
  )
}

export default Navbar
```

Next, head over to Footer.js and update all Links to AniLink. The updated code is marked in bold in Listing 3-56.

***Listing 3-56.*** The Footer.js File

```
import React from "react"
import styles from "../css/footer.module.css"
import links from "../constants/links"
import socialIcons from "../constants/social-icons"
//import { Link } from "gatsby"
import AniLink from "gatsby-plugin-transition-link/AniLink"

const Footer = () => {
return (
    <footer className={styles.footer}>
        <div className={styles.links}>
        {links.map((item, index) => {
            return (
            <AniLink paintDrip hex="#AEECEE" key={index} to={item.path}>
                {item.text}
            </AniLink>
            )
        })}
        </div>
```

```
        <div className={styles.icons}>
                    ...
                    ...
        </div>
        <div className={styles.copyright}>
            copyright &copy; Amazing Hampi {new Date().getFullYear()} all
            rights reserved
        </div>
    </footer>
)
}

export default Footer;
```

There is also a link in `index.js`. Let's update it. The updated code is marked in bold in Listing 3-57.

***Listing 3-57.*** The index.js File

```
...
...
import Tips from "../components/Home/Tips"
//import { Link } from "gatsby"
import AniLink from "gatsby-plugin-transition-link/AniLink"
import { graphql } from 'gatsby'

...
...

export default ({ data }) => (
    <Layout>
        <StyledHero home="true" img={data.defaultBcg.childImageSharp.fluid}>
            <Banner
                title="Amazing Hampi"
                info="Come and Explore Hampi, the city of ruins, which is a
                UNESCO World Heritage Site."
            >
```

```
        <AniLink paintDrip hex="#AEECEE" to="/places"
        className="btn-white">explore places</AniLink>
      </Banner>
    </StyledHero>
    <About />
    <Tips />
  </Layout>
)
```

Let's also update the link in the 404.js file. The updated code is marked in bold in Listing 3-58.

***Listing 3-58.*** The 404.js File

```
import React from "react"
import Layout from "../components/Layout"
import styles from "../css/error.module.css"
//import { Link } from "gatsby"
import AniLink from "gatsby-plugin-transition-link/AniLink"
import Banner from "../components/Banner"

export default function error() {
return (
    <Layout>
        <header className={styles.error}>
        <Banner title="oops it's a dead end">
            <AniLink paintDrip hex="#AEECEE" to="/" className="btn-white">
                back to home page
            </AniLink>
        </Banner>
        </header>
    </Layout>
)
}
```

If you move to a new page by clicking the link, you will get the transition animation.

# Adding a Contact Form

In this section, we add a contact form to our project. Head over to your code editor and add the `contact.module.css` file inside the `css` folder. The contents are shown in Listing 3-59.

*Listing 3-59.* The contact.module.css File

```css
.contact {
  padding: 4rem 0;
}
.center {
  width: 80vw;
  margin: 0 auto;
}
@media screen and (min-width: 992px) {
  .center {
    width: 50vw;
    margin: 0 auto;
  }
}
.contact label {
  text-transform: capitalize;
  display: block;
  margin-bottom: 0.5rem;
}
.formControl,
.submit {
  width: 100%;
  font-size: 1rem;
  margin-bottom: 1rem;
  padding: 0.375rem 0.75rem;
  border: 1px solid var(--darkGrey);
  border-radius: 0.25rem;
}
```

```css
.submit {
  background-color: var(--primaryColor);
  border-color: var(--primaryColor);
  text-transform: uppercase;
  color: var(--mainBlack);
  transition: var(--mainTransition);
  cursor: pointer;
}
.submit:hover {
  background: var(--darkGrey);
  color: var(--mainWhite);
  border-color: var(--darkGrey);
}
```

Next, create a folder called contact inside the components folder and add a Contact. js file inside it. This is a simple form with three fields for the name, email, and message. The contents of the Contact.js file are shown in Listing 3-60.

***Listing 3-60.*** Contact.js

```js
import React from "react"
import Title from "../Title"
import styles from "../../css/contact.module.css"
const Contact = () => {
  return (
    <section className={styles.contact}>
      <Title title="contact" subtitle="us" />
      <div className={styles.center}>
        <form className={styles.form}>
          <div>
            <label htmlFor="name">name</label>
            <input
              type="text"
              name="name"
              id="name"
```

```
        className={styles.formControl}
        placeholder="john smith"
      />
    </div>
    <div>
      <label htmlFor="email">email</label>
      <input
        type="email"
        name="email"
        id="email"
        className={styles.formControl}
        placeholder="email@email.com"
      />
    </div>
    <div>
      <label htmlFor="message">message</label>
      <textarea
        name="message"
        id="message"
        rows="10"
        className={styles.formControl}
        placeholder="hello there"
      />
    </div>
    <div>
      <input
        type="submit"
        value="submit here"
        className={styles.submit}
      />
    </div>
```

```
      </form>
    </div>
  </section>
  )
}

export default Contact
```

1

Next, add this Contact component to the contact.js page. The updated code is marked in bold in Listing 3-61.

***Listing 3-61.*** The Updated Contact.js File

```
import React from 'react'
import Layout from "../components/Layout"
import StyledHero from "../components/StyledHero"
import { graphql } from 'gatsby'
import Contact from '../components/Contact/Contact'

...
...

export default function contact({ data }) {
    return (
        <Layout>
            <StyledHero img={data.connectBcg.childImageSharp.fluid}>
            </StyledHero>
            <Contact />
        </Layout>
    )
}
```

The form appears on the Contact page, as shown in Figure 3-43.

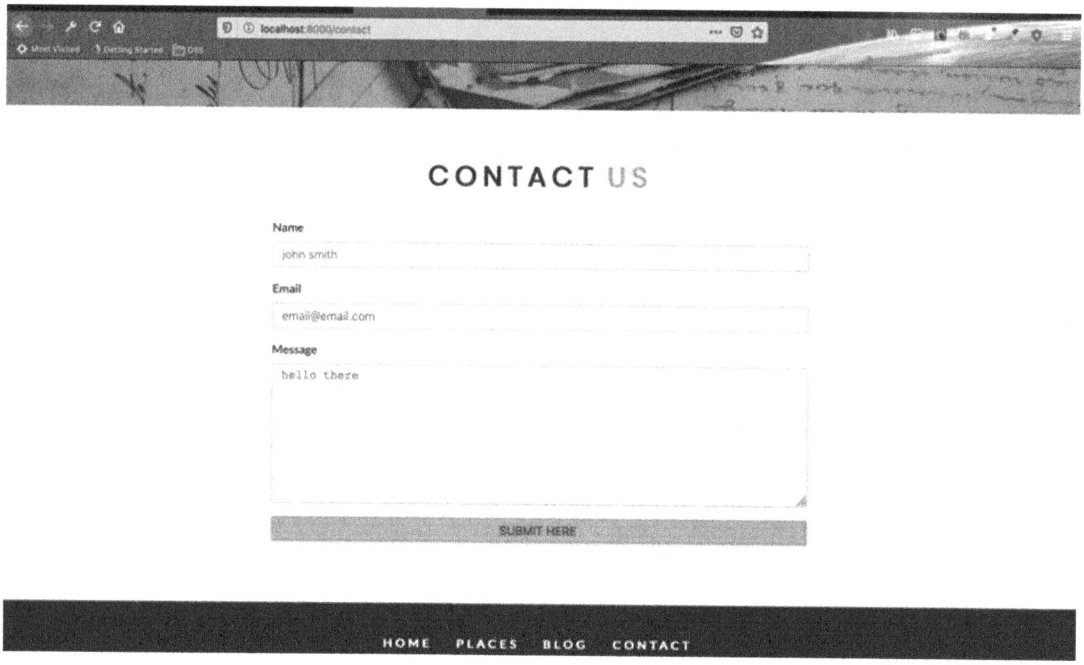

***Figure 3-43.***  *The Contact Us form*

We will be using an service called Formspree[20] to get user data from this form. Once you register and verify your email, you will see the screen in Figure 3-44.

---

[20]https://formspree.io

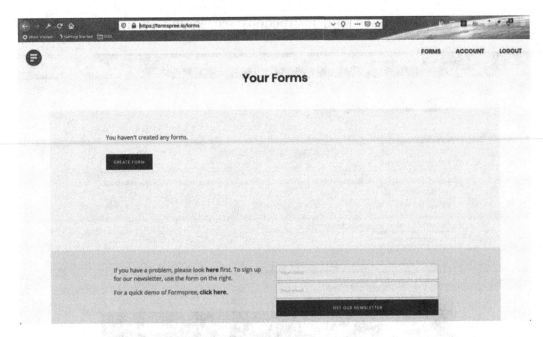

**Figure 3-44.** *Create a form using FormspreeFormspree*

Once you click the Create Form button, a popup will ask you to provide a name for your form, as shown in Figure 3-45. Add the name and click Create Form again.

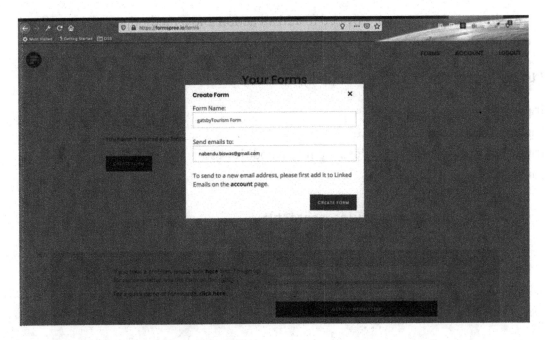

**Figure 3-45.** *The Create Form popup*

The next page will show the setup instructions; see Figure 3-46.

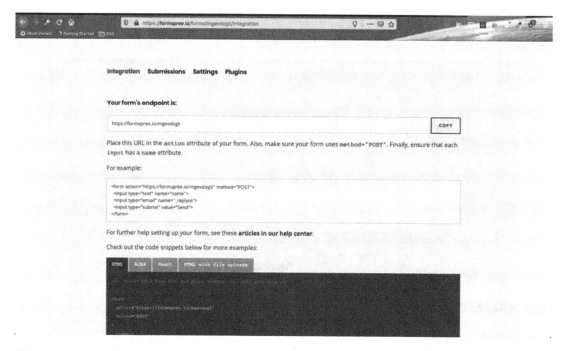

***Figure 3-46.*** *The setup instructions*

As shown in Figure 3-46, we need to add an action and a method to our form. Head over to `Contact.js` and add these. The change is marked in bold in Listing 3-62.

***Listing 3-62.*** The Updated Contact.js File

```
import React from "react"
import Title from "../Title"
import styles from "../../css/contact.module.css"
const Contact = () => {
  return (
    <section className={styles.contact}>
      <Title title="contact" subtitle="us" />
      <div className={styles.center}>
        <form action="https://formspree.io/mgevdogk" method="POST"
        className={styles.form}>
                      . . .
                      . . .
```

```
            </form>
        </div>
    </section>
  )
}
```

```
export default Contact
```

It's time to test our form. We can do that on a localhost also. Head over to the browser and add some values to all the fields. Click Submit Here, as shown in Figure 3-47.

***Figure 3-47.***  *Click the Submit Here button*

Next, you will be taken to the infamous I'm Not a Robot check box, as shown in Figure 3-48.

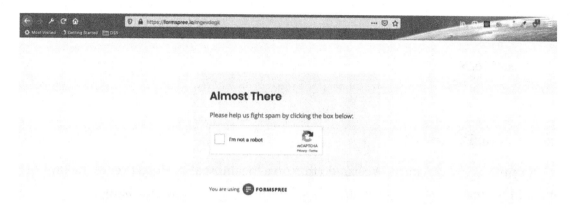

***Figure 3-48.*** *If you are not a robot, check the box*

After verification, it will open the page shown in Figure 3-49. From there, you can move back to the site.

***Figure 3-49.*** *The form was submitted successfully*

Once I log in to my Gmail account, I can see that the form was submitted (see Figure 3-50).

**Figure 3-50.** *The form was submitted*

I pushed the code to GitHub[21]. It will also start my automatic deployment to Netlify. It's time to check the form capabilities on the Internet as well. Once this is deployed, you can head over to `https://amazinghampi.netlify.com/contact`[22] and submit a form.

It will take you through the same process and I get a message in my Gmail (see Figure 3-51).

---

[21]`https://github.com/nabendu82/gatsbyTourism`
[22]`https://amazinghampi.netlify.com/contact`

**Figure 3-51.** *Verification from the Internet*

# Summary

This completes Chapter 3 and the first part of the tourism site with Contentful. We covered the following topics in this chapter:

- Creating the basic setup to create the Gatsby site

- Completing the Navbar and Footer components

- Completing the SimpleHero component, which shows the image in the site

- Adding two small sections—About Section and Hot Tips

- Deploying the site on the Internet using Netlify

- Optimizing the images using Gatsby plugins

- Doing page translation using the AniLink plugin

- Creating a fully working contact form with Formspree

In the next chapter, we will continue using Contentful to build the tourism site. We will set up Contentful and create the Places component in that chapter.

## CHAPTER 4

# Creating a Tourism Site with Contentful: Part Two

After completing much of the site in the previous chapter, it's time to set it up so it can accept data from the backend. We start this chapter by learning how to set up the Contentful CMS. Next, we will create the Places component. We are also going to use the data stored in the Contentful CMS in the Places component.

## Setting Up Contentful

It's time to display data in our project. We can do this with internal data, but we will use a headless CMS (Content Management System) to store our data and then consume it. We will use the Contentful CMS[1] for this project.

## CMS Setup

Go ahead and sign up. When you go to the dashboard the first time, you will get the screen shown in Figure 4-1.

---

[1]https://www.contentful.com/

© Nabendu Biswas 2021
N. Biswas, *Foundation Gatsby Projects*, https://doi.org/10.1007/978-1-4842-6558-1_4

**Figure 4-1.**  *Contentful space*

When you click Add a Space, you will see the popup in Figure 4-2. It shows that we have two free spaces and can have up to 5,000 records in the free account.

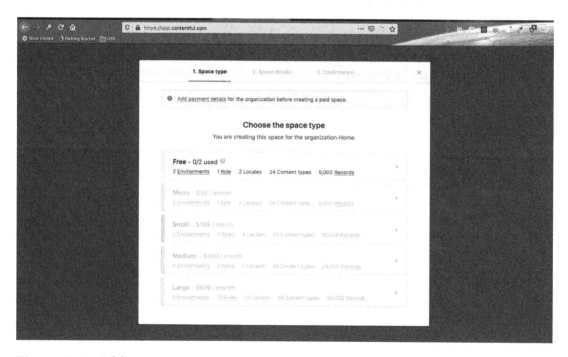

**Figure 4-2.**  *Add a space*

When you click the Free tab, it will open the popup shown in Figure 4-3. Here, you have to enter a Space Name.

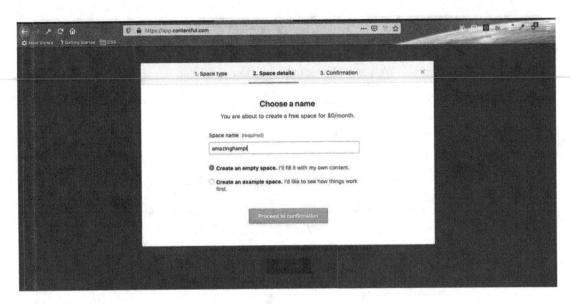

**Figure 4-3.**  *Name the space amazinghampi*

After you click the Proceed to Confirmation button, you will see the Confirmation screen shown in Figure 4-4.

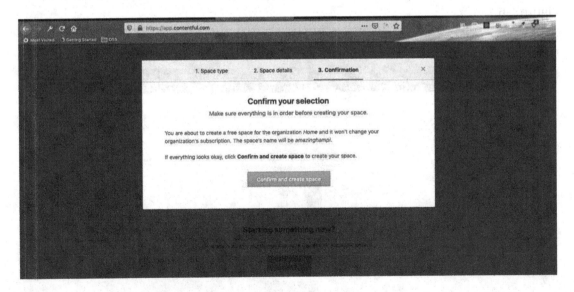

**Figure 4-4.**  *Confirm your selection*

Once you click Confirm and Create Space, it will take you to the screen in Figure 4-5. Here, Content Model and Content are the important tabs.

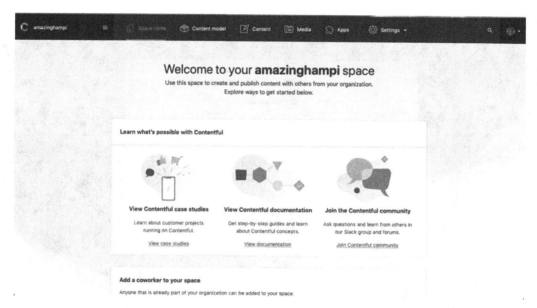

***Figure 4-5.*** *Home page*

The Content Model tab describes the fields of data and the Content tab describes the data. Head over to the Content Model tab and click Add Content Type, as shown in Figure 4-6.

***Figure 4-6.*** *Add content type*

Next, you have to provide a name and description and click Create, as shown in Figure 4-7.

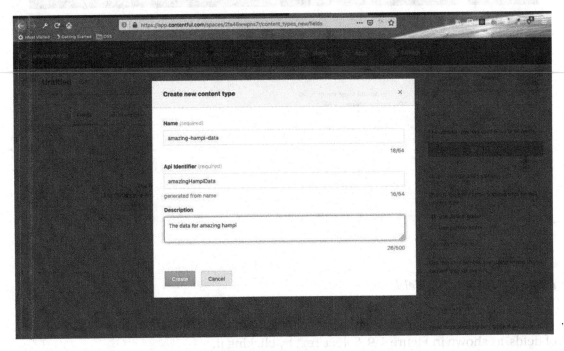

***Figure 4-7.*** *Provide a name and description*

We are basically creating data about different places to visit in Hampi. The next screen will ask us to add some fields, as shown in Figure 4-8.

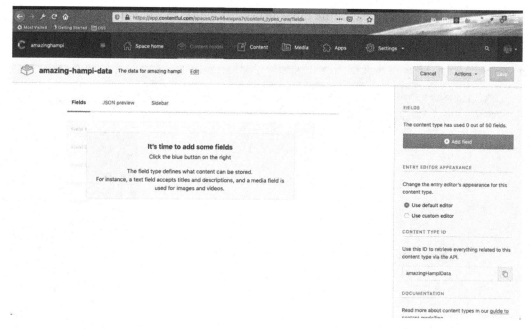

**Figure 4-8.** *Adding fields*

Let's add some fields by clicking the Add Field button. The next screen lists the types of fields, as shown in Figure 4-9. Select Text by clicking it.

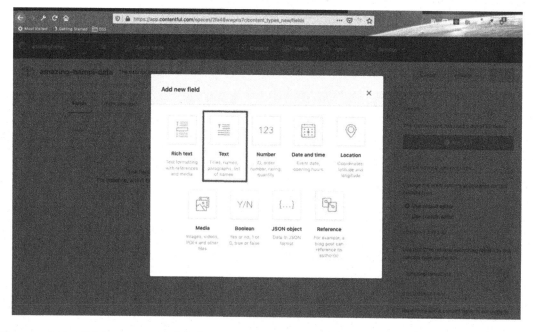

**Figure 4-9.** *Adding a new field*

In Figure 4-10, provide a name for this text field. In this case, it is simply called name. Click Create and Configure.

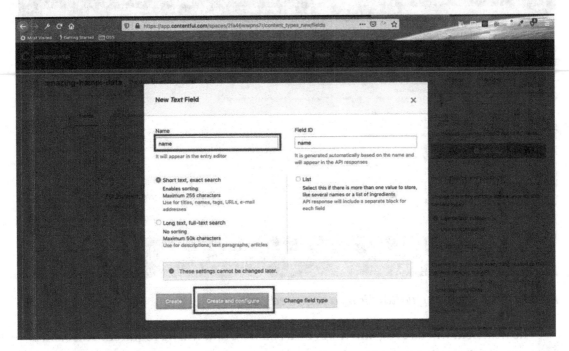

***Figure 4-10.*** *The New Text field*

Then in the next screen, shown in Figure 4-11, click the Validations tab and then check the Required Field option. We are doing this so that users cannot leave this field empty. After that, click the Save button.

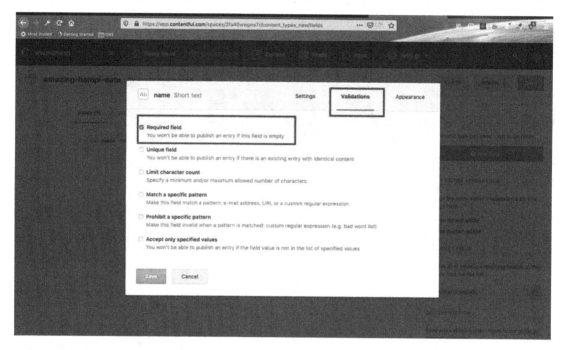

***Figure 4-11.*** *Making validations a required field*

The next field will be `slug` and it will be a text field and will be required. This field is for the text at the end of the URL, which represents each place. Follow the same process as for `name` and create the field. It is shown in Figure 4-12.

***Figure 4-12.*** *The slug field*

Next, we will create a Time Required field, as shown in Figure 4-14. This field tells the tourist the time required to visit a place. This will be an integer field, but not a required field. Once you click Add Field, choose Number from the popup, as shown in Figure 4-13.

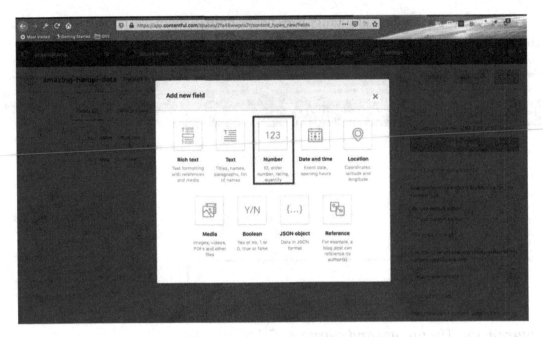

*Figure 4-13.* *The Number field*

Give it a name and then click Create, since it is not a required field. It is shown in Figure 4-14.

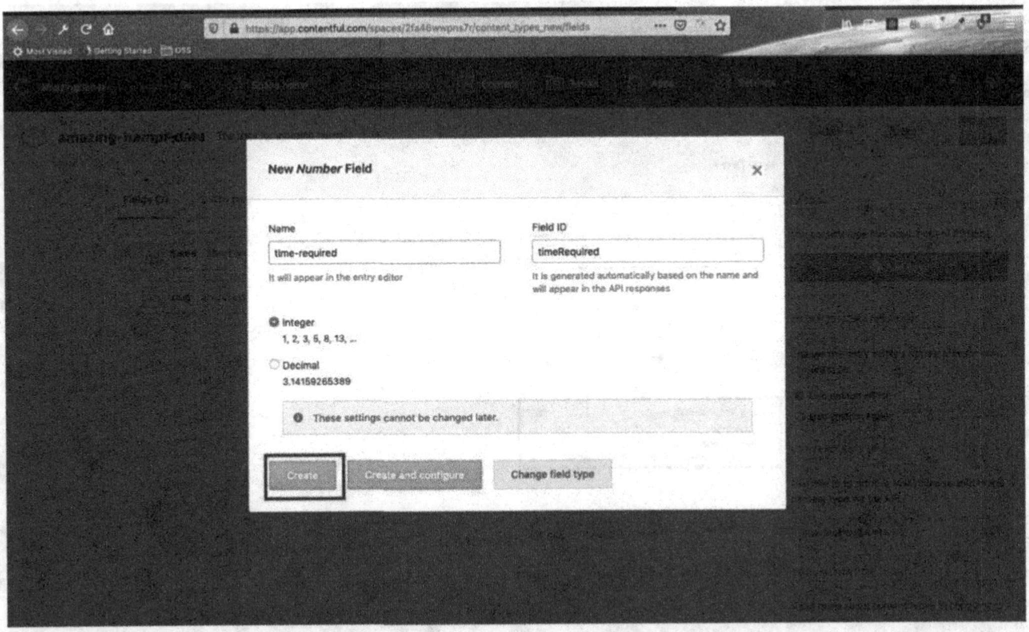

*Figure 4-14.* *Creating the time-required field*

Next, create the Timings and Entry Fees fields. Both of them will consist of short text and will not be required. This is shown in Figure 4-15.

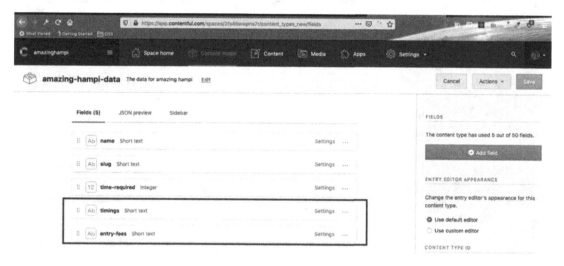

***Figure 4-15.*** *The timings and entry-fees fields*

Next, create the Description field, as shown in Figure 4-16. It will be long text and will be required.

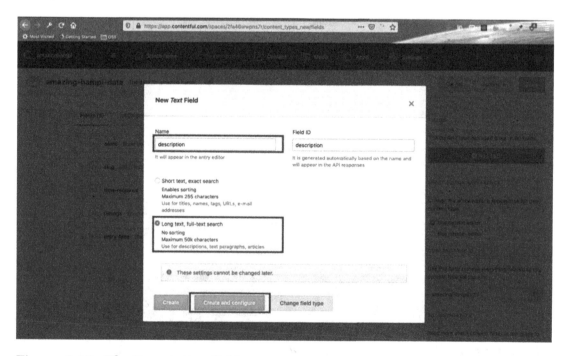

***Figure 4-16.*** *The Description field*

On the home page, we will have Featured Places, which will contain the top three places to visit in Hampi. Let's create a Boolean field for this. Click Add Field and choose Boolean, as shown in Figure 4-17.

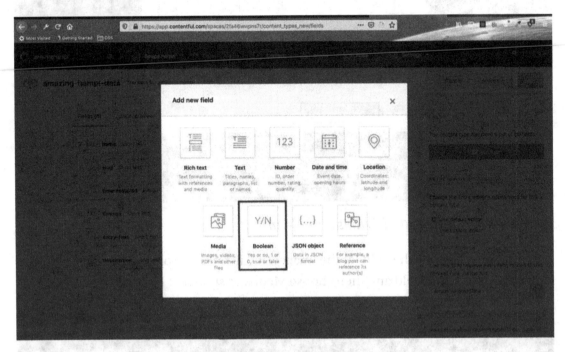

***Figure 4-17.*** *Adding a Boolean field*

Give it the name featured and click Create and Configure to make it a required field, as shown in Figure 4-18.

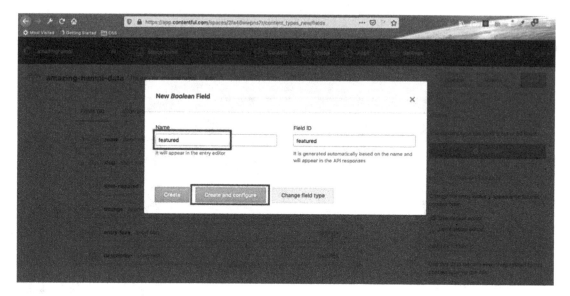

***Figure 4-18.*** *The featured field is a Boolean*

Next, we will create the field for the images. It will hold one or more images, required for a place. Click Add Field and then choose Media, as shown in Figure 4-19.

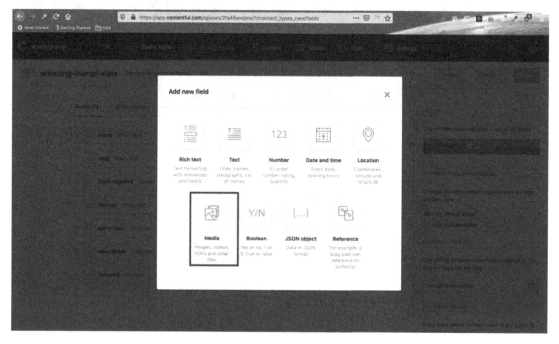

***Figure 4-19.*** *Media is selected*

Call this field images, then select the radio button for Many Files. Then click Create and Configure to make it a required field, before saving. This process is shown in Figure 4-20.

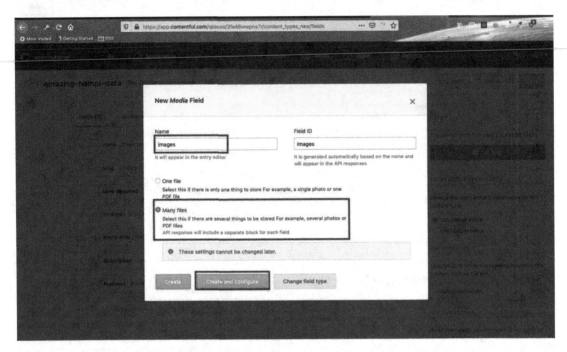

***Figure 4-20.***   *Creating a Media field called images*

We are done with all the models. Click the Save button on the top-right corner, as shown in Figure 4-21.

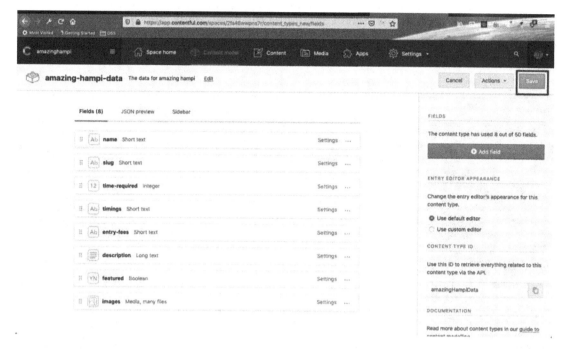

***Figure 4-21.*** *Save your efforts*

It's time to add some content. Head over to the Content tab. You will see the screen shown in Figure 4-22. Click the Add amazing-hampi-data button.

***Figure 4-22.*** *Adding data*

We will add data from the next screen, as shown in Figure 4-23.

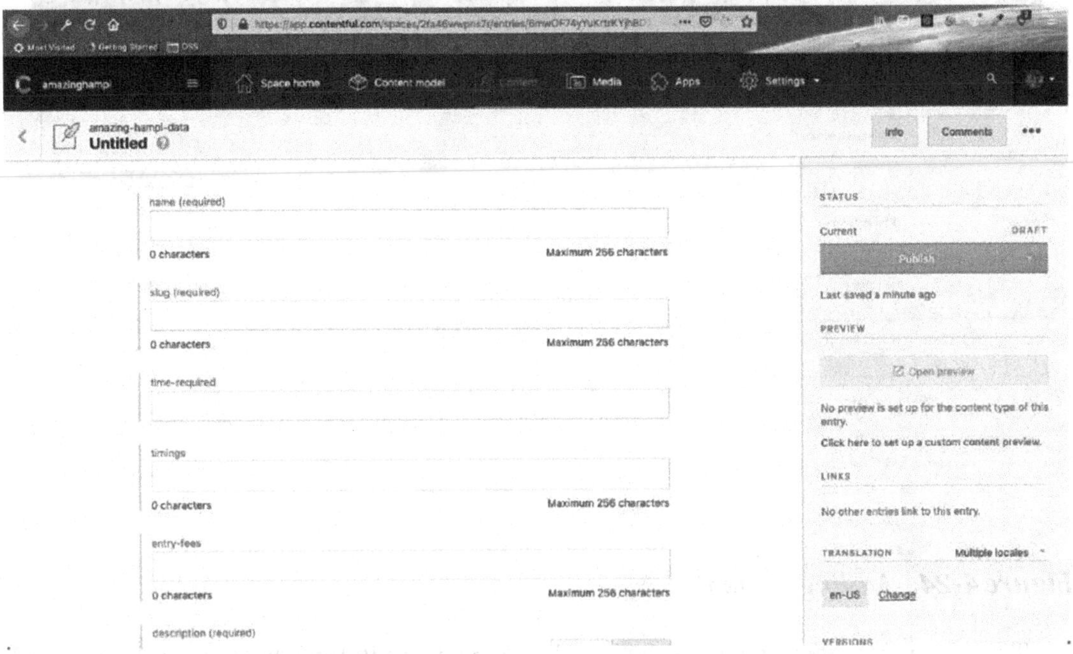

***Figure 4-23.*** *Adding data*

Let's add some content about our first place in Hampi, as shown in Figure 4-24.

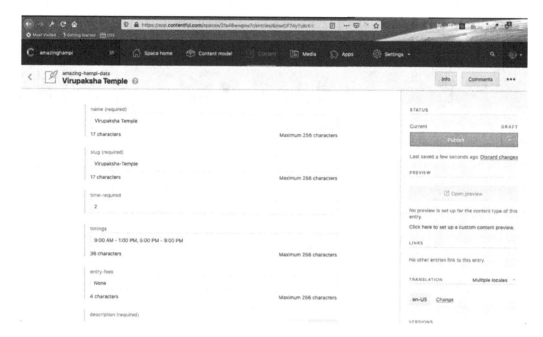

***Figure 4-24.*** *Adding content*

To add images, we select the image and then click the Publish button, as shown in Figure 4-25.

***Figure 4-25.*** *Publishing images*

I added two images, as shown in Figure 4-26.

***Figure 4-26.*** *Two images have been added*

Publish this on the main screen by clicking the Publish button, as shown in Figure 4-27.

***Figure 4-27.***  *Published*

Contentful will show these published items in the Content screen, as shown in Figure 4-28.

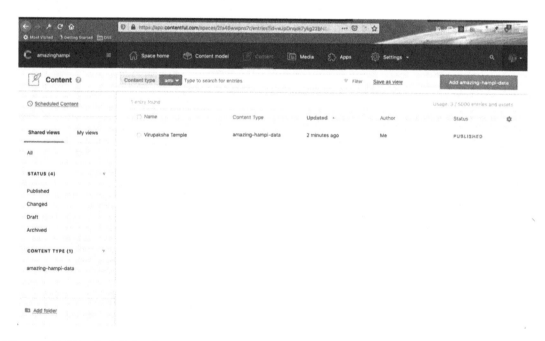

***Figure 4-28.***  *Published content*

Next, I will add more places to visit in Hampi by following the same steps. In fact, I added entries about 22 places in Contentful, as shown in Figure 4-29. You can add your own data.

*Figure 4-29.  Places to visit in Hampi added as content*

# Install the Gatsby Plugins

Next, we will import this data into our site. To do this, we will install the gatsby-source-contentful plugin. The docs can be found here[2].

As usual, we need to first npm install in our project directory, with the following command.

```
npm install --save gatsby-source-contentful
```

Next, in gatsby-config.js we had to add the plugin, which is highlighted in bold in Listing 4-1. As per the docs, let's add the object.

_____

[2]https://www.gatsbyjs.org/packages/gatsby-source-contentful/

***Listing 4-1.*** gatsby-config.js

```
module.exports = {
          plugins: [
          {
    resolve: `gatsby-source-filesystem`,
    options: {
      name: `images`,
      path: `${__dirname}/src/images/`,
    },
  },
          {
    resolve: `gatsby-source-contentful`,
    options: {
      spaceId: `your_space_id`,
 accessToken: process.env.CONTENTFUL_ACCESS_TOKEN,
    },
  },
          `gatsby-plugin-styled-components`,
          `gatsby-transformer-sharp`,
          `gatsby-plugin-sharp`,
          `gatsby-plugin-transition-link`
          ]
}
```

Let's get our API keys from Contentful. From the Contentful API, choose Settings ➤ API Keys, as shown in Figure 4-30.

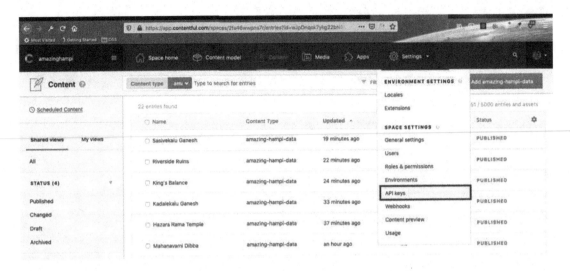

***Figure 4-30.*** *Getting the API keys*

It looks like a key has been created for us, as shown in Figure 4-31.

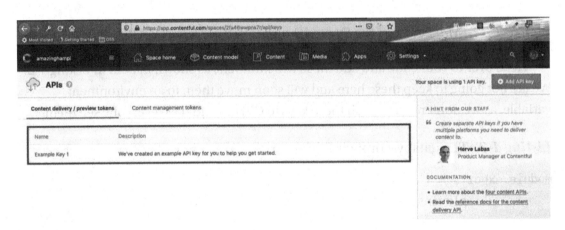

***Figure 4-31.*** *Example key 1*

Click Example Key 1 shown in Figure 4-31 to edit the name of the key. We need to note our Space ID and Content Delivery API - Access Token from here (see Figure 4-32).

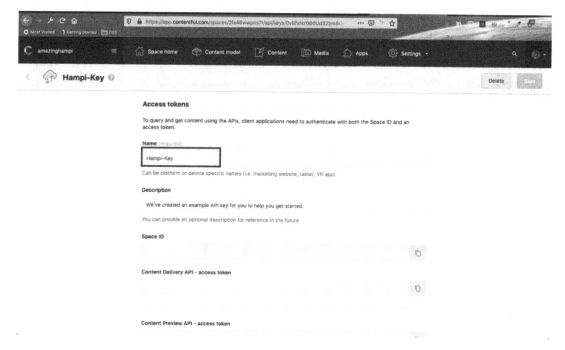

***Figure 4-32.*** *Make note of the Space ID and Content Delivery API - Access Token*

Head over to your code and add these two numbers, as shown in bold in Listing 4-2. We are not going to keep these here and will soon move them to an environment variable, as we don't need to push these keys to GitHub and have everyone see them.

***Listing 4-2.*** The gatsby-config.js File

```
module.exports = {
          plugins: [
          {
    resolve: `gatsby-source-filesystem`,
    options: {
      name: `images`,
      path: `${__dirname}/src/images/`,
    },
  },
```

```
      {
    resolve: `gatsby-source-contentful`,
    options: {
      spaceId: `2XXXXXXXXX2`,
      accessToken: `RXXXXXXXXXXXXXXXXXXXXE`,
    },
  },
        `gatsby-plugin-styled-components`,
        `gatsby-transformer-sharp`,
        `gatsby-plugin-sharp`,
        `gatsby-plugin-transition-link`
        ]
}
```

Let's head over to our terminal to check whether the setup was right, by running gatsby develop. The command runs without error and the connection also fetches the correct data from Contentful, as shown in Figure 4-33.

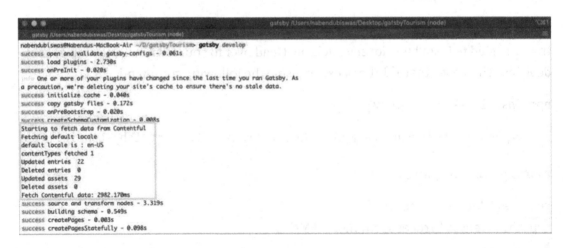

**Figure 4-33.**  *Fetching data from Contentful*

Let's go to GraphQL and refresh the browser. Click docs to see Contentful's queries, as shown in Figure 4-34.

*Figure 4-34.* *GraphQL*

Next, we will use environment variables to store the spaceId and accessToken. For that, we need to install the dotenv package. Head over to your terminal and stop gatsby develop. Then npm install the package, using the following command.

```
npm install --save dotenv
```

As per the docs,[3] we need to add the lines in Listing 4-3 to our gatsby-config.js file.

*Listing 4-3.* The gatsby-config.js File

```
require("dotenv").config({
  path: `.env.${process.env.NODE_ENV}`,
})
```

---

[3]https://www.gatsbyjs.org/docs/environment-variables/

```
module.exports = {
        plugins: [

                    ...

                    ...

            ]

}
```

We need to create an .env.development file in the root directory. Then take the keys from gatsby-config.js and add them (without quotation marks) to the two variables, as shown in Listing 4-4.

***Listing 4-4.*** The env.development File

```
CONTENTFUL_SPACE_ID=2XXXXXXXXX2
CONTENTFUL_ACCESS_TOKEN=RXXXXXXXXXXXXXXXXXXXXE
```

Next, in gatsby-config.js, add this using process.env, as highlighted in Listing 4-5.

***Listing 4-5.*** The gatsby-config.js File

```
require("dotenv").config({
  path: `.env.${process.env.NODE_ENV}`,
})

module.exports = {
        plugins: [
        ...
        ...
        {
    resolve: `gatsby-source-contentful`,
    options: {
      spaceId: process.env.CONTENTFUL_SPACE_ID,
      accessToken: process.env.CONTENTFUL_ACCESS_TOKEN,
    },
  },
        ...
        ...
        ]
}
```

225

Head over to `.gitignore` and add the `.env.development` file to it, as highlighted in Listing 4-6.

***Listing 4-6.*** The .gitignore File

```
# Logs
logs
*.log
npm-debug.log*
yarn-debug.log*
yarn-error.log*
.env.development
# Runtime data
pids
*.pid
*.seed
*.pid.lock
...
...
```

Once again, head over to the terminal and run `gatsby develop`, to check if all runs well. Figure 4-35 shows that it's running well.

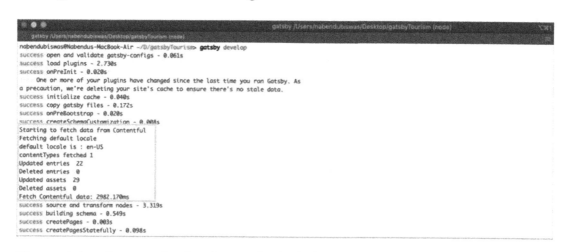

***Figure 4-35.*** *Run gatsby develop to check if it's running well*

Before pushing to GitHub, we need to add these variables to our Netlify deployment. Head over to your Netlify deployment, as shown in Figure 4-36.

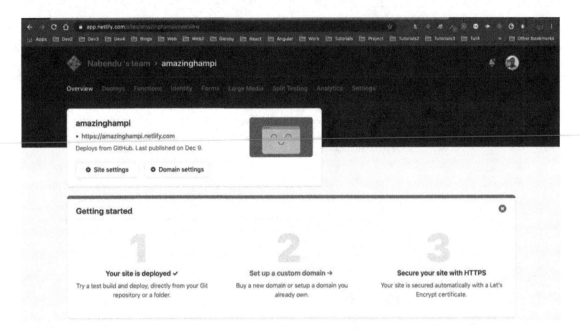

**Figure 4-36.** *The Netlify deployment*

Click the Site Settings button. On the left menu, click Build & Deploy and then choose Environment, as shown in Figure 4-37.

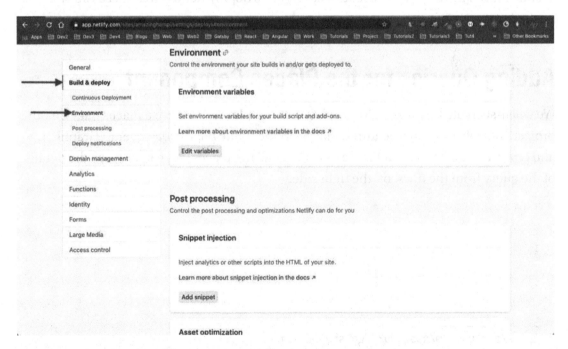

**Figure 4-37.** *Deploy the environment*

Click Edit Variables and add the two variables. After that, click Save, as shown in Figure 4-38.

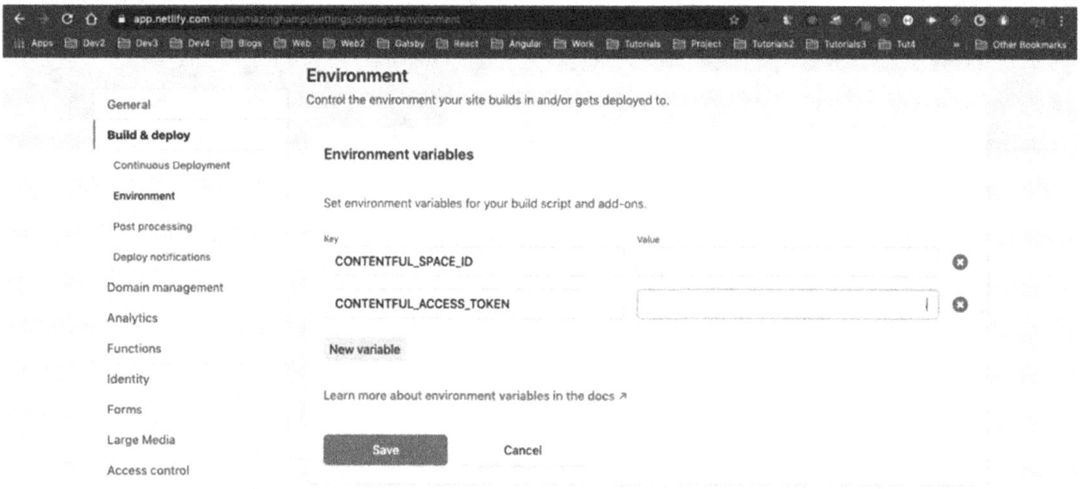

***Figure 4-38.*** *Adding two variables*

Commit your code and push it to GitHub. You can find my code in my GitHub account here[4]. In addition, because of continuous deployment, it was successfully pushed to the Netlify site[5].

# Adding Queries for the Places Component

We will first create the queries in GraphQL for our places. We have a Places page on our project and will also show Featured Places on the home page. Head over to GraphiQL and type the query shown in Figure 4-39 to get all the places. We can also see the details of the query from the docs, on the right side.

---

[4]https://github.com/nabendu82/gatsbyTourism
[5]https://amazinghampi.netlify.com/

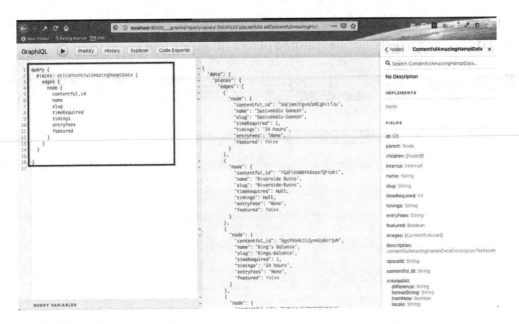

**Figure 4-39.**  *Using GraphiQL*

Let's also search for images. As per the docs, we can have fluid or fixed images. But we cannot use the fragment in GraphiQL as usual and we will use `src`, which we are going to later change in the code. This is shown in Figure 4-40.

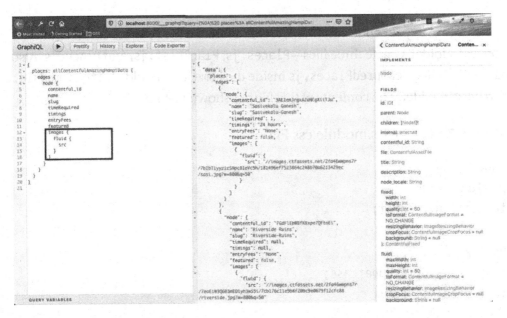

**Figure 4-40.**  *Searching for images*

Let's also add a query for Featured Places, as shown in Figure 4-41. Here we are using the `filter` option to get only the featured places (there are four).

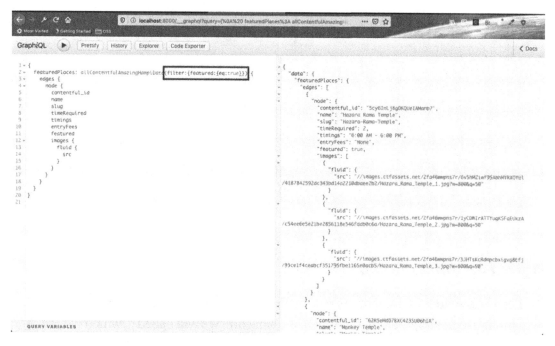

***Figure 4-41.*** *Getting only the featured places*

Next, move to your code editor and create a folder called `places` inside the `components` folder. Create three files—`Places.js`, `PlaceList.js`, and `Place.js`. Also, create a file called `FeaturedPlaces.js` inside the `home` folder. Add an `items.module.css` file to the `css` folder. The contents of this file are shown Listing 4-7.

***Listing 4-7.*** The items.module.css File

```css
.places {
  padding: 4rem 0;
  text-align: center;
}
.sub-text {
  text-transform: uppercase;
  font-size: 1.3rem;
```

```
    text-align: center;
    letter-spacing: 7px;
}
.sub-text span{
    color: var(--primaryColor);
}
.center {
    width: 80vw;
    margin: 3rem auto;
    display: grid;
    grid-template-columns: repeat(auto-fill, minmax(280px, 1fr));
    grid-column-gap: 2rem;
    grid-row-gap: 2rem;
}
@media screen and (min-width: 576px) {
    .center {
        grid-template-columns: repeat(auto-fill, minmax(368.66px, 1fr));
    }
}
@media screen and (min-width: 1200px) {
    .center {
        width: 100%;
        max-width: 1170px;
    }
}
```

## Adding the Featured Places Component

Next, let's update the FeaturedPlaces.js file. Here, we will add our query for featured places, which we created in GraphiQL. The only thing that changes is the GatsbyContent-fulFluid_tracedSVG fragment, instead of src. We also check to see if we are getting data correctly, by placing a console.log() in the code. The whole code is shown in Listing 4-8.

***Listing 4-8.*** The FeaturedPlaces.js File

```
import React from 'react'
import { useStaticQuery, graphql } from "gatsby"
import Title from "../Title"
import styles from "../../css/items.module.css"
import AniLink from "gatsby-plugin-transition-link/AniLink"

const getFeaturedPlaces = graphql`
query{
featuredPlaces: allContentfulAmazingHampiData(filter:{featured:{eq:true}})
{
    edges {
        node {
            contentful_id
            name
            slug
            timeRequired
            timings
            entryFees
            featured
        images {
            fluid {
                ...GatsbyContentfulFluid
                }
            }
        }
        }
    }
}
`;

const FeaturedPlaces = () => {
    const response = useStaticQuery(getFeaturedPlaces)
    const places = response.featuredPlaces.edges
            console.log(places);
```

```
    return (
        <section className={styles.places}>
            <Title title="featured" subtitle="places" />
            <AniLink fade to="/places" className="btn-primary">
                all places
            </AniLink>
        </section>
    )
}

export default FeaturedPlaces
```

Next, head over to index.js to add the FeaturedPlaces component, as highlighted in Listing 4-9.

*Listing 4-9.* FeaturedPlaces in the index.js File

```
...
...
import { graphql } from 'gatsby'
import FeaturedPlaces from "../components/Home/FeaturedPlaces"

...
...

export default ({ data }) => (
    <Layout>
        <StyledHero home="true" img={data.defaultBcg.childImageSharp.fluid}>
                    ...
                    ...
        </StyledHero>
        <About />
        <Tips />
        <FeaturedPlaces />
    </Layout>
)
```

In the browser, open the home page and choose Developer Tools ➤ Console. We can see data coming from Contentful, as shown in Figure 4-42.

*Figure 4-42.*  *We can see data coming from Contentful using the console*

Let's show the places array from the FeaturedPlaces component by adding the highlighted part in the FeaturedPlaces.js file, as shown in Listing 4-10.

*Listing 4-10.*  The Places Array in FeaturedPlaces.js

```
...
...
const FeaturedPlaces = () => {
    const response = useStaticQuery(getFeaturedPlaces)
    const places = response.featuredPlaces.edges

    return (
        <section className={styles.places}>
            <Title title="featured" subtitle="places" />
            <div className={styles.center}>
                {places.map(({ node }) => {
                    return <Place key={node.contentful_id} place={node} />
                })}
            </div>
```

```
        <AniLink fade to="/places" className="btn-primary">
            all places
        </AniLink>
    </section>
  )
}

export default FeaturedPlaces
```

We will create a simple `Place` component for now. Create a `Place.js` file inside the Places folder, using the content in Listing 4-11.

***Listing 4-11.*** The Place.js File

```
import React from 'react'
const Place = () => {
    return (
        <div>
            Single place
        </div>
    )
}

export default Place
```

When we move to the browser, we can see four single places, as shown in Figure 4-43.

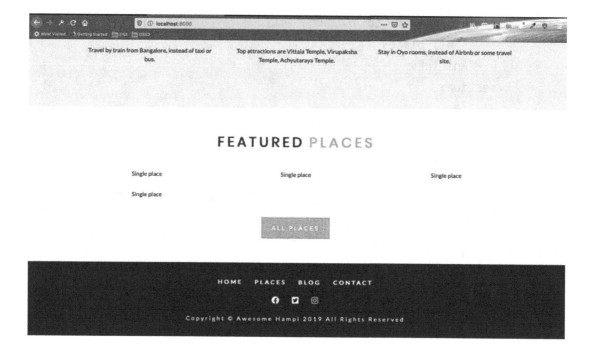

***Figure 4-43.*** *Four single places*

# Adding the Place Component

Next, we will start to work on our Place component. First, let's add `place.module.css` inside the `css` folder. The content of it is shown in Listing 4-12.

***Listing 4-12.*** The place.module.css File

```
.place {
  box-shadow: var(--lightShadow);
  transition: var(--mainTransition);
}
.place:hover {
  box-shadow: var(--darkShadow);
}

.img-container {
  position: relative;
```

```css
  background: var(--primaryColor);
  transition: var(--mainTransition);
}
.img {
  transition: var(--mainTransition);
}
.img-container:hover .img {
  opacity: 0.3;
}

.link {
  position: absolute;
  top: 50%;
  left: 50%;
  transform: translate(-50%, -50%);
  opacity: 0;
  text-transform: uppercase;
  letter-spacing: var(--mainSpacing);
  color: var(--mainWhite);
  border: 2px solid var(--mainWhite);
  padding: 0.9rem 1.6rem;
  display: inline-block;
  transition: var(--mainTransition);
  cursor: pointer;
}
.link:hover {
  background: var(--mainWhite);
  color: var(--primaryColor);
}
.img-container:hover .link {
  opacity: 1;
}

.footer {
  padding: 1rem;
  text-align: left;
}
```

```css
.footer h3 {
  text-transform: capitalize;
  margin-bottom: 0;
}
.info {
  display: flex;
  flex-wrap: wrap;
  justify-content: space-between;
  text-transform: uppercase;
  align-items: center;
  margin-top: 0.5rem;
}
.info h6,
.info h4 {
  margin-bottom: 0;
}
.country {
  text-transform: capitalize;
  color: var(--primaryColor);
  display: flex;
  align-items: center;
}
.icon {
  margin-right: 0.4rem;
}
.details {
  color: var(--darkGrey);
  text-transform: uppercase;
  text-align: right;
}
```

Next, let's add some code to Place.js to show the images. The content is shown in Listing 4-13.

***Listing 4-13.*** Code in Place.js

```
import React from 'react'
import Image from "gatsby-image"
import styles from "../../css/place.module.css"
import AniLink from "gatsby-plugin-transition-link/AniLink"

const Place = ({ place }) => {
    const { name, slug, images } = place;
    let mainImage = images[0].fluid;

    return (
        <article className={styles.place}>
            <div className={styles.imgContainer}>
                <Image fluid={mainImage} className={styles.img} alt="single
                place" />
            </div>
        </article>
    )
}

export default Place
```

This code will show all our three images on the Featured Places page, as shown in Figure 4-44.

*Figure 4-44.* *Images of the featured places*

Let's complete the code by adding the AniLink, as highlighted in Listing 4-14, which will take visitors to the slug when they click it. We also show the name after the image.

*Listing 4-14.* AniLink in Place.js

```
import React from 'react'
import Image from "gatsby-image"
import styles from "../../css/place.module.css"
import AniLink from "gatsby-plugin-transition-link/AniLink"

const Place = ({ place }) => {
    const { name, slug, images } = place;
    let mainImage = images[0].fluid;

    return (
        <article className={styles.place}>
            <div className={styles.imgContainer}>
                <Image fluid={mainImage} className={styles.img} alt="single
                place" />
```

```
        <AniLink fade className={styles.link}
        to={`/places/${slug}`}>details</AniLink>
      </div>
      <div className={styles.footer}>
          <h3>{name}</h3>
      </div>
    </article>
  )
}

export default Place
```

This code will show the Featured Places with the names of the places below them, as shown in Figure 4-45.

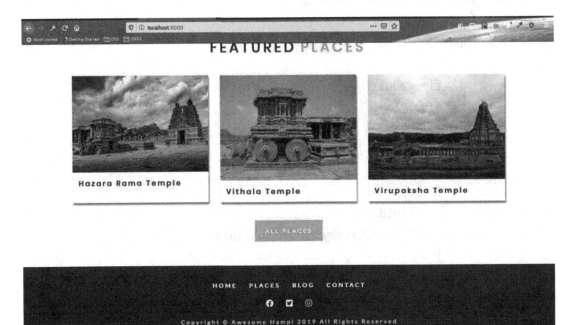

***Figure 4-45.*** *Featured places with descriptive names*

# Creating the Places Component

Let's start by creating our Places component. Open your `Places.js` file and update it as shown in Listing 4-15. We are basically using the GraphQL query, which we created in GraphiQL in the previous section.

***Listing 4-15.*** The Places.js File

```
import React from "react"
import PlaceList from "./PlaceList"
import { useStaticQuery, graphql } from "gatsby"

const getPlaces = graphql`
query {
    places: allContentfulAmazingHampiData {
        edges {
            node {
                name
                timeRequired
                slug
                timings
                contentful_id
                entryFees
                images {
                    fluid {
                        ...GatsbyContentfulFluid
                    }
                }
            }
        }
    }
}
`
```

```
const Places = () => {
    const { places } = useStaticQuery(getPlaces)
    return <PlaceList places={places} />
}

export default Places
```

As we are getting the places, we are passing them to the PlaceList component. Let's create a simple PlaceList component now. Create a PlaceList.js file inside the places folder and add the content from Listing 4-16 to it.

***Listing 4-16.*** The PlaceList.js File

```
import React, { Component } from 'react'

class PlaceList extends Component {
    render() {
        return (
                        <div>
                                PlaceList...
                    </div>
        )
    }
}
export default PlaceList
```

Next, we will show the places component in the places.js page. It is highlighted in Listing 4-17.

***Listing 4-17.*** The Places component in places.js

```
import React from 'react'
import Layout from "../components/Layout"
import StyledHero from "../components/StyledHero"
import { graphql } from 'gatsby'
import Places from '../components/Places/Places'

...
...
```

```
export default function places({ data }) {
    return (
        <Layout>
            <StyledHero img={data.defaultBcg.childImageSharp.fluid}>
            </StyledHero>
            <Places />
        </Layout>
    )
}
```

Let's now update `PlaceList.js` to show all the places. Here we are using a class-based component and accessing the `places` passes from the Places component, by `this.props.places`.

We also have two local states of `places` and `sortedPlaces`. This is updated by `this.props.places` once the components loads and is updated by a React lifecycle called `componentDidMount()`.

After that, we sort over `sortedPlaces` and pass its value to an already created Place component. The contents are shown in Listing 4-18.

***Listing 4-18.*** The Code in PlaceList.js

```
import React, { Component } from 'react'
import styles from "../../css/items.module.css"
import Place from "./Place"
import Title from "../Title"

class PlaceList extends Component {
    state = {
        places: [],
        sortedPlaces: [],
    }

    componentDidMount() {
        this.setState({
            places: this.props.places.edges,
            sortedPlaces: this.props.places.edges
        })
    }
```

```
    render() {
        return (
        <section className={styles.tours}>
            <Title title="hampi" subtitle="places" />
            <div className={styles.center}>
                {this.state.sortedPlaces && this.state.sortedPlaces.map(({
                node }) => {
                    return <Place key={node.contentful_id} place={node} />
                })}
            </div>
        </section>
        )
    }
}
export default PlaceList
```

When we move to the Places page[6], it will show all 22 places, as shown in Figure 4-46.

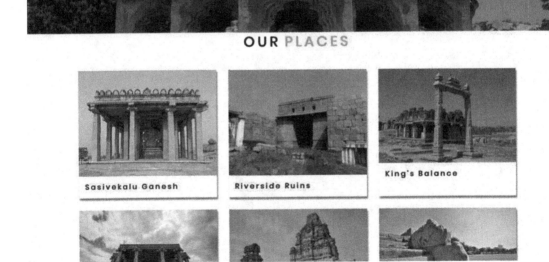

*Figure 4-46.* *All 22 places are shown on this page*

---

[6]http://localhost:8000/places

# Create a Place Template

Next, we will create a template to show when we go to a single place. Head over to your code editor and create a `templates` folder inside the `src` folder. Create a file called **place-template.js** inside that folder. Add the basic code shown in Listing 4-19 to it.

***Listing 4-19.*** The place-template.js File

```
import React from 'react'

const placeTemplate = () => {
      return (
                        <div>
                            Dummy Place
                        </div>
      )
}

export default placeTemplate
```

We are basically creating our pages programmatically through the templates. Create a file called `gatsby-node.js` in the root directory.

Let's first create the query in GraphiQL. Head over to GraphQL[7] and create the query shown in Figure 4-47, which lists all the slugs.

---

[7]http://localhost:8000/graphql

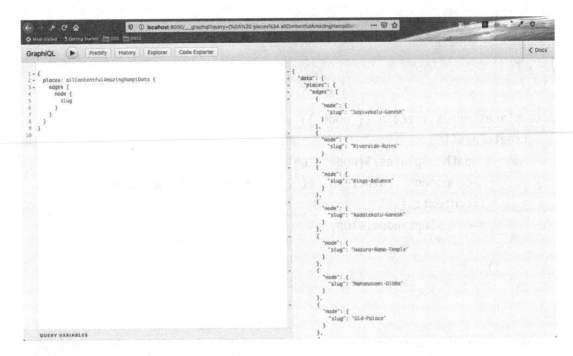

***Figure 4-47.*** *The slugs query*

Head over to the gatsby-node.js file and add the content in Listing 4-20. Here, we are using async-await syntax to make the call. We are using the GraphQL query we created in the GraphiQL playground.

Once we receive the data, we loop over it and create the pages with the slug and template.

***Listing 4-20.*** The gatsby-node.js File

```
const path = require("path")

exports.createPages = async ({ graphql, actions }) => {
const { createPage } = actions

const { data } = await graphql(`
query {
    places: allContentfulAmazingHampiData {
        edges {
        node {
                slug
            }
```

```
        }
      }
  }
`)

data.places.edges.forEach(({ node }) => {
    createPage({
            path: `places/${node.slug}`,
            component: path.resolve("./src/templates/place-template.js"),
            context: {
                slug: node.slug,
            },
        })
    })
}
```

After saving the file, we need to restart the server. After restarting the browser, go to any nonexistent page and you will be shown the 404 page with all pages. We can see all the pages dynamically created, as shown in Figure 4-48.

*Figure 4-48. All pages*

If we click any area of the page, it will show us data from `place-template.js`, as shown in Figure 4-49.

*Figure 4-49.* *Dummy place*

We will create the `place-template.js` file next. In this part, we will start by creating the query for the template page. We will first create the query to get data of a single slug, as shown in Figure 4-50.

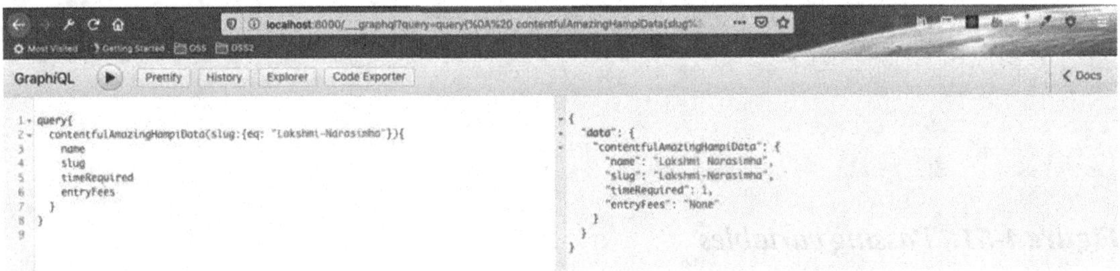

*Figure 4-50.* *Single slug*

We need to dynamically pass a variable to this query from our code. To test this, we will update the query and pass the variable from the Query Variables screen. This is shown in Figure 4-51.

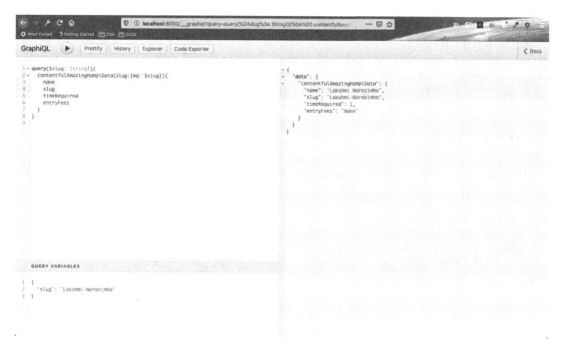

**Figure 4-51.** *Passing variables*

Let's complete this query by adding all the fields, as shown in Figure 4-52.

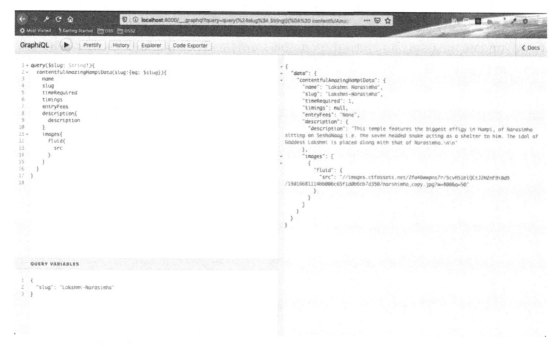

**Figure 4-52.** *All fields added to the query*

Next, we will add the query to `place-template.js` and display it. We are destructuring the data, which we receive from the query.

Some of our places have multiple images, so we are destructuring the images. We keep the first image as `mainImage` and the rest of the images in the array as `placeImages`. The code is shown in Listing 4-21.

*Listing 4-21.* The Code in place-template.js

```
import React from "react"
import { graphql } from "gatsby"

const Template = ({ data }) => {
    const { name, timeRequired, timings, entryFees, description: {
    description }, images } = data.place;
            console.log(images);
    const [mainImage, ...placeImages] = images
            console.log(mainImage);
            console.log(placeImages);
    return <h1>{name}</h1>
}
export const query = graphql`
query($slug: String!){
    place: contentfulAmazingHampiData(slug:{eq: $slug}){
        name
        slug
        timeRequired
        timings
        entryFees
        description{
            description
        }
        images{
            fluid{
                src
            }
        }
```

```
    }
  }
`

export default Template
```

Once we move to a place with multiple images and open the console, we can see the variables. The name is also displayed on the page, as shown in Figure 4-53.

***Figure 4-53.*** *The variables at work*

Let's add the styles for the templates by creating a file called `template.module.css` inside the `css` folder. The file's contents are shown in Listing 4-22.

***Listing 4-22.*** The template.module.css File

```css
.template {
  padding: 4rem 0;
}
.center {
  width: 80vw;
  margin: 0 auto;
}
```

```css
.images {
  display: grid;
  grid-template-columns: repeat(auto-fit, minmax(250px, 1fr));
  grid-column-gap: 1rem;
  grid-row-gap: 1rem;
  margin-bottom: 2rem;
}
.image {
  box-shadow: var(--lightShadow);
}
.template h2 {
  text-transform: capitalize;
  letter-spacing: var(--mainSpacing);
  margin-bottom: 1rem;
}
.info {
  display: flex;
  flex-wrap: wrap;
}
.info p {
  display: flex;
  align-items: center;
  margin-right: 2rem;
  text-transform: capitalize;
}
.icon {
  color: var(--primaryColor);
  font-size: 1.4rem;
  margin-right: 0.5rem;
}
.desc {
  line-height: 2;
}
.template h4 {
  text-transform: capitalize;
}
```

```css
.template h2 {
  margin: 2rem 0;
}
.journey {
  margin: 3rem 0;
}
@media screen and (min-width: 992px) {
  .journey,
  .desc {
    width: 70vw;
  }
}
@media screen and (min-width: 1200px) {
  .center {
    width: 95vw;
    max-width: 1170vw;
  }
  .images {
    grid-template-columns: repeat(auto-fit, minmax(340px, 1fr));
    grid-column-gap: 50px;
  }
}
```

Next, we need to update `place-template.js` to show more fields. Also, we need to change our `src` in the query to a fragment or the code will give an error. The updated code is marked in bold in Listing 4-23.

***Listing 4-23.*** More Fields in place-template.js

```js
import React from "react"
import { graphql } from "gatsby"
import Layout from "../components/Layout"
import StyledHero from "../components/StyledHero"
import styles from "../css/template.module.css"
import Img from "gatsby-image"
import { FaMoneyBillWave } from "react-icons/fa"
```

```
const Template = ({ data }) => {
    const { name, timeRequired, timings, entryFees, description: {
    description }, images } = data.place;
    const [mainImage, ...placeImages] = images

    return (
        <Layout>

            <StyledHero img={mainImage.fluid} />
            <section className={styles.template}>
                <div className={styles.center}>
                    <div className={styles.images}>
                        {placeImages && placeImages.map((item,index) =>{
                            return <Img key={index} fluid={item.fluid}
                            alt="single" className={styles.image}/>
                        })}
                    </div>
                    <h2>{name}</h2>
                    <div className={styles.info}>
                        <p>
                            <FaMoneyBillWave className={styles.icon} />
                            Entry Fees - {entryFees}
                        </p>
                    </div>
                </div>
            </section>
        </Layout>
    )
}

export const query = graphql`
query($slug: String!){
    place: contentfulAmazingHampiData(slug:{eq: $slug}){
        name
        slug
        timeRequired
        timings
```

```
    entryFees
    description{
        description
    }
    images{
        fluid{
            ...GatsbyContentfulFluid_tracedSVG
        }
    }
  }
}
`

export default Template
```

Once we go to a page, we can see our images and the text, as shown in Figure 4-54.

Hazara Rama Temple

Entry Fees - None

***Figure 4-54.*** *Images and text are now displayed*

Next, let's add all the fields to the `place-template.js` for our places. It will contain the `timeRequired`, `timings`, and `description` fields. The updated code is marked in bold in Listing 4-24.

***Listing 4-24.*** Time Fields in place-template.js

```
...
...
import { FaMoneyBillWave, FaClock, FaTypo3 } from "react-icons/fa"

const Template = ({ data }) => {
    const { name, timeRequired, timings, entryFees, description: {
description }, images } = data.place;
    const [mainImage, ...placeImages] = images

    return (
        <Layout>
            <SEO title={name} />
            <StyledHero img={mainImage.fluid} />
            <section className={styles.template}>
                <div className={styles.center}>
                    <div className={styles.images}>
                        {placeImages && placeImages.map((item,index) =>{
                            return <Img key={index} fluid={item.fluid}
                            alt="single" className={styles.image}/>
                        })}
                    </div>
                    <h2>{name}</h2>
                    <div className={styles.info}>
                        <p>
                            <FaMoneyBillWave className={styles.icon} />
                            Entry Fees - {entryFees}
                        </p>
                        <p>
                            <FaClock className={styles.icon} />Time
                            Required - {timeRequired} hours
                        </p>
```

```
                {timings ?
                    <p>
                        <FaTypo3 className={styles.icon} />
                        Timings - {timings}
                    </p>:

                }
                </div>
            <p className={styles.desc}>{description}</p>
                </div>
            </section>
        </Layout>
    )
}

...
```

Our page now looks almost complete, as shown in Figure 4-55.

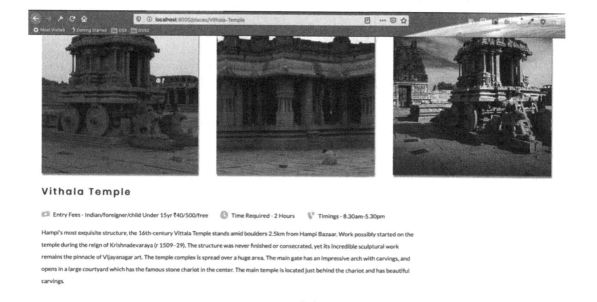

*Figure 4-55.* *The page is nearly complete*

One last thing to do is to add a button that allows visitors to go back to the Places page. Add an AniLink to place-template.js. The updated code is marked in bold in Listing 4-25.

***Listing 4-25.*** AniLink in place-template.js

```
...
...
import { FaMoneyBillWave, FaClock, FaTypo3 } from "react-icons/fa"
import AniLink from "gatsby-plugin-transition-link/AniLink"

const Template = ({ data }) => {
    const { name, timeRequired, timings, entryFees, description: {
    description }, images } = data.place;
    const [mainImage, ...placeImages] = images

    return (
        <Layout>
            <SEO title={name} />
            <StyledHero img={mainImage.fluid} />
            <section className={styles.template}>
                <div className={styles.center}>
                                            ...
                                            ...
                    <h2>{name}</h2>
                    <div className={styles.info}>
                                    ...
                                    ...
                    </div>
                <p className={styles.desc}>{description}</p>
                    <AniLink fade to="/places" className="btn-primary">back
                    to places</AniLink>
                </div>
            </section>
        </Layout>
    )
}

...
```

This will display a nice return button (called Back to Tours), as shown in Figure 4-56.

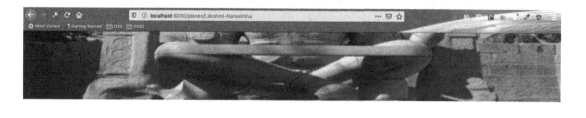

**Lakshmi Narasimha**

Entry Fees - None          Time Required - 1 Hours

This temple features the biggest effigy in Hampi, of Narasimha sitting on SeshaNaag i.e. the seven headed snake acting as a shelter to him. The idol of Goddess Lakshmi is placed along with that of Narasimha.

BACK TO TOURS

***Figure 4-56.*** *The Back to Tours button is displayed*

Once it has pushed the code to GitHub, it starts the automatic deployment to Netlify. My Netlify build failed because of the `GatsbyContentfulFluid_tracedSVG` fragment that's used in three places (see Figure 4-57).

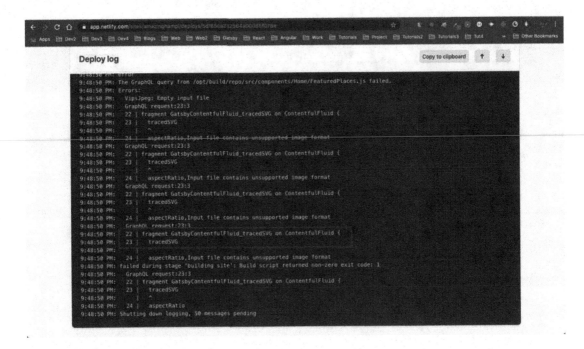

*Figure 4-57.* The Netlify error

I fixed the error by changing the fragment from GatsbyContentfulFluid_tracedSVG to GatsbyContentfulFluid in all three files, as shown in Figure 4-58.

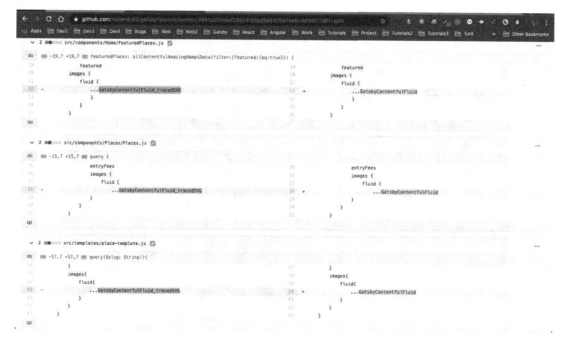

***Figure 4-58.*** *Changing this fragment fixes the error*

You can find my code in my GitHub account here[8]. The site is successfully live here[9].

# Summary

This completes Chapter 4 and the second part of the tourism site using Contentful. We covered the following topics in this chapter:

- Setting up the Contentful CMS and connecting to the project

- Creating the Places component, which shows data stored in the Contentful CMS

In the next chapter, we continue with the tourism site using Contentful. We will create the Blog and Photos components in that chapter.

---

[8]https://github.com/nabendu82/gatsbyTourism
[9]https://amazinghampi.netlify.com/

# Creating a Tourism Site with Contentful: Part Three

Welcome to Chapter 5. In this chapter, we will add two more components to the tourism site: the Blog and Photos components. They will show data stored in the Contentful CMS. Let's start by creating a new content model for the blog on the site.

## Creating the Blog Component

From the Contentful dashboard, click the Content Model tab and then click the Add Content Type button. This is shown in Figure 5-1.

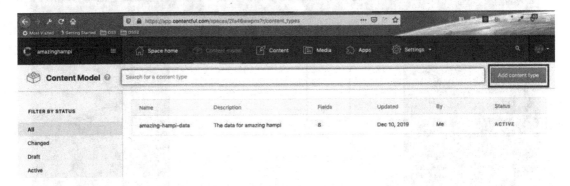

***Figure 5-1.*** *Choose to add content type from the Contentful dashboard*

In the popup window shown in Figure 5-2, provide a name and description and then click Create.

© Nabendu Biswas 2021
N. Biswas, *Foundation Gatsby Projects*, https://doi.org/10.1007/978-1-4842-6558-1_5

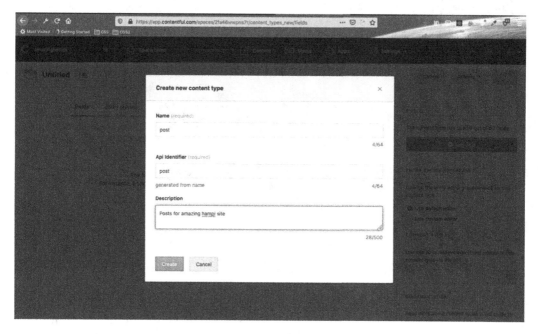

***Figure 5-2.*** *Create new content type*

After you click Add Field, you will get the popup shown in Figure 5-3. Click Text in this window.

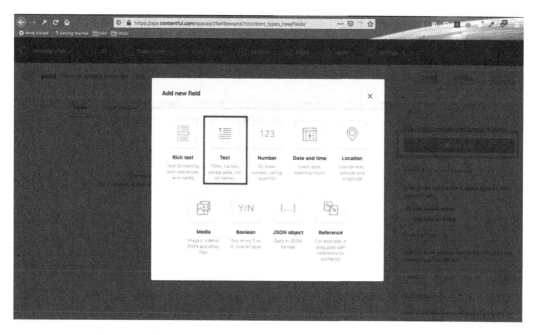

***Figure 5-3.*** *Add a Text field*

Provide a name and click Create and Configure, as shown in Figure 5-4.

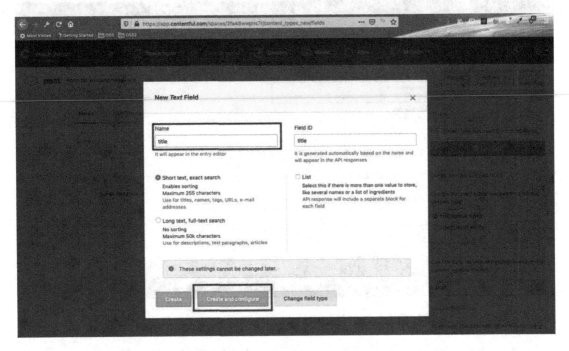

***Figure 5-4.***  *Choose a name for your Text field*

In the next window, click the Validations tab. After that click, check the Required Field button and then click Save, as shown in Figure 5-5.

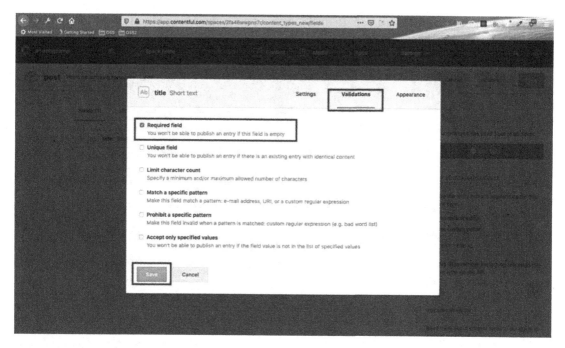

***Figure 5-5.***  *Make this field required*

Follow this exact same process to create a Slug field. It is shown in Figure 5-6.

***Figure 5-6.***  *Create a slug field*

Next, add a Date and Time field, as shown in Figure 5-7.

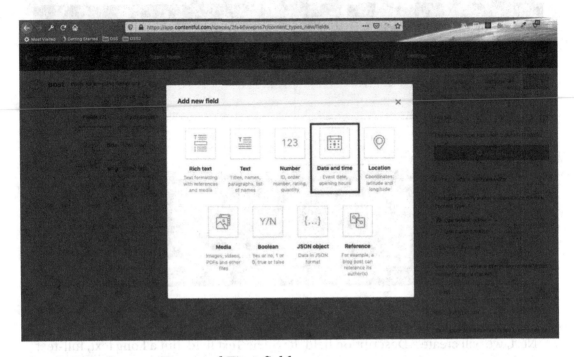

**Figure 5-7.**  *Create a Date and Time field*

Give this field a name and click Create and Configure. You need to follow the process to make it a required field. This is shown in Figure 5-8.

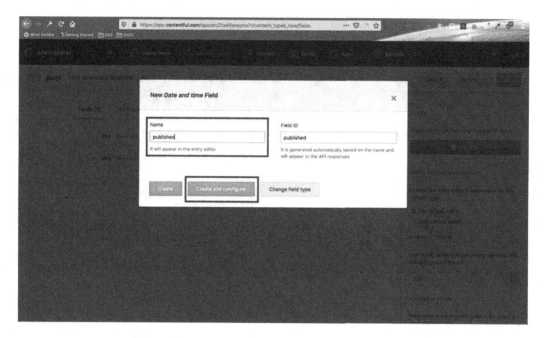

***Figure 5-8.***  *The Published field*

Next, we will create a Description field. It will be Text field, but a Long text, full-text search. As usual, make it a required field, as shown in Figure 5-9.

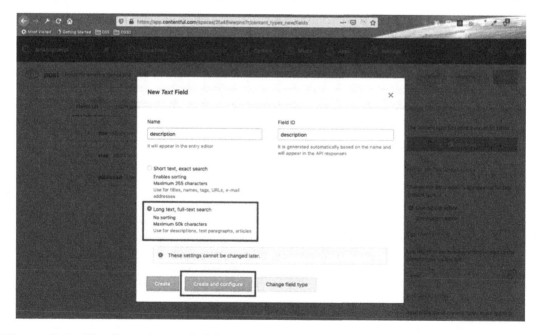

***Figure 5-9.***  *The Description field*

Next, create an Author field. But don't make it required; simply click Create. This is shown in Figure 5-10.

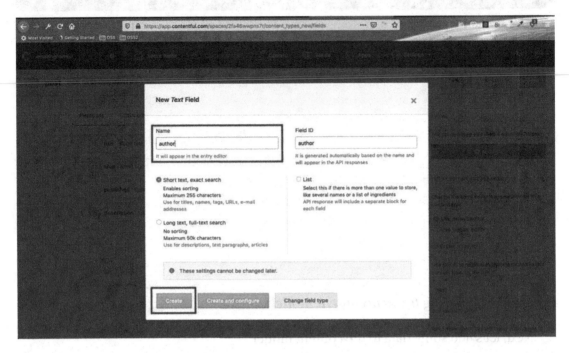

***Figure 5-10.*** *The Author field*

After adding all these fields, click Save in the top-right corner to save this content model, as shown in Figure 5-11.

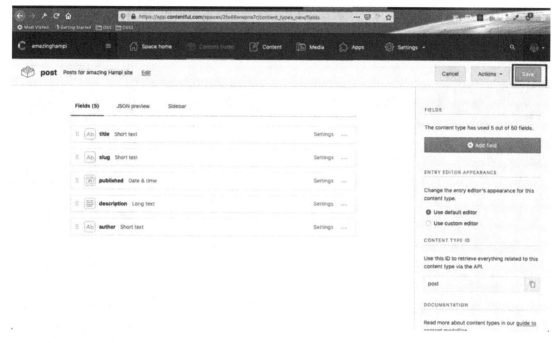

**Figure 5-11.** *Saving the new content model*

Next, let's add some data to the content model.

# Adding Data to the Content Model

Go to the Content tab and click the Add Entry button. Then choose Post, as shown in Figure 5-12.

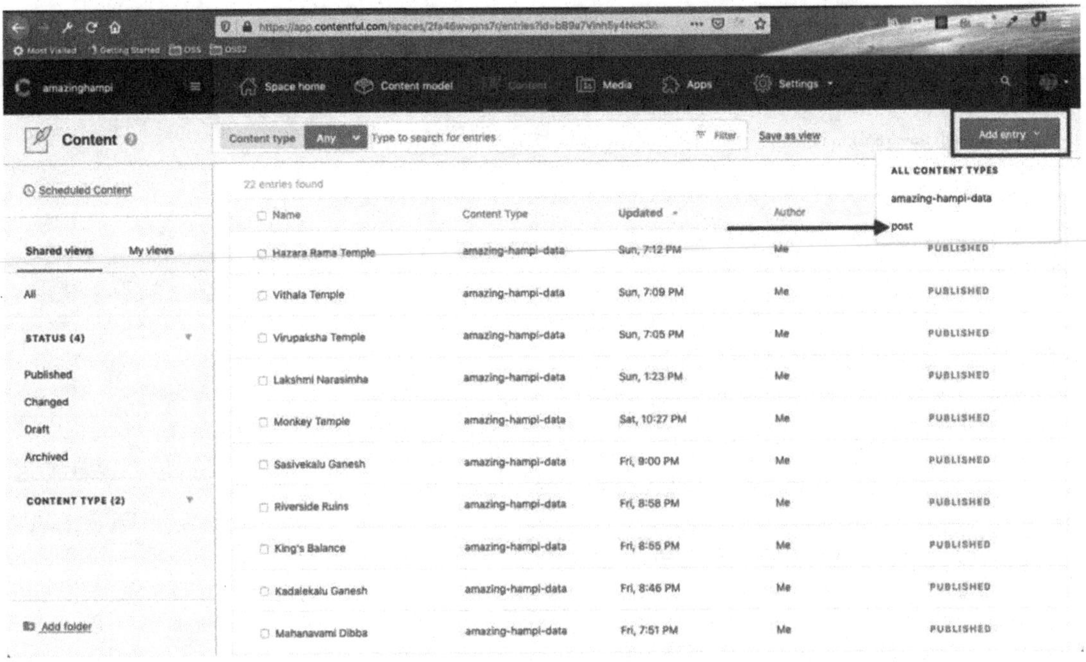

**Figure 5-12.** *Choose Post to add to the content model*

For this post I am taking real blogs from Medium. We will put them in the Description field, but it requires a Markdown file. We can convert the Medium post to Markdown with this[1] awesome npm package. It is shown in Figure 5-13.

---

[1]https://medium.com/@macropus/export-your-medium-posts-to-markdown-b5ccc8cb0050

**Figure 5-13.**  *The content*

I added four original blogs from Medium.com, as shown in Figure 5-14. I'll add more later, as I am also planning to visit Hampi soon.

**Figure 5-14.** *Hippy Hampi blogs*

One thing I forgot to add to the content model is an Image field. I will head over to the Content Model - Post and add a Media field. See Figure 5-15.

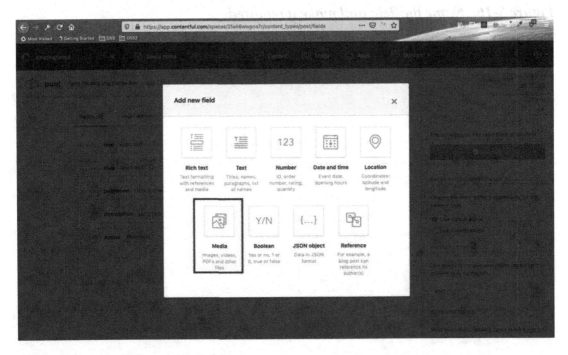

**Figure 5-15.** *Add a Media field*

Give it the name image and then click on Create and Configure to make it a required field, as shown in Figure 5-16.

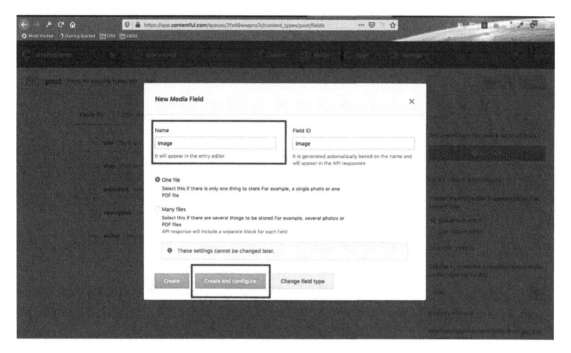

***Figure 5-16.***  *Name the field and make it required*

Next, save it by clicking the Save button, as shown in Figure 5-17.

**Figure 5-17.** *Save the new field*

I also added the required image to all the posts. After that, to access these new posts, we need to restart the server. Go ahead and stop `gatsby develop` from the terminal and re-run it.

Also, refresh the GraphQL in the browser and write the query in Figure 5-18 to display all posts.

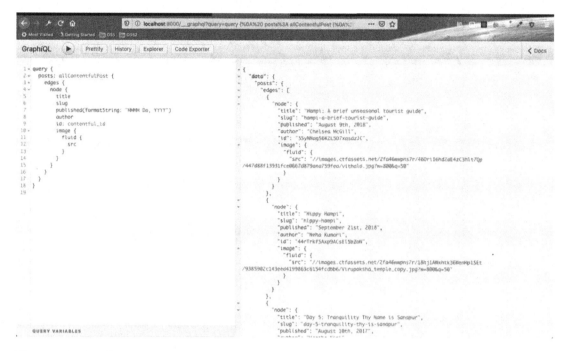

***Figure 5-18.***  *Our query*

Before moving forward, I want to create another GraphQL query. Generally the blogs are posted in descending order, meaning that the newer blogs should come up. This is shown in Figure 5-19.

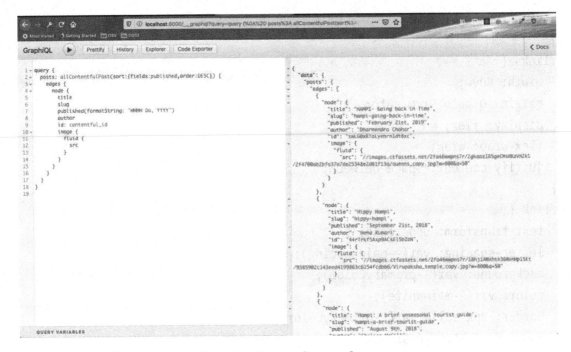

**Figure 5-19.** *The posts are listed in descending order*

# Displaying the Blog Component

It's time to write the code to display the Blog component. Create a new blog folder inside the **components** folder. Inside it, create two files called BlogList.js and BlogCard.js.

Let's first add the CSS required for this component in the css folder. Add a file called blog.module.css to the css folder and add the contents in Listing 5-1 to it.

*Listing 5-1.* The blog.module.css File

```
.blog {
  padding: 4rem 0;
}
.center {
  width: 80vw;
  margin: 3rem auto;
  display: grid;
  grid-template-columns: repeat(auto-fill, minmax(280px, 1fr));
  grid-column-gap: 2rem;
```

```css
  grid-row-gap: 2rem;
}
.links {
  width: 80vw;
  margin: 0 auto 5rem auto;
  display: flex;
  flex-wrap: wrap;
  justify-content: space-between;
}
.link {
  text-transform: uppercase;
  letter-spacing: var(--mainSpacing);
  background: var(--primaryColor);
  color: var(--mainWhite);
  border: 2px solid var(--primaryColor);
  padding: 0.25rem 0.5rem;
  border-radius: 0.5rem;
  display: inline-block;
  transition: var(--mainTransition);
  cursor: pointer;
}
.link:hover {
  background: transparent;
  color: var(--primaryColor);
}
.active {
  background: var(--mainWhite);
  color: var(--primaryColor);
}

@media screen and (min-width: 576px) {
  .center {
    grid-template-columns: repeat(auto-fill, minmax(368.66px, 1fr));
  }
```

```css
  .links {
    width: 60vw;
  }
}
@media screen and (min-width: 1200px) {
  .center {
    width: 100%;
    max-width: 1170px;
  }
}
```

For now, add this dummy content to BlogCard.js, which we will change soon. The code is shown in Listing 5-2.

***Listing 5-2.*** Dummy Content for BlogCard.js

```javascript
import React from "react"

const BlogCard = () => {
    return <div>This is a blog card</div>
}

export default BlogCard
```

Next, add the content in Listing 5-3 to the BlogList.js file. Here, we are using the GraphQL query we created earlier in our GraphiQL playground. We are mapping through the responses we are getting from this query.

***Listing 5-3.*** The BlogList.js File

```javascript
import React from "react"
import BlogCard from "./BlogCard"
import Title from "../Title"
import { useStaticQuery, graphql } from "gatsby"
import styles from "../../css/blog.module.css"

const getPosts = graphql`
query {
posts: allContentfulPost(sort:{fields:published,order:DESC}) {
```

```
    edges {
        node {
            title
            slug
            published(formatString: "MMMM Do, YYYY")
            author
            id: contentful_id
            image {
                fluid {
                    ...GatsbyContentfulFluid
                }
            }
        }
    }
}
}
`

const BlogList = () => {
    const { posts } = useStaticQuery(getPosts)

    return (
        <section className={styles.blog}>
            <Title title="hampi" subtitle="blogs" />
            <div className={styles.center}>
                {posts.edges.map(({ node }) => {
                    return <BlogCard key={node.id} blog={node} />
                })}
            </div>
        </section>
    )
}

export default BlogList
```

Finally, add this component to the blog.js file so that it can be rendered when we click on the Blog page. The component's code is highlighted in bold in Listing 5-4.

***Listing 5-4.*** The BlogList in blog.js

```
import React from 'react'
import Layout from "../components/Layout"
import StyledHero from "../components/StyledHero"
import { graphql } from 'gatsby'
import BlogList from '../components/Blog/BlogList'

export const query = graphql`
query {
    blogBcg: file(relativePath: {eq: "blogBcg.jpeg"}) {
        childImageSharp {
            fluid(quality: 90, maxWidth: 4160) {
                ...GatsbyImageSharpFluid_withWebp
            }
        }
    }
}
`;

export default function blog({ data }) {
    return (
        <Layout>
            <StyledHero img={data.blogBcg.childImageSharp.fluid} />
            <BlogList />
        </Layout>
    )
}
```

# Creating the BlogCard Component

We will work on the BlogCard component now. Let's start by adding some styles to it. Create a new file called blog-card.module.css inside the css folder. Add the content in Listing 5-5 to it.

***Listing 5-5.*** The blog-card.module.css File

```css
.blog {
  box-shadow: var(--lightShadow);
  transition: var(--mainTransition);
}
.blog:hover {
  box-shadow: var(--darkShadow);
}

.img-container {
  position: relative;
  background: var(--primaryColor);
  transition: var(--mainTransition);
}
.img {
  transition: var(--mainTransition);
}
.img-container:hover .img {
  opacity: 0.3;
}

.link {
  position: absolute;
  top: 50%;
  left: 50%;
  transform: translate(-50%, -50%);
  opacity: 0;
  text-transform: uppercase;
  letter-spacing: var(--mainSpacing);
  color: var(--mainWhite);
  border: 2px solid var(--mainWhite);
  padding: 0.5rem 0.7rem;
  display: inline-block;
  transition: var(--mainTransition);
  cursor: pointer;
}
```

```css
.link:hover {
  background: var(--mainWhite);
  color: var(--primaryColor);
}
.img-container:hover .link {
  opacity: 1;
}

.footer {
  padding: 1rem;
  text-align: left;
}
.footer h4 {
  text-transform: capitalize;
  margin-bottom: 0;
}
.date {
  position: absolute;
  left: 0;
  top: 75%;
  background: var(--primaryColor);
  padding: 0.3rem 0.5rem;
  border-top-right-radius: 1rem;
  border-bottom-right-radius: 1rem;
}
```

Next, let's update the `BlogCard.js` file with real code, as shown in Listing 5-6. Here, we are just adding some styles from the `css` folder. We are getting the `blog` props from the `BlogList` component. We are destructuring it by taking the title image and publishing it to show the blog.

Once we click on the post, we will use the slug to display it. (We will do that in the next section.)

***Listing 5-6.***  Code in BlogCard.js

```
import React from "react"
import styles from "../../css/blog-card.module.css"
import Image from "gatsby-image"
import AniLink from "gatsby-plugin-transition-link/AniLink"

const BlogCard = ({ blog }) => {
    const { slug, title, image, published } = blog
    return (
        <article className={styles.blog}>
            <div className={styles.imgContainer}>
                <Image fluid={image.fluid} className={styles.img}
                alt="single post" />
                <AniLink fade className={styles.link} to={`/blog/${slug}`}>
                    read more
                </AniLink>
                <h6 className={styles.date}>{published}</h6>
            </div>
            <div className={styles.footer}>
                <h4>{title}</h4>
            </div>
        </article>
    )
}

export default BlogCard
```

This code will show all four blogs from Contentful, as shown in Figure 5-20.

**Figure 5-20.**   *Hampi blogs shown in a browser*

## Creating the Single Blog Page

We will now show the blog pages when a user clicks on them. To do this, we will follow the same template approach that we followed on the tour. Create a file called blog-template.js inside the templates folder. For now, add the dummy data from Listing 5-7 to it.

*Listing 5-7.*   The Dummy Code for blog-template.js

```
import React from "react"

const Blog = () => {
    return <div>this is single blog page</div>
}

export default Blog
```

Let's write our GraphQL query in the GraphiQL playground, as shown in Figure 5-21.

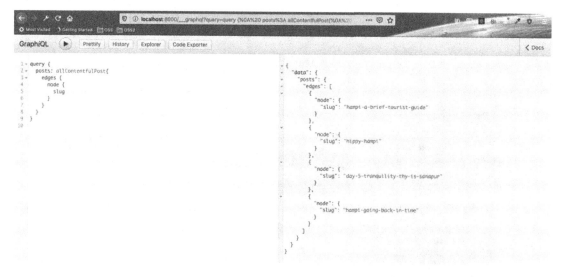

**Figure 5-21.** *The GraphQL query*

Next, open gatsby-node.js and add this new query. We will also loop through the node and create the page. The updated code is marked in bold in Listing 5-8.

***Listing 5-8.*** Blog in gatsby-node.js

```
const path = require("path")

exports.createPages = async ({ graphql, actions }) => {
const { createPage } = actions

const { data } = await graphql(`
query {
    places: allContentfulAmazingHampiData {
        edges {
        node {
                slug
            }
        }
    }
```

```
      posts: allContentfulPost {
         edges {
            node {
               slug
            }
         }
      }
   }
`)

data.places.edges.forEach((({ node }) => {
   createPage({
            path: `places/${node.slug}`,
            component: path.resolve("./src/templates/place-template.js"),
            context: {
               slug: node.slug,
            },
         })
   })
   data.posts.edges.forEach((({ node }) => {
      createPage({
         path: `blog/${node.slug}`,
         component: path.resolve("./src/templates/blog-template.js"),
         context: {
            slug: node.slug,
         },
      })
   })
}
```

To test whether everything is working, we need to stop and start gatsby develop in the terminal. After that, move to any nonexistent page in the browser and you can see that those pages have been created. See Figure 5-22.

***Figure 5-22.*** *New pages were created*

Click on any one of them and you will see the dummy text, as shown in Figure 5-23.

***Figure 5-23.*** *The dummy text is shown for now*

Let's create the query to show the single blog post in the playground, as shown in Figure 5-24.

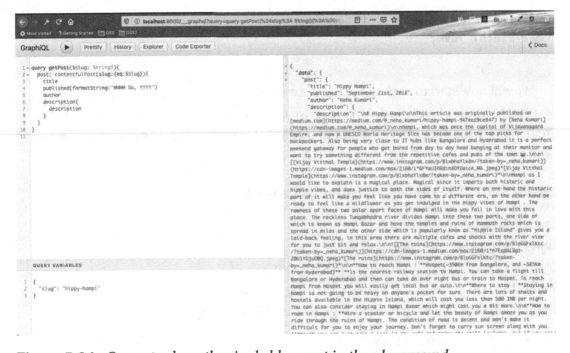

***Figure 5-24.*** *Query to show the single blog post in the playground*

Let's also add the styles to the css folder and call it single-blog.module.css. The contents are shown in Listing 5-9.

***Listing 5-9.*** The single-blog.module.css File

```css
.blog {
  padding: 4rem 0;
}
.center {
  width: 80vw;
  margin: 0 auto;
}
.blog h1,
.blog h4 {
  text-transform: capitalize;
}
.post {
  margin: 2rem 0;
}
```

```
.post img {
  max-width: 70vw;
}
```

We will now start to update our `blog-template.js` file. We are using the query
we created in the playground. After that, we destructure the data we are receiving. We
are right now showing the Title and Published fields in the blog. The code is shown in
Listing 5-10.

*Listing 5-10.*  The Updated blog-template.js File

```
import React from "react"
import { graphql } from "gatsby"
import Layout from "../components/Layout"
import styles from "../css/single-blog.module.css"
import AniLink from "gatsby-plugin-transition-link/AniLink"

const Blog = ({ data }) => {
    const { title, published, author, description: {description}} = data.post;
    return <Layout>
                <section className={styles.blog}>
                    <div className={styles.center}>
<h1>{title}</h1>
                        <h4>Published at: {published}</h4>
                    </div>
                </section>
        </Layout>
}

export const query = graphql`
    query getPost($slug: String!){
    post: contentfulPost(slug:{eq:$slug}){
    title
    published(formatString:"MMMM Do, YYYY")
    author
    description{
        description
    }
```

```
}
}
`;
```

```
export default Blog
```

When we head over to a blog post, we can see that it is rendered properly, as shown in Figure 5-25.

***Figure 5-25.*** *Hippy hampi is being properly rendered*

Let's also add an Author field and a link to go back to the Blog page. The updated code is marked in bold in Listing 5-11.

***Listing 5-11.*** Author and Link in the blog-template.js File

```
...
import styles from "../css/single-blog.module.css"
import AniLink from "gatsby-plugin-transition-link/AniLink"

const Blog = ({ data }) => {
    const { title, published, author, description: {description}} = data.post;
    return <Layout>
                <section className={styles.blog}>
                    <div className={styles.center}>
                <h1>{title}</h1>
                        <h4>Published at: {published}</h4>
                        <h4>Author: {author}</h4>
```

```
                    <AniLink fade to="/blog" className="btn-
                    primary">all blogs</AniLink>
            </div>
        </section>
    </Layout>
}
...
```

To display the Markdown file that we are getting in the Description field, we need to do some configuration. I found this[2] blog, which was helpful to me to do the setup.

To display Markdown files, we need to npm install the gatsby-transformer-remark plugin. Head over to the terminal and stop the gatsby develop. Then install the plugin by running the npm install --save gatsby-transformer-remark command. Finally, add it to the gatsby-config.js file, as shown in Listing 5-12.

***Listing 5-12.*** The gatsby-transformer-remark Plugin Added to gatsby-config.js

```
require("dotenv").config({
  path: `.env.${process.env.NODE_ENV}`,
})

  plugins: [
...
...

    ,
    `gatsby-plugin-sitemap`,
    `gatsby-plugin-styled-components`,
    `gatsby-transformer-sharp`,
    `gatsby-plugin-sharp`,
    `gatsby-plugin-transition-link`,
    `gatsby-transformer-remark`
  ]
}
```

Next, move back to your blog-template.js file. Here we need to update the query for description a bit to add a transformer plugin. The updated code is highlighted in Listing 5-13.

---

[2]https://codebushi.com/gatsby-with-contentful-cms/

***Listing 5-13.*** Markdown in blog-template.js

```
const Blog = ({ data }) => {
    const { title, published, author, description: {childMarkdownRemark}} =
    data.post;
    return <Layout>
                    <section className={styles.blog}>
                        <div className={styles.center}
            <h1>{title}</h1>
                            <h4>Published at: {published}</h4>
                            <h4>Author: {author}</h4>
                            <div dangerouslySetInnerHTML={{__
                            html:childMarkdownRemark.html}} />
                            <AniLink fade to="/blog" className="btn-primary">
                            all blogs</AniLink>
                        </div>
                    </section>
        </Layout>
}

export const query = graphql`
    query getPost($slug: String!){
            post: contentfulPost(slug:{eq:$slug}){
    title
    published(formatString:"MMMM Do, YYYY")
    author
    description{
        childMarkdownRemark{
            html
        }
    }
}
}
`;

export default Blog
```

Start your `gatsby develop` from the terminal and then head over to a blog post. You can see that the Markdown rendered successfully, as shown in Figure 5-26.

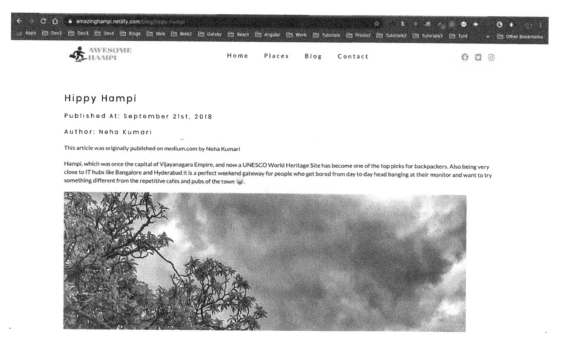

***Figure 5-26.*** *Awesome Hampi has rendered properly*

I have been in Hampi for the past four days and created six blogs on Hampi. The four day blogs can be found here[3]. My other blogs (on saving money during your Hampi stay) can be found here[4]. Yet another blog on Rama and Shiva in Hampi can be found here[5]. I added these blogs in Contentful so they are reflected on the site, as shown in Figure 5-27.

---

[3]https://medium.com/@nabendu82/my-hampi-vacation-day1-b0a2b7e26cbf

[4]https://medium.com/@nabendu82/how-to-save-money-and-travel-in-hampi-495a5d3f2415

[5]https://medium.com/@nabendu82/rama-and-shiva-in-hampi-b5cce3ac5496

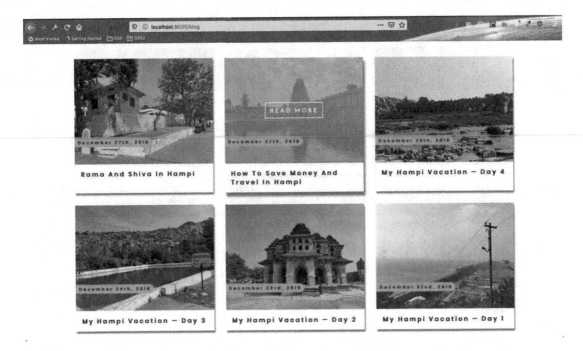

**Figure 5-27.** *Blogs have been added*

Similarly, I added many new places and some missing pictures for all the places, as shown in Figure 5-28.

***Figure 5-28.*** *Places and images were also added*

Upon checking the blog, I found that it will look nice if it contained the header image like the place.

As we did with the place-template.js file, we need to add StyledHero to blog-template.js. The updated code is marked in bold in Listing 5-14.

***Listing 5-14.*** StyledHero in blog-template.js

```
...
...
import AniLink from "gatsby-plugin-transition-link/AniLink"
import StyledHero from "../components/StyledHero"

const Blog = ({ data }) => {
    const { title, published, author, description: {childMarkdownRemark},
    image} = data.post;
    return <Layout>
                <h1 className={styles.center}>{title}</h1>
                <StyledHero img={image.fluid} />
                <section className={styles.blog
```

```
                  <div className={styles.center}>
                  <h4>Published at: {published}</h4>
                  <h4>Author: {author}</h4>
                  ...
                  </div>
              </section>
        </Layout>
}

export const query = graphql`
    query getPost($slug: String!){
        post: contentfulPost(slug:{eq:$slug}){
    title
    published(formatString:"MMMM Do, YYYY")
    author
    description{
        childMarkdownRemark{
            html
        }
    }
    image {
            fluid {
                ...GatsbyContentfulFluid
            }
        }
}
}
`;

export default Blog
```

This code will show a nice header image with every blog post, as shown in Figure 5-29.

***Figure 5-29.*** *This header image is shown with every blog post*

Next, we will commit and push the changes to GitHub for the automatic deployment in Netlify to start. Our site is live at `https://amazinghampi.netlify.com/`,[6] as shown in Figure 5-30.

---

[6]`https://amazinghampi.netlify.com/`

***Figure 5-30.*** *The live amazinghampi site*

# Creating the Photos Component

In this section, we'll create a new page called Photos. It will contain most of the photos that I took during my Hampi vacation[7]. All of these photos are royalty free, so feel free to use them. To create a new link in the navbar and footer components, we just need to add it to the links.js file. The changed code is marked in bold in Listing 5-15.

***Listing 5-15.*** Photos in links.js

```
export default [
  {
    path: "/",
    text: "home",
  },
  {
    path: "/places",
```

---

[7]https://medium.com/@nabendu82/my-hampi-vacation-day1-b0a2b7e26cbf

```
    text: "places",
  },
  {
    path: "/blog",
    text: "blog",
  },
  {
    path: "/photos",
    text: "photos",
  },
  {
    path: "/contact",
    text: "contact",
  }
]
```

This code will be added to the navbar and the footer on the website, as shown in Figure 5-31.

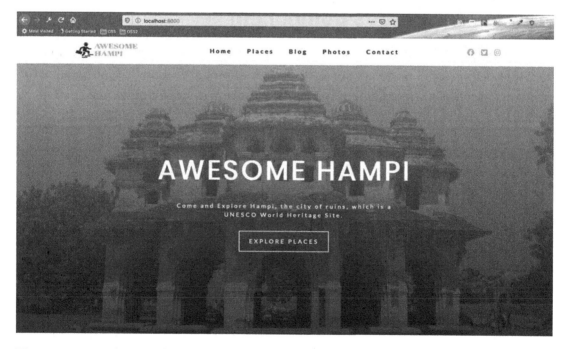

*Figure 5-31.*  *The new link is added*

Let's create a photos.js file inside the pages folder. It is similar to the blog.js page, except the image is hampiPhoto.jpg in this case. The code is shown in Listing 5-16.

*Listing 5-16.* The photos.js File

```
import React from 'react'
import Layout from "../components/Layout"
import StyledHero from "../components/StyledHero"
import { graphql } from 'gatsby'
import PhotoList from '../components/Photos/PhotoList'

export const query = graphql`
query {
    blogBcg: file(relativePath: {eq: "hampiPhoto.jpg"}) {
        childImageSharp {
            fluid(quality: 90, maxWidth: 4160) {
                ...GatsbyImageSharpFluid_withWebp
            }
        }
    }
}
`;

export default function photos({ data }) {
    return (
        <Layout>
            <StyledHero img={data.blogBcg.childImageSharp.fluid} />
            <PhotoList />
        </Layout>
    )
}
```

Next, let's create a folder called photos inside the components directory. Then create a file called PhotoList.js inside it. The dummy code we use for now is shown in Listing 5-17.

***Listing 5-17.*** Dummy Code for PhotoList.js

```
import React from 'react'

const PhotoList = () => {
    return (
            <div>PhotoList component</div>
        )
}
export default PhotoList;
```

When we open the Photos page, it displays everything correctly, as shown in Figure 5-32.

***Figure 5-32.***  *The Photos page works as expected*

## Setting Up Contentful for the Photos Component

Before adding code to the file, we need to create content in Contentful and test the query. Head over to Contentful and create a new content model, as shown in Figure 5-33.

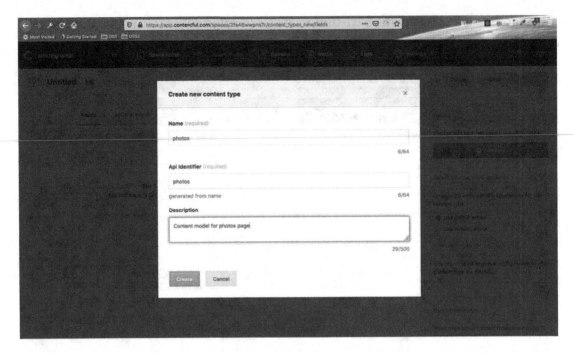

**Figure 5-33.**  *Create a new content model*

I added four fields, all of them required. See Figure 5-34.

**Figure 5-34.**  *Four required fields*

After saving by clicking the Save button, let's add some content from the Content tab, as shown in Figure 5-35.

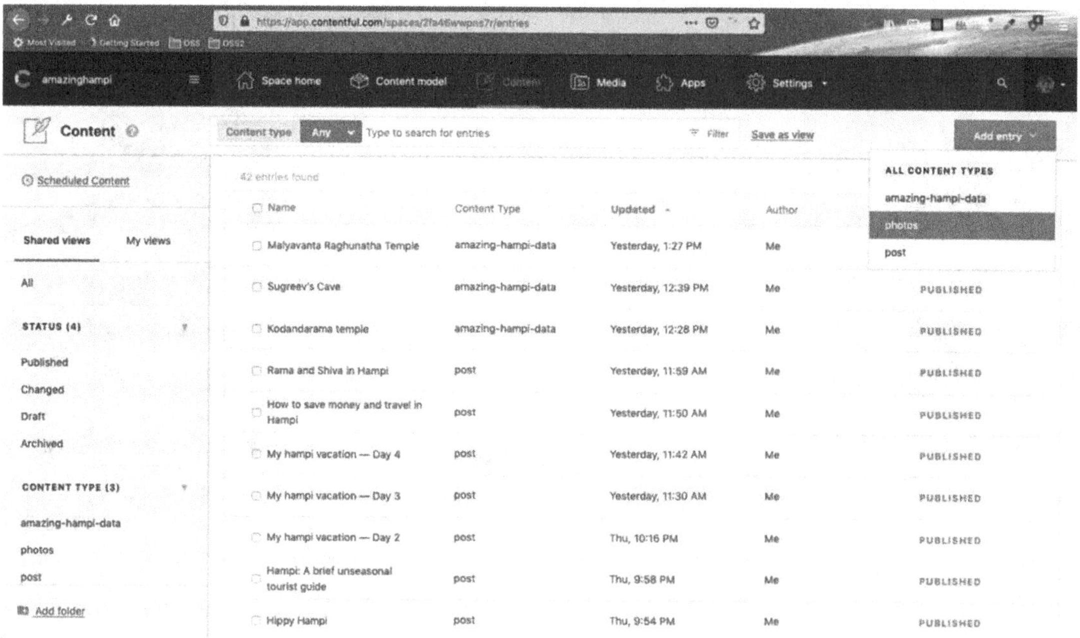

**Figure 5-35.** *Adding content*

On the content page, I provide a name, slug, brief description, and two photos. They are the same image, but the first one is smaller and 650x487 pixels and will be displayed on the Photos page. The larger, original photo will be displayed once we go to the new page using the slug mechanism. The photo, which anyone can download for personal use, is shown in Figure 5-36.

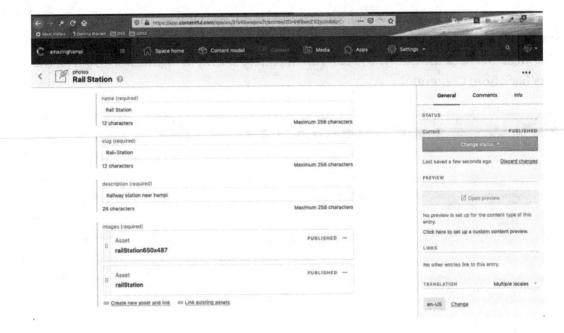

**Figure 5-36.**  *The content is added*

I added some content from my Hampi trip, as shown in Figure 5-37. I will add hundreds more items later.

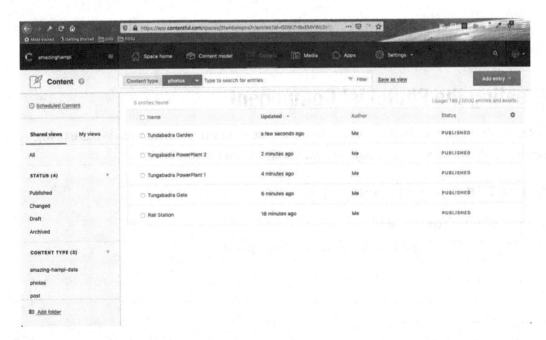

**Figure 5-37.**  *Content from my Hampi trip*

After any change in Contentful, you have to restart the DEV server by closing and starting `gatsby develop` from the terminal. Also, refresh your GraphiQL playground at GraphQL[8] to check the query. You can run the query shown in Figure 5-38 to get all the data back from Contentful.

***Figure 5-38.*** *All the data from Contentful*

## Creating the PhotoList Component

Let's add the query to `PhotoList.js` to get all the data from Contentful. We are using similar code we used with `BlogList.js.` It's shown in Listing 5-18.

***Listing 5-18.*** Updated PhotoList.js

```
import React from 'react'
import { useStaticQuery, graphql } from "gatsby"
```

---

[8]http://localhost:8000/graphql

```
const getPhotos = graphql`
query {
            photos: allContentfulPhotos {
        edges{
            node {
                id: contentful_id
                name
                slug
                description
                images{
                    fluid{
                        src
                    }
                }
            }
        }
    }
}
`;

const PhotoList = () => {
    const { photos } = useStaticQuery(getPhotos);
    console.log(photos);
    return (
            <div>PhotoList component</div>
        )
}
export default PhotoList;
```

Let's check whether we are receiving the data by opening the console and going to the Photos page, as shown in Figure 5-39.

***Figure 5-39.*** *The data is being received from Contentful*

Now that we are receiving the data, it's time to show it in the component. First, let's add some more imports at the top of the PhotoList.js file. Next, let's update inside the return statement to pass each node through a map to the PhotoCard component. The updated code is highlighted in Listing 5-19.

***Listing 5-19.*** PhotoCard Component in PhotoList.js

```
import React from 'react'
import { useStaticQuery, graphql } from "gatsby"
import Title from "../Title"
import styles from "../../css/items.module.css"
import PhotoCard from './PhotoCard'

const getPhotos = graphql`
query {
        photos: allContentfulPhotos {
    edges{
        node {
            id: contentful_id
```

```
            name
            slug
            description
            images{
                fluid{
                    ...GatsbyContentfulFluid
                }
            }
        }
    }
}
}
`;

const PhotoList = () => {
    const { photos } = useStaticQuery(getPhotos);
    return (
        <section className={styles.tours}>
            <Title title="hampi" subtitle="photos" />
            <div className={styles.center}>
                {photos.edges.map(({ node }) => {
                    return <PhotoCard key={node.id} photo={node} />
                })}
            </div>
        </section>
    )
}
export default PhotoList;
```

## Creating the PhotoCard Component

Create PhotoCard.js inside the photos folder. Add the content in Listing 5-20 to it.

***Listing 5-20.*** PhotoCard.js

```
import React from 'react'
import Image from "gatsby-image"
import styles from "../../css/place.module.css"
import AniLink from "gatsby-plugin-transition-link/AniLink"

const PhotoCard = ({ photo }) => {
    const { name, slug, images } = photo;
    let mainImage = images[0].fluid;

    return (
        <article className={styles.place}>
            <div className={styles.imgContainer}>
                <Image fluid={mainImage} className={styles.img} alt="single
                photo" />
                <AniLink fade className={styles.link}
                to={`/photos/${slug}`}>open</AniLink>
            </div>
            <div className={styles.footer}>
                <h3>{name}</h3>
            </div>
        </article>
    )
}

export default PhotoCard
```

When we go to our Photos page in the browser, we get all the five photos, as shown in Figure 5-40.

*Figure 5-40.* *All five photos are shown*

# Creating the Photos Template

In this section, we will start adding code to display the larger image. It will appear when we click the Open button inside the photo on the Photos page.

To do this, we will follow the process we used earlier in this chapter. Create a file called photos-template.js inside the templates folder and add the contents of Listing 5-21. For now, use dummy data, which we are going to replace soon.

*Listing 5-21.* The photos-template.js File

```
import React from 'react'
const Photos = () => {
    return (
        <div>
            This is Photos template
        </div>
    )
}
export default Photos
```

Let's write our GraphQL query in the GraphiQL playground, as shown in Figure 5-41.

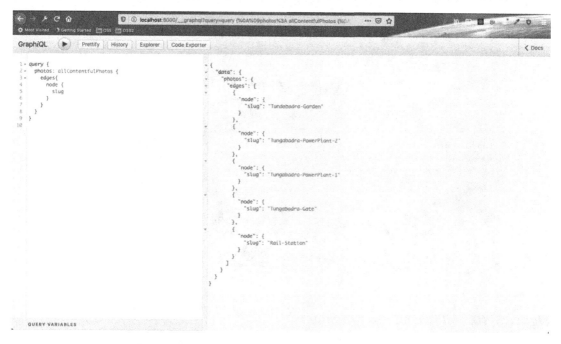

***Figure 5-41.*** *The GraphiQL playground*

Next, open `gatsby-node.js` and add this new query. Next, we will loop through the node and create the page. The updated code is marked in bold in Listing 5-22.

***Listing 5-22.*** Photos in gatsby-node.js

```
const path = require("path")

exports.createPages = async ({ graphql, actions }) => {
const { createPage } = actions

const { data } = await graphql(`
query {
    places: allContentfulAmazingHampiData {
        edges {
        node {
                slug
            }
        }
```

```
    }
    posts: allContentfulPost {
        edges {
            node {
                slug
            }
        }
    }
    photos: allContentfulPhotos {
        edges{
            node {
                slug
            }
        }
    }
}
`)

data.places.edges.forEach(({ node }) => {
    createPage({
            path: `places/${node.slug}`,
            component: path.resolve("./src/templates/place-template.js"),
            context: {
                slug: node.slug,
            },
        })
    })
    data.posts.edges.forEach(({ node }) => {
        createPage({
            path: `blog/${node.slug}`,
            component: path.resolve("./src/templates/blog-template.js"),
            context: {
                slug: node.slug,
            },
        })
    })
```

```
    data.photos.edges.forEach(({ node }) => {
        createPage({
            path: `photos/${node.slug}`,
            component: path.resolve("./src/templates/photos-template.js"),
            context: {
                slug: node.slug,
            },
        })
    })
}
```

To test whether everything is working, we need to stop and start `gatsby develop` in the terminal. Then move to any nonexistent page in the browser. You can see those pages being created, as shown in Figure 5-42.

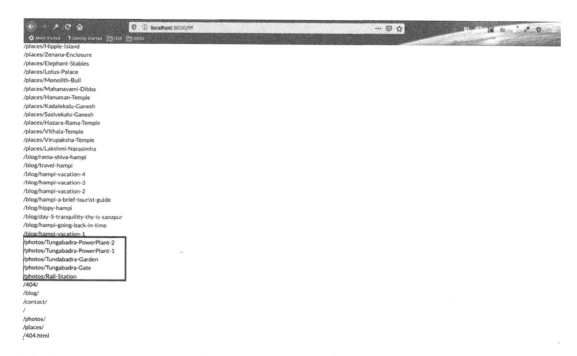

***Figure 5-42.***  *New pages are being created*

Click any one of the pages and you will get the dummy text, as shown in Figure 5-43.

**Figure 5-43.** *The dummy data*

Let's create the query to show the single blog photo in our playground, as shown in Figure 5-44.

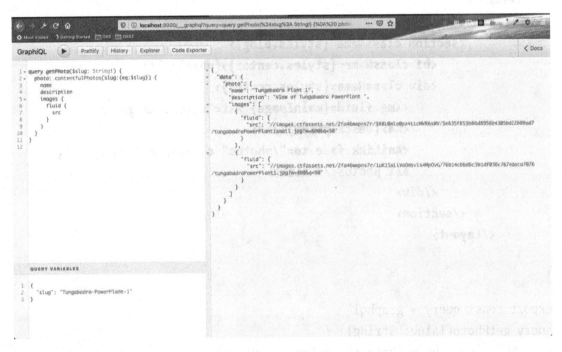

**Figure 5-44.** *The GraphiQL playground*

Next, let's add this query to the `photos-template.js` file. Don't forget to change `src` in `images` to `...GatsbyContentfulFluid`. Next, we will display the image along with the name and description. We need to import some components, as we did earlier, and we are also using the `css` from our Blog module. We are showing the image through the `img` from `gatsby-image`. The updated code is marked in bold in Listing 5-23.

**Listing 5-23.** Query in photos-template.js

```
import React from 'react'
import { graphql } from "gatsby"
import Layout from "../components/Layout"
import styles from "../css/single-blog.module.css"
```

315

```
import AniLink from "gatsby-plugin-transition-link/AniLink"
import Img from "gatsby-image"

const Photos = ({ data }) => {
    const { name, description, images } = data.photo;
    let mainImage = images[1].fluid;

    return (
        <Layout>
            <section className={styles.blog}>
                <h1 className={styles.center}>{name}</h1>
                <div className={styles.center}>
                    <Img fluid={mainImage} alt="single image" />
                    <h4>{description}</h4>
                    <AniLink fade to="/photos" className="btn-primary">
                    all photos</AniLink>
                </div>
            </section>
        </Layout>
    )
}

export const query = graphql`
query getPhoto($slug: String!) {
    photo: contentfulPhotos(slug:{eq:$slug}) {
        name
        description
        images {
            fluid {
                ...GatsbyContentfulFluid
            }
        }
    }}
`;

export default Photos
```

When we click any photo on the Photos page, we get the amazing full photo, as shown in Figure 5-45. Feel free to use these photos in any of your personal work.

*Figure 5-45. The Hampi rail station*

You can find the code here[9].

# Summary

This completes Chapter 5 and the third part of creating the tourism site using Contentful. We covered the following topics in this chapter:

- Creating the Blog component, which shows data stored in the Contentful CMS

- Creating the Photos component, which also shows data stored in the Contentful CMS

In the next chapter, we will complete the tourism site using Contentful. We will add Gatsby plugins and advertisements to the site.

---

[9]https://github.com/nabendu82/gatsbyTourism

# Creating a Tourism Site with Contentful: Part Four

Welcome to Chapter 6. In this chapter, we will add Gatsby plugins and advertisements to our site. Doing so will add functionality and advertising to our site, and this process is more complex than when adding these options to a normal HTML, CSS, or JS site.

## Adding Gatsby Plugins

To complete this section, you need to buy a domain name and add the details to Netlify. This process is described in Chapter 2. After you're done with the setup, go to `https://amazinghampi.com/`[1] to access the project, as shown in Figure 6-1.

---

[1]`https://amazinghampi.com/`

© Nabendu Biswas 2021
N. Biswas, *Foundation Gatsby Projects*, https://doi.org/10.1007/978-1-4842-6558-1_6

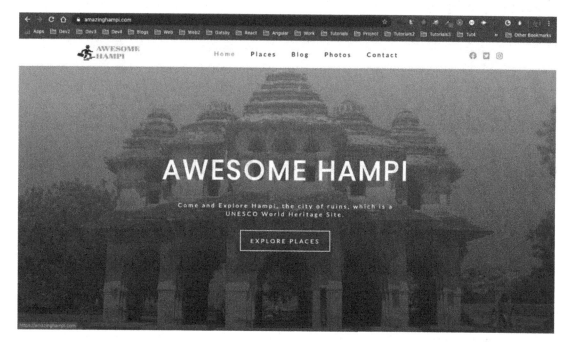

**Figure 6-1.** *The Hampi site, finally live*

## The SEO Plugin

In this section, you'll add plugins for SEO purposes. You need to first install the gatsby-plugin-react-helmet plugin, which will help you control the head element of each page.

As per the documentation,[2] npm install the package first. Head back to the project and stop any gatsby develop that's running. After that, npm install the packages using the following command.

```
npm install --save gatsby-plugin-react-helmet react-helmet
```

As per the documentation, we need to add the code highlighted in Listing 6-1 to the gatsby-config.js file.

**Listing 6-1.**  Add react-helmet to the gatsby-config.js File

```
require("dotenv").config({
  path: `.env.${process.env.NODE_ENV}`,
})
```

---

[2]https://www.gatsbyjs.org/packages/gatsby-plugin-react-helmet/

```
plugins: [
        ...
...
    `gatsby-plugin-sitemap`,
    `gatsby-plugin-styled-components`,
    `gatsby-transformer-sharp`,
    `gatsby-plugin-sharp`,
    `gatsby-plugin-transition-link`,
    `gatsby-transformer-remark`,
    `gatsby-plugin-react-helmet`
  ]
}
```

We also need to add site metadata to the `gatsby-config.js` file, as it will be used by the next plugins. One thing to notice is the `image` tag. The image mentioned in it needs to be placed in a static folder. The updated code is marked in bold in Listing 6-2.

*Listing 6-2.* Add the Site's Metadata to the gatsby-config.js File

```
require("dotenv").config({
  path: `.env.${process.env.NODE_ENV}`,
})

module.exports = {
  siteMetadata: {
    title: "AmazingHampi",
    description: "Tips, information, blogs and photos on Hampi, the city of
    ruins, is a UNESCO World Heritage Site.",
    author: "Nabendu Biswas",
    twitterUsername: "@nabendu82",
    image:'/VirupakshaTemple20.jpg',
    siteUrl:'https://amazinghampi.com'
  },
  plugins: [
          ...
          ...
    `gatsby-plugin-sitemap`,
```

```
`gatsby-plugin-styled-components`,
`gatsby-transformer-sharp`,
`gatsby-plugin-sharp`,
`gatsby-plugin-transition-link`,
`gatsby-transformer-remark`,
`gatsby-plugin-react-helmet`
  ]
}
```

After this, start your `gatsby develop` and head over to the code editor. Add an `SEO.js` file inside the `components` folder. The initial contents of the file are shown in Listing 6-3. It accepts two props—`title` and `description`—from any component.

***Listing 6-3.*** The SEO.js File

```
import React from "react"
import { Helmet } from "react-helmet"
import { useStaticQuery, graphql } from "gatsby"

const SEO = ({ title, description }) => {
    return (
        <Helmet htmlAttributes={{ lang: "en" }} title={title}>
            <meta name="description" content={description} />
        </Helmet>
        )
}

export default SEO
```

Next, head over the home page `index.js` file and import the SEO component. Use it to pass the title and description. The updated code is marked in bold in Listing 6-4.

***Listing 6-4.*** The SEO Component in index.js

```
...
...
import FeaturedPlaces from "../components/Home/FeaturedPlaces"
import SEO from "../components/SEO"
```

```
...
...

export default ({ data }) => (
    <Layout>
        <SEO title="Home" description="Tips, information, blogs and photos
        on Hampi" />
        <StyledHero home="true" img={data.defaultBcg.childImageSharp.fluid}>
            ...
            ...
        </StyledHero>
        <About />
        <Tips />
        <FeaturedPlaces />
    </Layout>
)
```

When we head over to the localhost, we can see the title and meta tags inside the head tag, as shown in Figure 6-2.

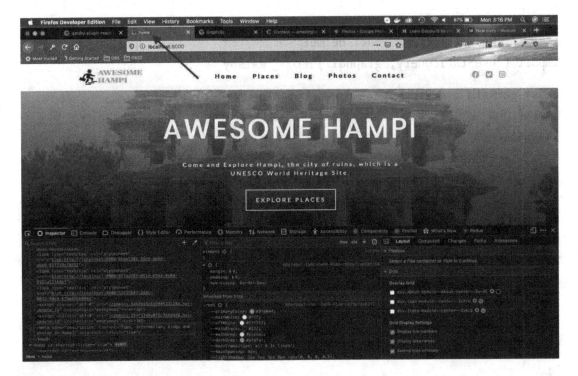

***Figure 6-2.***  *The title and meta tags*

To be able to introduce GraphQL into our SEO.js file, we must create the query in the GraphiQL playground, as shown in Figure 6-3.

*Figure 6-3.* *The query in the playground*

Let's add the query to the SEO.js file and change the title to also include the siteTitle that we are getting from our query. We also need to add a new meta for images. The updated code is marked in bold in Listing 6-5.

*Listing 6-5.* Updated SEO.js File

```
import React from "react"
import { Helmet } from "react-helmet"
import { useStaticQuery, graphql } from "gatsby"

const getData = graphql`
query{
    site{
        siteMetadata {
            siteTitle: title
            siteDesc: description
            author
            siteUrl
            image
            twitterUsername
        }
    }
}
`;
```

```
const SEO = ({ title, description }) => {
    const { site } = useStaticQuery(getData);
    const { siteTitle, siteDesc, siteUrl, image, twitterUsername } = site.
    siteMetadata;
    return (
        <Helmet htmlAttributes={{ lang: "en" }} title={`${title} |
        ${siteTitle}`}>
            <meta name="description" content={description || siteDesc} />
            <meta name="image" content={image} />
        </Helmet>
    )
}

export default SEO
```

In the updated SEO.js file, we made description props optional, so if we don't pass anything, we will be using siteDesc, which we defined in gatsby-config.js. Let's delete the description from index.js, as we will use the longer and more accurate siteDesc. The update is shown in Listing 6-6.

***Listing 6-6.*** Delete Description from index.js

```
...

export default ({ data }) => (
    <Layout>
        <SEO title="Home" />
        <StyledHero home="true" img={data.defaultBcg.childImageSharp.fluid}>
            ...

                ...
        </StyledHero>
        <About />
        <Tips />
        <FeaturedPlaces />
    </Layout>
)
```

In our localhost, we can now see these changes (see Figure 6-4).

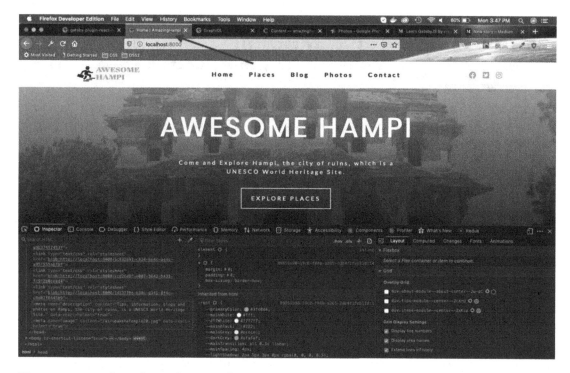

***Figure 6-4.***  *The title and meta changes*

Next, we will add a Twitter Card to our project. When we share our project on Twitter, the Twitter Card will show a nice image with the description. The updated code is marked in bold in Listing 6-7.

***Listing 6-7.***  Twitter Card in SEO.js

```
...

const SEO = ({ title, description }) => {
    const { site } = useStaticQuery(getData);
    const { siteTitle, siteDesc, siteUrl, image, twitterUsername } = site.
    siteMetadata;
    return (
        <Helmet htmlAttributes={{ lang: "en" }} title={`${title} |
        ${siteTitle}`}>
            <meta name="description" content={description || siteDesc} />
            <meta name="image" content={image} />
            <meta name="twitter:card" content="summary_large_image" />
```

```
        <meta name="twitter:creator" content={twitterUsername} />
        <meta name="twitter:title" content={siteTitle} />
        <meta name="twitter:description" content={siteDesc} />
        <meta name="twitter:image" content={`${siteUrl}${image}`} />
    </Helmet>
    )
}

export default SEO
```

Next, we will add a Facebook Card to our project. When we share our project on Facebook, the Facebook Card will show a nice image with the description. The updated code is marked in bold in Listing 6-8.

***Listing 6-8.*** Facebook Card in SEO.js

```
...
const SEO = ({ title, description }) => {
    const { site } = useStaticQuery(getData);
    const { siteTitle, siteDesc, siteUrl, image, twitterUsername } = site.
    siteMetadata;
    return (
        <Helmet htmlAttributes={{ lang: "en" }} title={`${title} |
        ${siteTitle}`}>
            <meta name="description" content={description || siteDesc} />
            <meta name="image" content={image} />
            <meta name="twitter:card" content="summary_large_image" />
            <meta name="twitter:creator" content={twitterUsername} />
            <meta name="twitter:title" content={siteTitle} />
            <meta name="twitter:description" content={siteDesc} />
            <meta name="twitter:image" content={`${siteUrl}${image}`} />
            <meta property="og:url" content={siteUrl} />
            <meta property="og:type" content="website" />
            <meta property="og:title" content={siteTitle} />
            <meta property="og:description" content={siteDesc} />
```

```
    <meta property="og:image" content={`${siteUrl}${image}`} />
    <meta property="og:image:width" content="400" />
    <meta property="og:image:height" content="300" />
  </Helmet>
  )
}

export default SEO
```

To test the cards, we need to push the code to GitHub so that it is deployed in Netlify.

Next, let's test this on the Twitter Card Validator and the Facebook Card Validator, to check how it will look on both social networks. The results are shown in Figures 6-5 and 6-6.

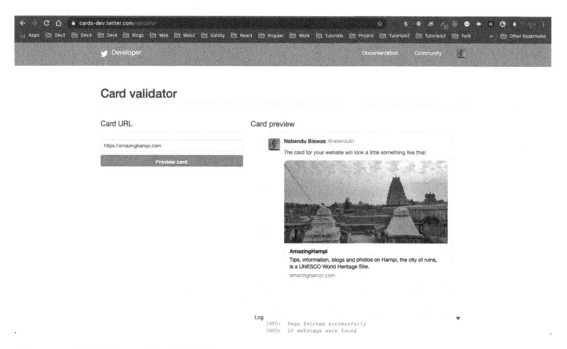

***Figure 6-5.*** *Twitter Card validator*

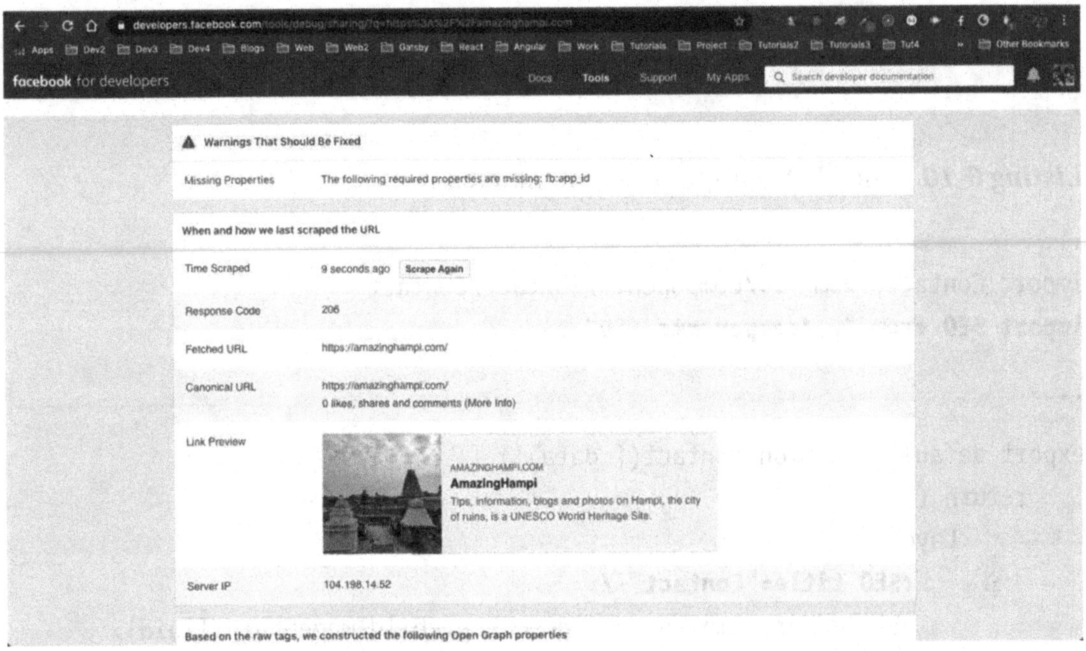

**Figure 6-6.** *Facebook Card validator*

It looks great on both networks. Let's now add SEO to all the pages in our project.

First, we will add an SEO component to 404.js and contact.js. These components will also have default descriptions like index.js, so we are not passing the description prop. The updated code is marked in bold in Listings 6-9 and 6-10.

**Listing 6-9.** The SEO Component in 404.js

```
...
...
import Banner from "../components/Banner"
import SEO from "../components/SEO"

export default function error() {
return (
    <Layout>
        <SEO title="Error" />
        <header className={styles.error}>
            ...
        </header>
```

```
        </Layout>
    )
}
```

***Listing 6-10.***  The SEO Component in contact.js

```
...
import Contact from '../components/Contact/Contact'
import SEO from "../components/SEO"

...

export default function contact({ data }) {
    return (
        <Layout>
            <SEO title="Contact" />
            <StyledHero img={data.connectBcg.childImageSharp.fluid}>
            </StyledHero>
            <Contact />
        </Layout>
    )
}
```

The next three pages (blog.js, photos.js, and places.js) will have different descriptions. We will be passing the description props. The updated code is marked in bold in Listings 6-11 through 6-13.

***Listing 6-11.***  The SEO Component in blog.js

```
...
import BlogList from '../components/Blog/BlogList'
import SEO from "../components/SEO"

...

export default function blog({ data }) {
    return (
        <Layout>
            <SEO title="Blog" description="Real experiences blogs on Hampi,
            the city of ruins, is a UNESCO World Heritage Site." />
```

```
            <StyledHero img={data.blogBcg.childImageSharp.fluid} />
            <BlogList />
        </Layout>
    )
}
```

*Listing 6-12.* The SEO Component in photos.js

```
...
import PhotoList from '../components/Photos/PhotoList'
import SEO from "../components/SEO"

...

export default function photos({ data }) {
    return (
        <Layout>
            <SEO title="Photos" description="Royalty free image of Hampi,
            the city of ruins, is a UNESCO World Heritage Site." />
            <StyledHero img={data.blogBcg.childImageSharp.fluid} />
            <PhotoList />
        </Layout>
    )
}
```

*Listing 6-13.* The SEO Component in places.js

```
...
import Places from '../components/Places/Places'
import SEO from "../components/SEO"

...

export default function places({ data }) {
    return (
        <Layout>
            <SEO title="Places" description="Places to visit in Hampi, the
            city of ruins, is a UNESCO World Heritage Site." />
```

```
                <StyledHero img={data.defaultBcg.childImageSharp.fluid}>
                </StyledHero>
                <Places />
            </Layout>
        )
}
*
```

We have three templates that auto-generate pages for us. We will be using the page name as the title in all three. The updated code is marked in bold in Listings 6-14 through 6-16.

***Listing 6-14.*** The SEO Component in blog-template.js

```
...
import StyledHero from "../components/StyledHero"
import SEO from "../components/SEO"

const Blog = ({ data }) => {
    const { title, published, author, description: {childMarkdownRemark},
    image} = data.post;
    return <Layout>
                <SEO title={title} />
                <h1 className={styles.center}>{title}</h1>
                <StyledHero img={image.fluid} />
                <section className={styles.blog}>
                    <div className={styles.center}>
                        ...
                    </div>
                </section>
            </Layout>
}

...

export default Blog
```

***Listing 6-15.*** The SEO Component in place-template.js

```
...
import AniLink from "gatsby-plugin-transition-link/AniLink"
import SEO from "../components/SEO"

const Template = ({ data }) => {
    const { name, timeRequired, timings, entryFees, description: {
    description }, images } = data.place;
    const [mainImage, ...placeImages] = images

    return (
        <Layout>
            <SEO title={name} />
            <StyledHero img={mainImage.fluid} />
            <section className={styles.template}>
                ...
            </section>
        </Layout>
    )
}

...
export default Template
```

***Listing 6-16.*** The SEO Component in photos-template.js

```
...
import Img from "gatsby-image"
import SEO from "../components/SEO"

const Photos = ({ data }) => {
    const { name, description, images } = data.photo;
    let mainImage = images[1].fluid;

    return (
        <Layout>
            <SEO title={name} description={`Royalty free image of ${name}`}/>
            <section className={styles.blog}>
```

```
            <h1 className={styles.center}>{name}</h1>
            ...
        </section>
      </Layout>
  )
}

...

export default Photos
```

## Other Plugins

We will add two more plugins for SEO—gatsby-plugin-robots-txt and gatsby-plugin-sitemap. The details for installing both can be found in Chapter 2.

After the required npm installs, add the code in Listing 6-17 to the gatsby-config.js file. The updated code is marked in bold.

*Listing 6-17.* Plugins in gatsby-config.js

```
plugins: [
  {
    resolve: `gatsby-source-filesystem`,
    options: {
      name: `images`,
      path: `${__dirname}/src/images/`,
    },
  },
  {
    resolve: `gatsby-source-contentful`,
    options: {
      spaceId: process.env.CONTENTFUL_SPACE_ID,
      accessToken: process.env.CONTENTFUL_ACCESS_TOKEN,
    },
  },
```

```
  {
    resolve: 'gatsby-plugin-robots-txt',
    options: {
      host: 'https://amazinghampi.com',
      sitemap: 'https://amazinghampi.com/sitemap.xml',
      policy: [{ userAgent: '*', allow: '/' }]
    }
  },
  `gatsby-plugin-sitemap`,
  `gatsby-plugin-styled-components`,
  `gatsby-transformer-sharp`,
  `gatsby-plugin-sharp`,
  `gatsby-plugin-transition-link`,
  `gatsby-transformer-remark`,
  `gatsby-plugin-react-helmet`
]
```

I will also add Google Analytics to the site, so that I can keep count and do other analyses on my visitors. The installation process is similar to what we did in Chapter 2.

After following the required steps on the Google Analytics page and npm installing the plugin, the changes shown in Listing 6-18 need to be made to the `gatsby-config.js` file. The updated code is marked in bold.

*Listing 6-18.* Google Analytics in gatsby-config.js

```
plugins: [
        ...
  {
    resolve: 'gatsby-plugin-robots-txt',
    options: {
      host: 'https://amazinghampi.com',
      sitemap: 'https://amazinghampi.com/sitemap.xml',
      policy: [{ userAgent: '*', allow: '/' }]
    }
  },
```

```
{
  resolve: `gatsby-plugin-google-analytics`,
  options: {
    trackingId: "UA-XXXXXXXXX-2",
  }
},
  `gatsby-plugin-sitemap`,
        ...
]
```

After pushing and successfully deploying to Netlify, the site is live at `https://amazinghampi.com/`[3] and the project is complete! See Figure 6-7.

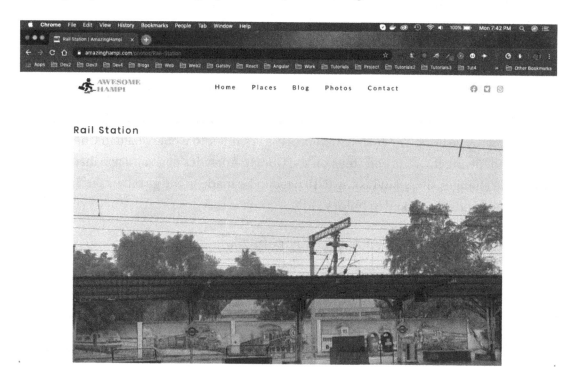

***Figure 6-7.***  *The live amazinghampi.com site*

Feel free to use this code to create amazing sites by cloning or forking from my GitHub at `https://github.com/nabendu82/gatsbyTourism`.[4]

---

[3]`https://amazinghampi.com/`
[4]`https://github.com/nabendu82/gatsbyTourism`

# Adding Advertisements to the Site

I decided to include advertisements on the site built in this series. I had just learned how to include ads on a Gatsby-powered site and added this information to my blog site at https://nabendu.blog/[5].

## Using Media.net Ads

I have approval to use Media.net ads. You can learn more about that process in Chapter 2. After you log in to the Media.net console, you need to click the Add New button, as shown in Figure 6-8.

*Figure 6-8.*   *The Media.net site*

It will show the popup in Figure 6-9, where you have to enter the domain name, average daily traffic, and current ad revenue.

---

[5]https://nabendu.blog/

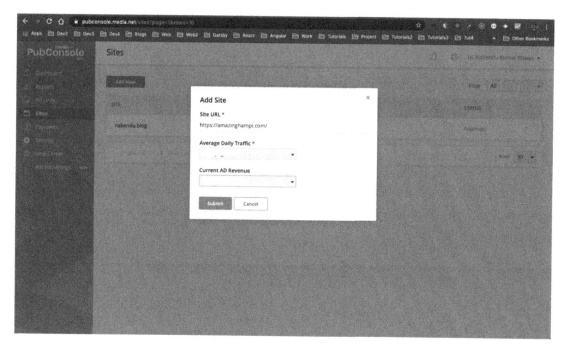

**Figure 6-9.** *The Add Site dialog box*

After you click the Submit button, it will show the status as Pending, as shown in Figure 6-10.

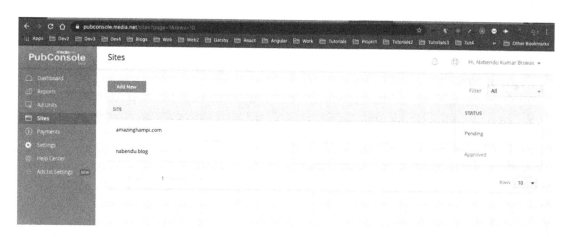

**Figure 6-10.** *Your status will be pending for a while*

Next, move to the Ads.txt Settings tab. Click the Set Up Now button on the newly added site, as shown in Figure 6-11.

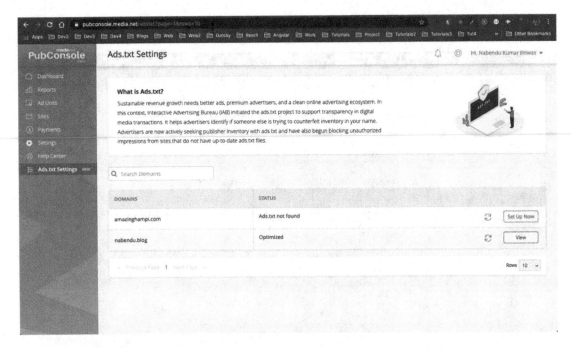

***Figure 6-11.*** *The Ads.txt settings*

You will get a popup to download the Ads.txt file, as shown in Figure 6-12.

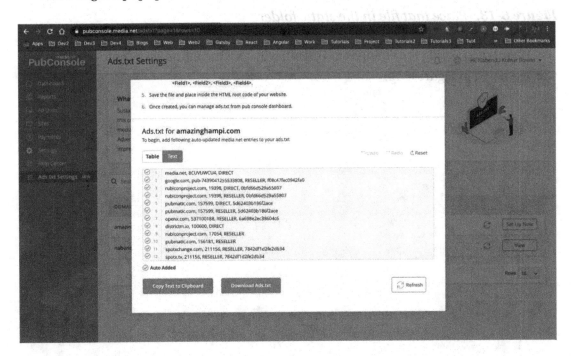

***Figure 6-12.*** *Download the Ads.txt file*

Place the Ads.txt file in the static folder of the project, as shown in Figure 6-13.

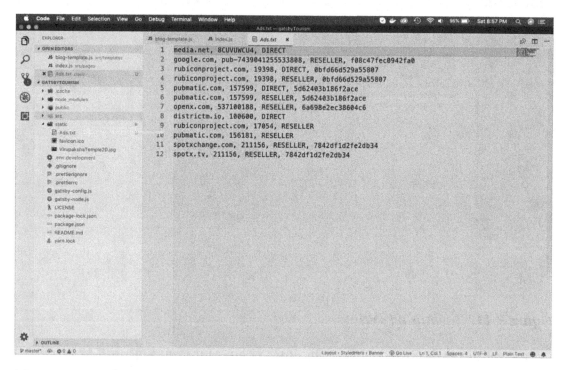

***Figure 6-13.***  *Place that file in the static folder*

After that, pushing the changes to GitHub will start the automatic deployment of the site, as shown in Figure 6-14.

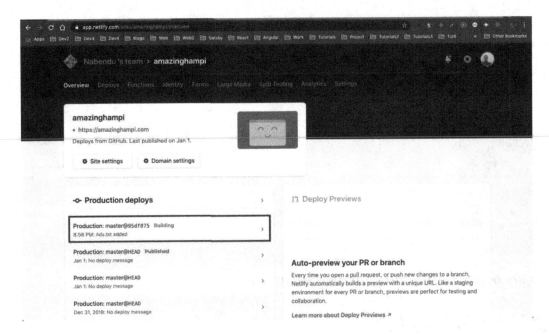

***Figure 6-14.*** *Automatic deployment begins*

Once the deployment is complete, you will see that it has Optimized status in the Ads.txt Settings tab. This is shown in Figure 6-15.

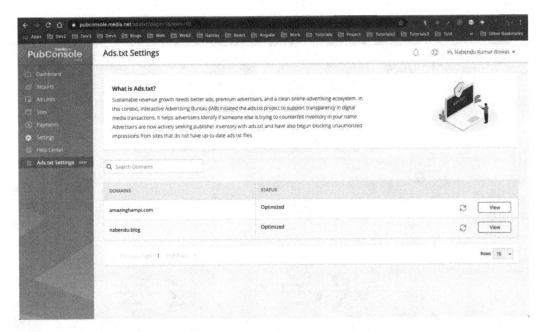

***Figure 6-15.*** *The domain is optimized*

Media.net rejected my site, so I was not able to show ads from this network. This message is shown in Figure 6-16.

***Figure 6-16.***   *The amazinghampi site was rejected*

## Using Infolinks Ads

I thought it would be smart to show another ad network, in this case Infolinks. After logging in to this site, I provided my site name. They also asked me to place an `ads.txt` on the site. See Figure 6-17.

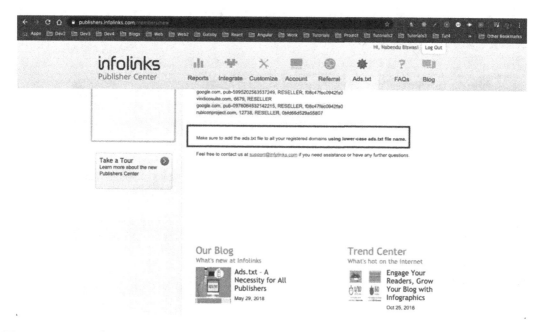

***Figure 6-17.***   *The new ads.txt*

I added the new `ads.txt` file and pushed it to Netlify. It is shown in Figure 6-18.

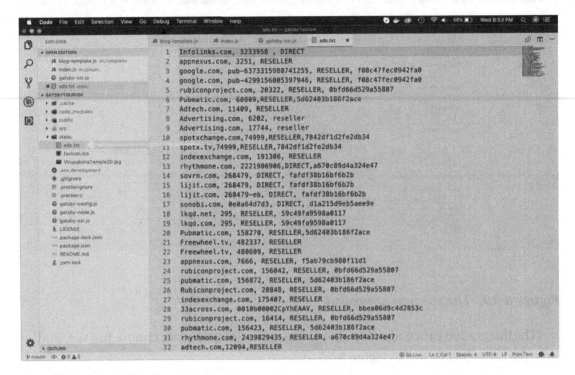

***Figure 6-18.*** *The ads.txt file*

After waiting a day, they approved my site, as shown in Figure 6-19.

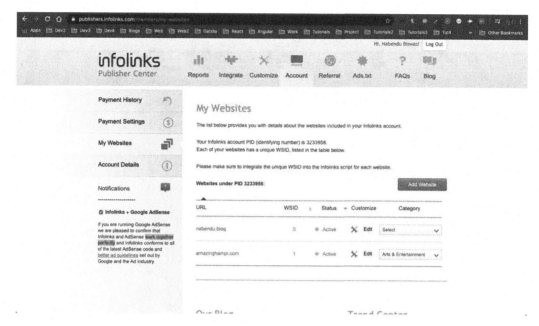

***Figure 6-19.*** *The site was approved*

The integration process is very simple. Go to the Integrate tab, choose the site, and copy the code. It is shown in Figure 6-20.

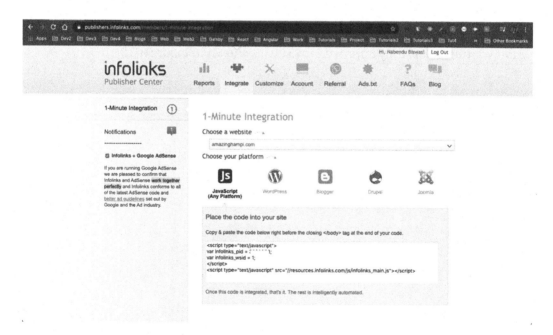

***Figure 6-20.*** *The Integrate tab*

The way to include ads on a Gatsby site is a bit different; we also need to put this code in the gatsby-ssr.js file, as shown in Listing 6-19.

***Listing 6-19.*** Ad Code in gatsby-ssr.js

```
const React = require("react");

exports.onRenderBody = function({ setHeadComponents, setPostBodyComponents }) {
    setHeadComponents([

    ]);

    setPostBodyComponents([
            <script
                dangerouslySetInnerHTML={{
                    __html:`
                    var infolinks_pid = XXXXXXX;
                    var infolinks_wsid = 1;

                    `
                }}
            />,
            <script type="text/javascript" src="//resources.infolinks.
            com/js/infolinks_main.js"></script>
    ]);
};
```

Unlike with Media.net, you don't need to worry about placing your ads in Infolinks. You do it using the Customize tab (see Figure 6-21).

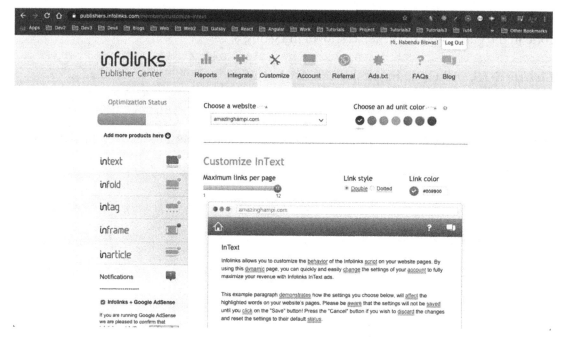

***Figure 6-21.*** *Use the Customize tab*

I pushed my code to Netlify and it was deployed. Now the ads are live on `https://amazinghampi.com/`[6]. You get a floating ad and text ads (see Figure 6-22).

---

[6]`https://amazinghampi.com/`

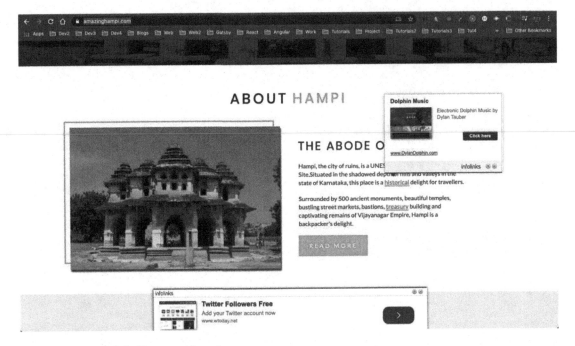

**Figure 6-22.** *Ads live on the site*

I hope you adequately learned how to add advertisements to your Gatsby site in this section.

# Summary

This completes Chapter 6 and the last part of creating the tourism site using Contentful. We covered the following topics in this chapter:

- Adding various Gatsby plugins to add functionality to our Gatsby site

- Adding advertising to our Gatsby site, which is more complex than adding it to a normal HTML, CSS, or JS site

In the next chapter, we will create a video chat site in Gatsby using Twilio.

# CHAPTER 7

# Creating a Video Chat Site

On April 2, 2020 one of my favorite sites, dev.to, announced a Twilio hackathon. The link is found here[1]. In this hackathon, participants had to make anything with the Twilio API and submit it before April 30, 2020. I decided to make a simple video app with Gatsby and the Twilio API. One of the main categories of this hackathon was Covid-19 communications, so it will be simple enough for anyone to use, including elderly people.

I got help from a YouTube tutorial in order to build this[2] web app. You need a Twilio account for this project. We will go through the whole process, from setting up the account to writing Twilio functions for the video chat app, in this chapter.

## The Setup

In a new folder called SimpleVideoApp, create a new Gatsby project with the default starter, using the gatsby new command. The commands are shown in Listing 7-1.

*Listing 7-1.* Creating a New Gatsby Project

```
mkdir SimpleVideoApp
cd SimpleVideoApp
gatsby new .
```

Once the installation is done, it's time to install twilio and twilio-video. Use the command in Listing 7-2 from the terminal to do this.

---

[1]https://dev.to/devteam/announcing-the-twilio-hackathon-on-dev-21h8
[2]https://www.youtube.com/embed/KO2SnxY6c_0

© Nabendu Biswas 2021
N. Biswas, *Foundation Gatsby Projects*, https://doi.org/10.1007/978-1-4842-6558-1_7

***Listing 7-2.*** Twilio Install

```
npm i twilio
npm i twilio-video
```

It's time to create a Twilio account.

# Creating a Twilio Account

Go to https://www.twilio.com/try-twilio to create an account. Enter the details on this page and click the Start Your Free Trial button (see Figure 7-1).

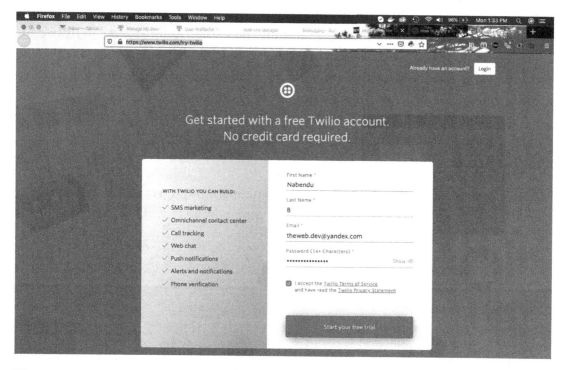

***Figure 7-1.*** *Twilio account*

You will get the usual verification email on the next page (see Figure 7-2).

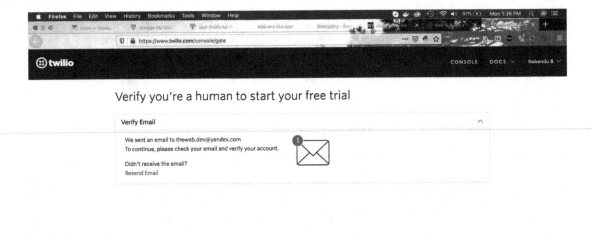

*Figure 7-2.*  *Verification email*

Upon checking my mailbox, I found the mail. Click the Confirm Your Email link to continue (see Figure 7-3).

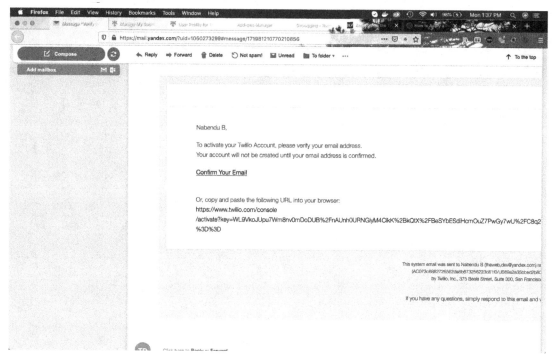

**Figure 7-3.** *Confirm your email*

After that, you have to do mobile number verification. Provide a valid mobile number and click the check box; then click the Verify button (see Figure 7-4).

***Figure 7-4.*** *Mobile verification*

We will get a verification code on our mobile phone, which you need to enter here and then click Submit (see Figure 7-5).

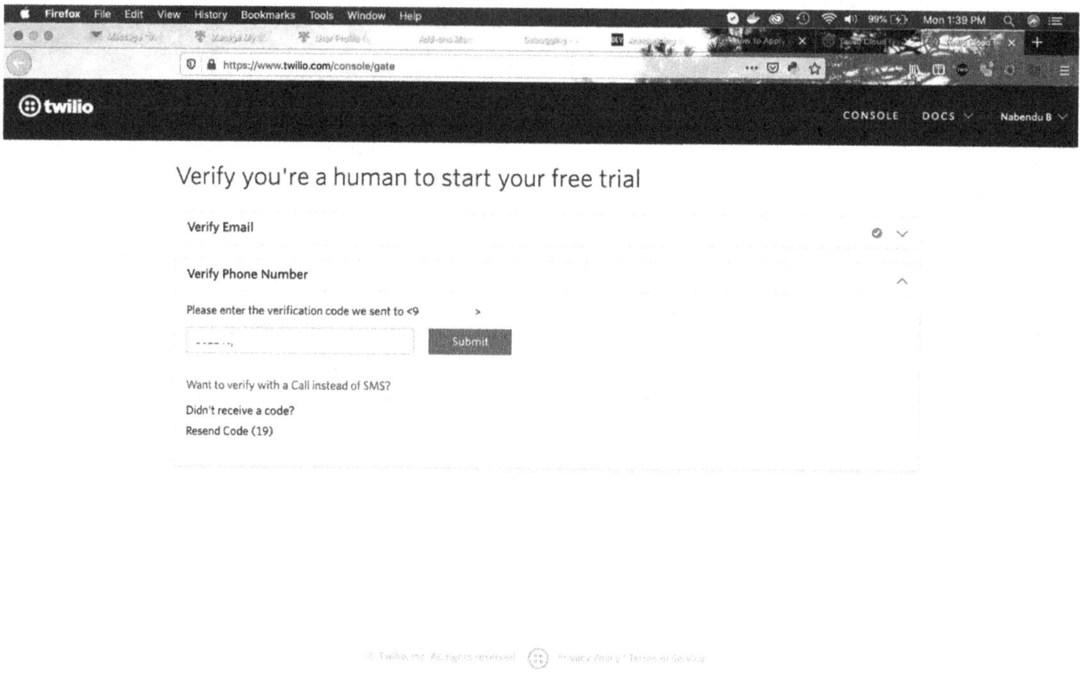

***Figure 7-5.*** *Verification code*

After that, you'll see the screen in Figure 7-6, in which you have to state whether you code. I chose Yes.

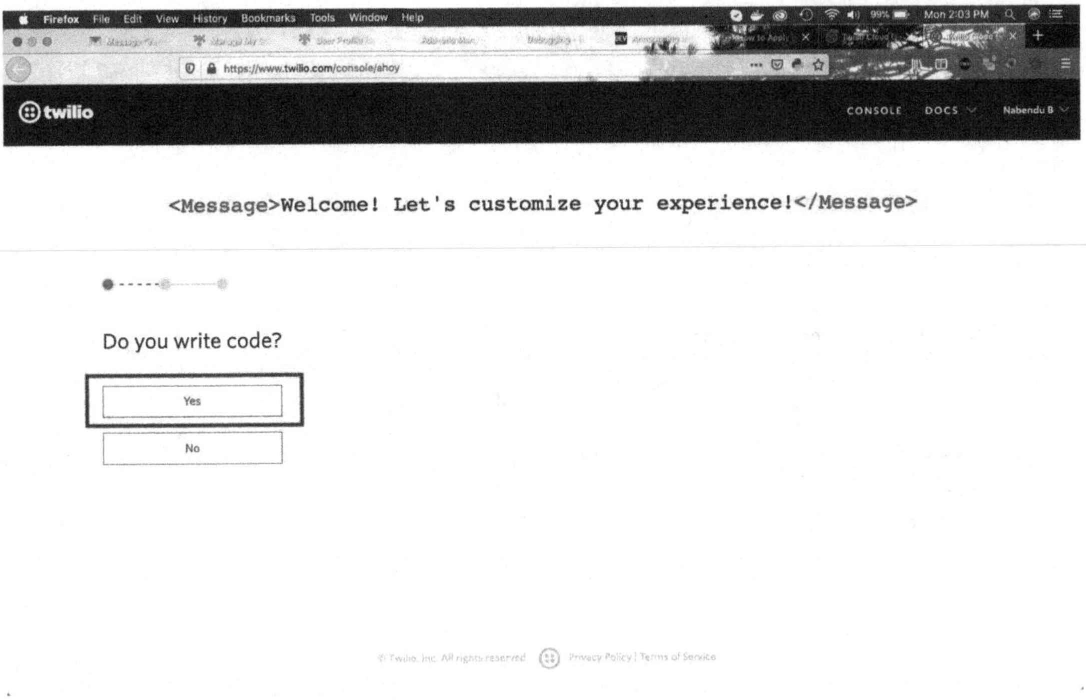

`<Message>Welcome! Let's customize your experience!</Message>`

Do you write code?

| Yes |
| --- |

| No |
| --- |

**Figure 7-6.** *Choose yes when asked if you write code*

In the next screen we have to choose the framework. We need to choose NodeJS here (see Figure 7-7).

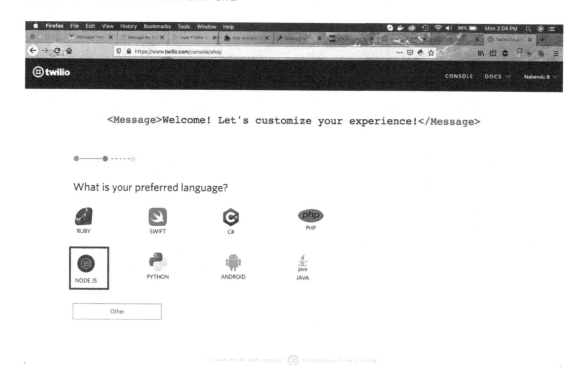

***Figure 7-7.***  *Choose NodeJS*

Next, click the Skip to Dashboard button, as shown in Figure 7-8.

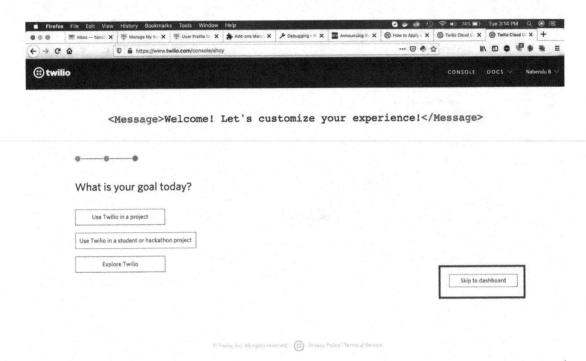

**Figure 7-8.**  *Skip to the dashboard*

This will take you to the dashboard (see Figure 7-9).

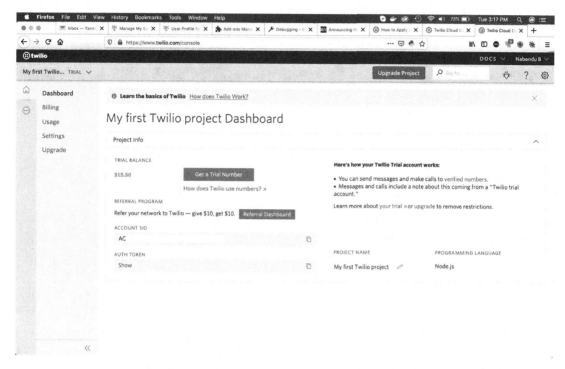

*Figure 7-9.*  *The Twilio dashboard*

# Working in the Dashboard

There are a lot of settings in the dashboard, including creating a Twilio function. We logged into the Twilio dashboard earlier. Click the three dots on the left menu, as shown in Figure 7-10.

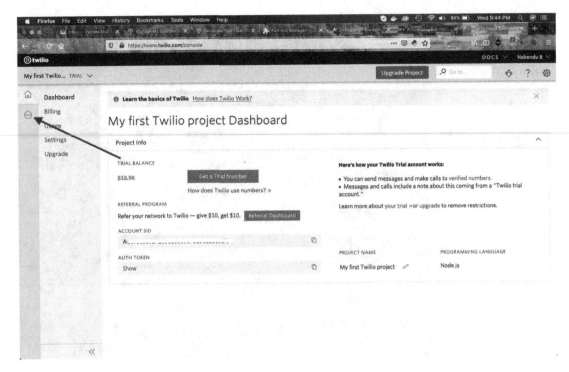

***Figure 7-10.*** *Click the three dots*

Next, click Programmable Video from the menu (see Figure 7-11).

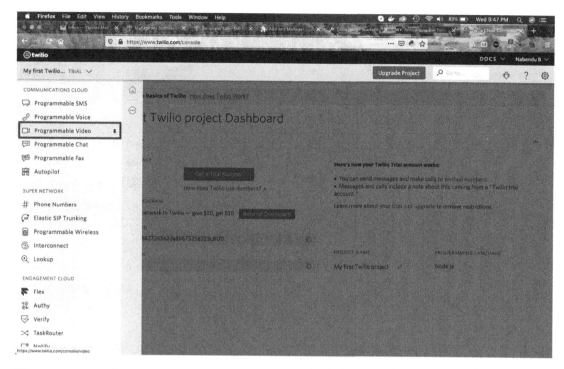

***Figure 7-11.*** *Choose Programmable Video*

On the next screen, click the Show API Credentials link (see Figure 7-12).

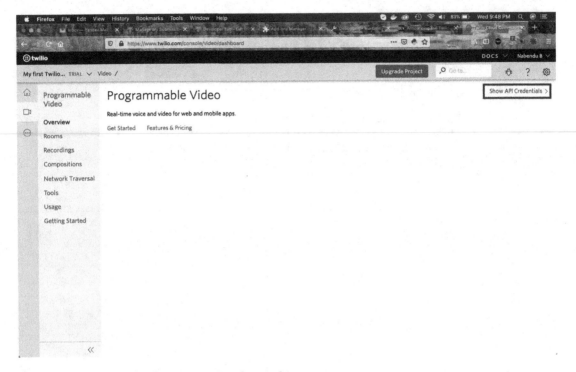

**Figure 7-12.** *Click Show API Credentials*

On the next page, note your Account SID and Auth Token (see Figure 7-13).

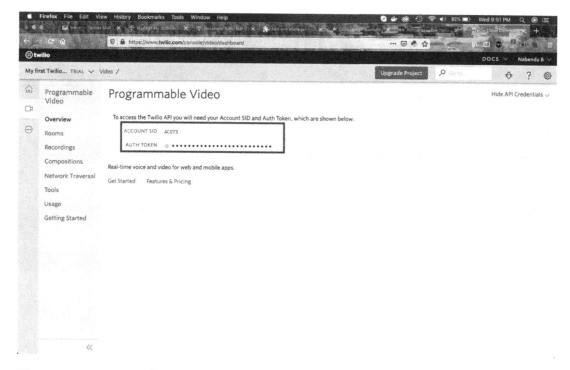

***Figure 7-13.*** *Write down these credentials somewhere safe*

# Updating the API Key Settings

It's time to put these secrets in an .env file. Create an .env file in the root directory and put the account SID and auth token into the TWILIO_ACC_SID and TWILIO_AUTH_TOKEN variables, respectively. The content is shown in Listing 7-3.

***Listing 7-3.*** The Environment File

```
TWILIO_ACC_SID=XXXXXXXXXXXX
TWILIO_AUTH_TOKEN=XXXXXXXXXX
```

Then choose Tools from the left menu (see Figure 7-14).

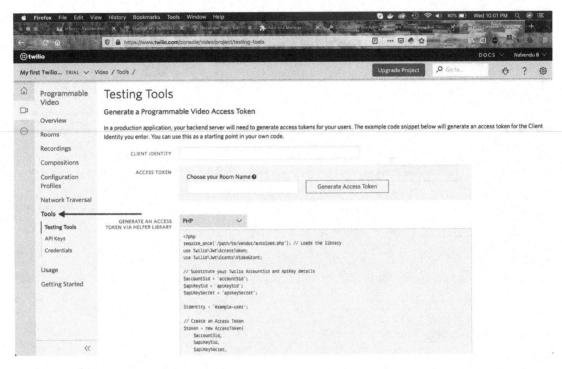

***Figure 7-14.*** *Tools*

After that, click the API Keys submenu link. Next, we have to click the Create New API Key button (see Figure 7-15).

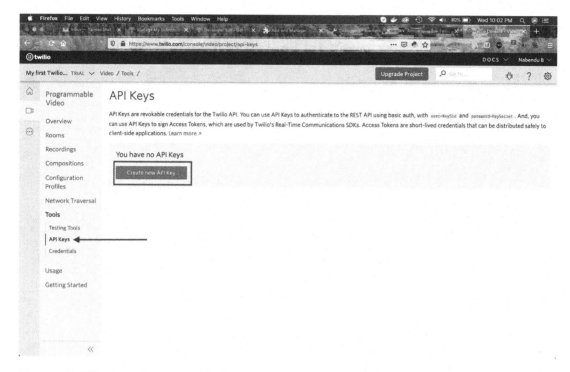

***Figure 7-15.***  *Create a new API key*

On the next screen, we have to give the new API key a name and then click the Create API Key button (see Figure 7-16).

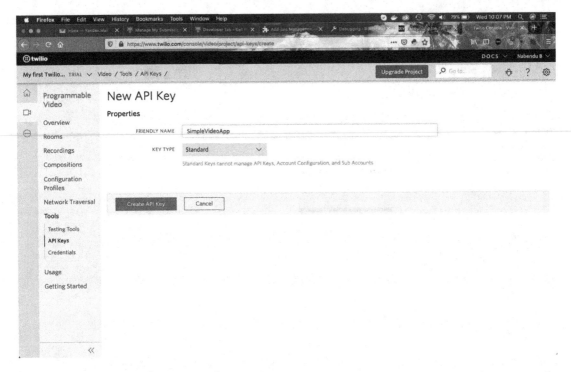

***Figure 7-16.*** *Provide a name here*

On the next screen, we will be shown the SID and the SECRET. We need to note them both (see Figure 7-17).

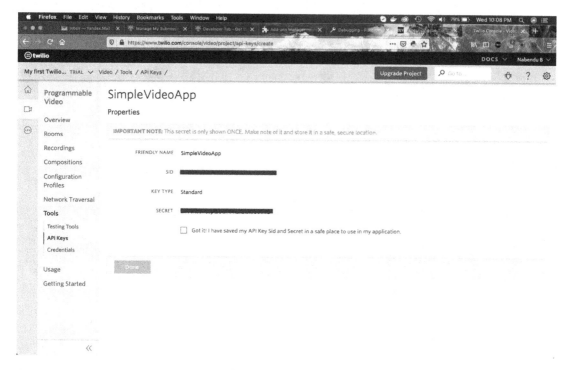

**Figure 7-17.** *Note the SID and secret*

Then click the check box and the Done button (see Figure 7-18).

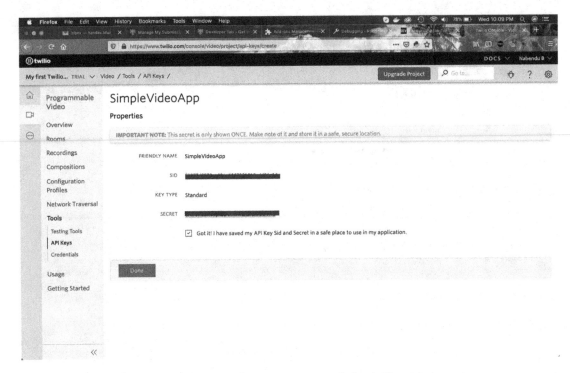

***Figure 7-18.*** *Check the box to indicate you saved the information*

On the next screen, the secret won't be visible. This means our API keys have been saved (see Figure 7-19).

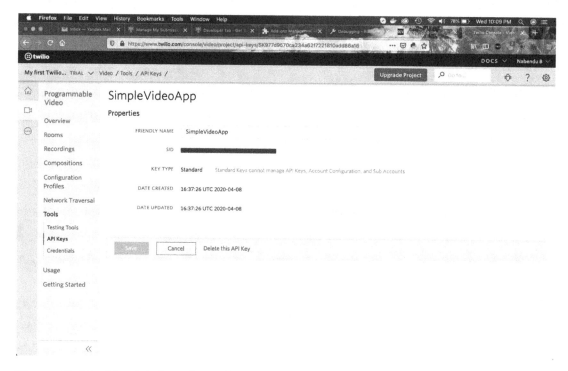

**Figure 7-19.** *The API keys have been saved*

Again, go to the .env file and save the two variables in Listing 7-4.

**Listing 7-4.** Environment File with Additional Keys

```
TWILIO_ACC_SID=XXXXXXXXXXXX
TWILIO_AUTH_TOKEN=XXXXXXXXXX
TWILIO_API_SID=XXXXXXXXXXXX
TWILIO_API_SECRET=XXXXXXXXXX
```

The settings of the API keys took a lot of time, so we will start with Twilio functions in the next section.

# Creating Twilio Functions

We will finally start creating Twilio functions. First, click the three dots on the left side of the Twilio dashboard (see Figure 7-20).

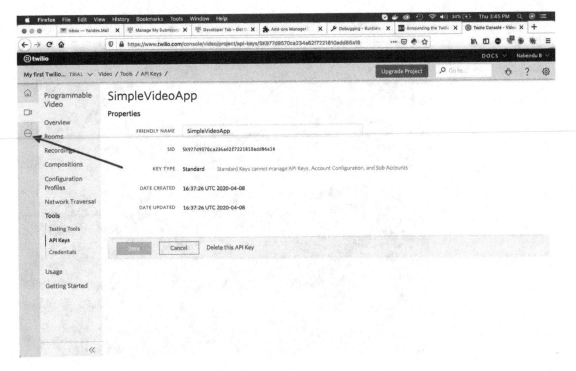

***Figure 7-20.***  *The Twilio dashboard*

Next, if you scroll down a bit, you will find the Functions menu; click it (see Figure 7-21).

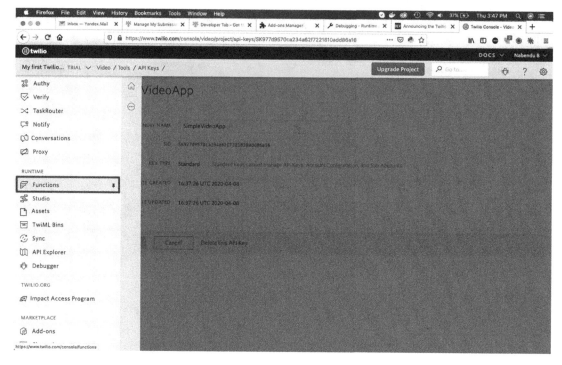

***Figure 7-21.*** *Functions*

On the next screen, click the Create a Function button (see Figure 7-22).

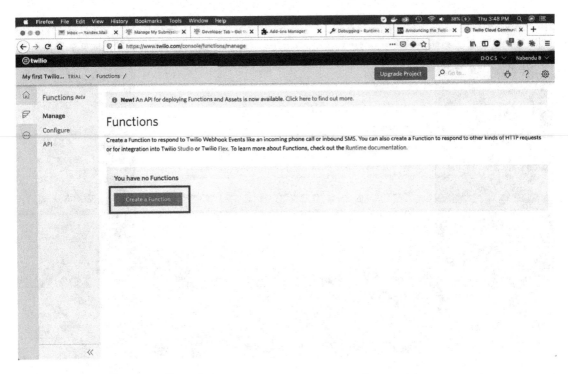

***Figure 7-22.*** *Create a function*

A popup will appear in which you need to click Blank and then click the Create button (see Figure 7-23).

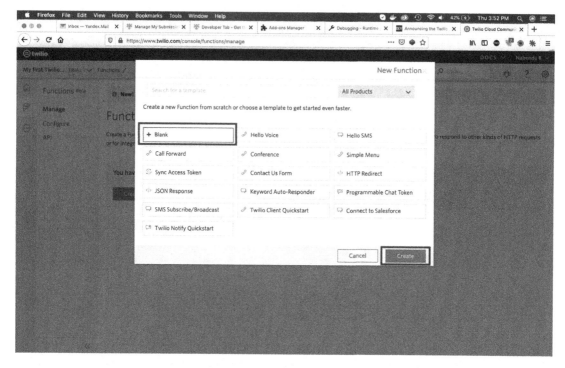

***Figure 7-23.*** *Create a blank function*

On the next page, we need to give our function a name and a path. I named them Create Token and /`create-token`, respectively (see Figure 7-24).

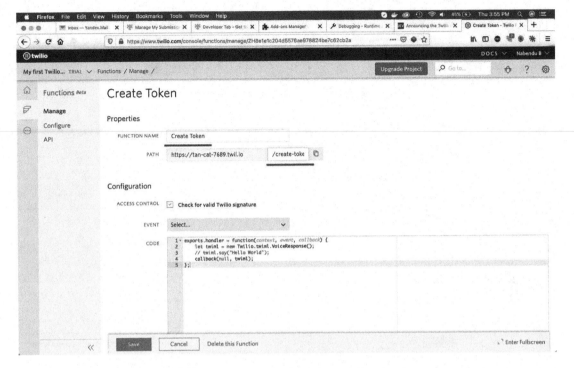

***Figure 7-24.*** *Create a token*

Next, we need to remove the check box and then remove everything inside the function (see Figure 7-25).

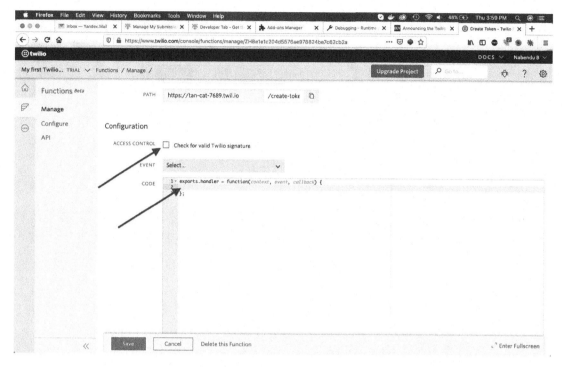

***Figure 7-25.*** *Remove everything inside the function*

Next, we will write some code in the function. This code will use built-in Twilio variables and get a new access token from our stored variables. The code is shown in Listing 7-5.

***Listing 7-5.*** Twilio Functions

```
exports.handler = function(context, event, callback) {
    let accessToken = Twilio.jwt.AccessToken;
    let videoGrant = accessToken.VideoGrant;
    let token = new accessToken(process.env.ACCOUNT_SID, process.env.API_
    KEY, process.env.API_SECRET);
};
```

After writing these three lines of code, click the Save button. After that, click the Configure link in the left menu. It will open the page shown in Figure 7-26.

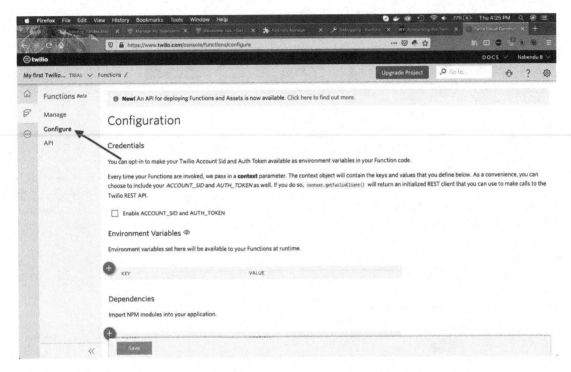

*Figure 7-26.*   *Configuration page*

We need to check the Enable ACCOUNT_SID and AUTH_TOKEN check box. After that, click the + button next to KEY twice and enter API_KEY and API_SECRET in the Key column.

You get their values from TWILIO_API_SID and TWILIO_API_SECRET, which will be saved in the previous .env file (see Figure 7-27).

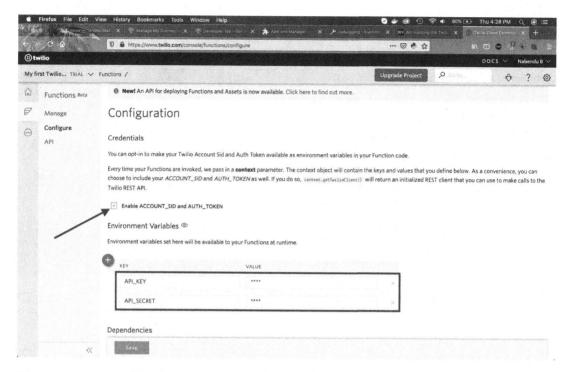

***Figure 7-27.***  *Enable the API keys*

After clicking the Save button, click the Manage link (see Figure 7-28).

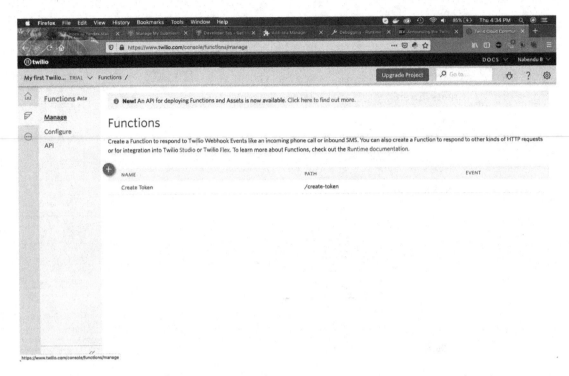

**Figure 7-28.** *Choose the Manage option*

We need to click the function name (such as Create Token) to go to the edit page. Next, we add the four lines in Figure 7-29 to the function. We are doing a callback with the token with JWT.

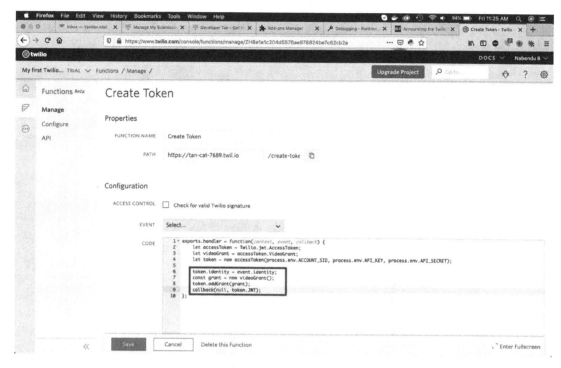

*Figure 7-29.  Configuring the function*

# Adding the Code

We will do some coding now, but first start the project by moving to the directory and running the gatsby develop command.

## Basic Setup

The command to start the server is shown in Listing 7-6.

***Listing 7-6.*** Server Start Command

```
cd SimpleVideoApp
gatsby develop
```

If we go to http://localhost:8000/,[3] we will get the default page (see Figure 7-30).

---

[3]http://localhost:8000/

***Figure 7-30.*** *Default starter*

Time to change the default starter, so open the index.js file and add the code in Listing 7-7.

***Listing 7-7.*** The index.js File

```
import React from "react"
import Layout from "../components/layout"
import SEO from "../components/seo"

const IndexPage = () => {
  return (
    <Layout>
        <SEO title="Home" />
    </Layout>
  )
}

export default IndexPage
```

We will remove all the unnecessary things. Remove the `page-2.js` file, as we don't need it.

It's also time to change some things in this Gatsby starter. Open the `layout.js` file in the `components` folder and change the footer text. The updated code is marked in bold in Listing 7-8.

***Listing 7-8.*** The layout.js File

```
...
...
return (

    <Header siteTitle={data.site.siteMetadata.title} />
    <div
      style={{
        margin: `0 auto`,
        maxWidth: 960,
        padding: `0 1.0875rem 1.45rem`,
      }}
    >
      <main>{children}</main>
      <footer>
        Copyright © <a href="https://thewebdev.tech">SimpleVideoApp</a>,
        {new Date().getFullYear()},
          All rights reserved
      </footer>
    </div>

  )
...
...
```

Also, let's change the site's title. Head over to the `gatsby-config.js` file and change it. The updated code is marked in bold in Listing 7-9.

*Listing 7-9.* Site Metadata Change in gatsby-config.js

```
module.exports = {
  siteMetadata: {
    title: `Simple Video App`,
    description: `A simple video app, created using gatsby and twilio,
    for twilio hackathon on dev.to`,
    author: `Nabendu Biswas`,
  },
  plugins: [
              ...
              ...
  ],
}
```

When we go to `http://localhost:8000/`,[4] we will see the updated app (see Figure 7-31).

*Figure 7-31.*  *Updated app*

## Create a Login Form

Let's create a simple functional login form. Create a file called `login-form.js` inside the `components` folder and put the code from Listing 7-10 in it. It is a simple form with a text field that allows you to enter the name and a button to submit the form.

---

[4] `http://localhost:8000/`

***Listing 7-10.*** The login-form.js File

```
import React, { useState } from "react"

const LoginForm = () => {
    const [name, setName] = useState("")

    return (
            <form>
                    <label htmlFor="name">
                      Display Name: <br />
                        <input
                        type="text"
                        id="name"
                        name="name"
                        value={name}
                        onChange={e => setName(e.target.value)}
                        />
                    </label>
                <br />
                <button type="submit">Join Video Chat</button>
            </form>
    )
}

export default LoginForm
```

Next, let's show this component in the index.js file. Import it and use it. The updated code is marked in bold in Listing 7-11.

***Listing 7-11.*** LoginForm in index.js

```
import React from "react"
import Layout from "../components/layout"
import SEO from "../components/seo"
import LoginForm from "../components/login-form"

const IndexPage = () => {
  return (
```

```
    <Layout>
            <SEO title="Home" />
            <LoginForm />
    </Layout>
    )
}
```

```
export default IndexPage
```

The web app now shows our not-so-beautiful login form (see Figure 7-32).

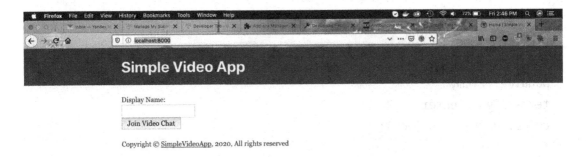

***Figure 7-32.*** *Simple login form*

Let's style this web app a bit, as I like web apps to look nice. First update all the primary styles in `layout.css`. Remove all the content and replace it with Listing 7-12.

***Listing 7-12.*** The New layout.css File

```css
@import url("https://fonts.googleapis.com/css?family=Quicksand&display=swap");

* {
    box-sizing: border-box;
    margin: 0;
}

:root {
    --primaryColor:#243e36;
    --mainGrey: #F9F9FA;
    --mainWhite: #fff;
    --mainBlack: #0A0A0A;
    --darkGrey: #8e8e8e;
```

```css
    --mainTransition: all 0.3s linear;
    --mainSpacing: 4px;
}

body {
    font-family: "Quicksand", sans-serif;
    background: var(--mainGrey);
    color: var(--mainBlack);
    font-size: 18px;
    overflow-x: hidden;
}

footer {
  margin-top: auto;
  padding: 2rem;
  text-align: center;
  color: var(--mainBlack);
}
```

Next, let's update the header.js file to use a new color scheme. I had updated the background and also removed the line margin: 0 auto from maxWidth: 960. The updated code is marked in bold in Listing 7-13.

***Listing 7-13.*** The Updated header.js File

```js
import { Link } from "gatsby"
import PropTypes from "prop-types"
import React from "react"

const Header = ({ siteTitle }) => (
  <header
    style={{
      background: `#243e36`,
      marginBottom: `1.45rem`,
    }}
  >
```

```
<div
  style={{
    maxWidth: 960,
    padding: `1.45rem 1.0875rem`,
  }}
>
    <h1 style={{ margin: 0 }}>
        ...
        ...
    </h1>
  </div>
</header>
)
...
...

export default Header
```

Next, create a file called login.module.css in the components folder and put the code in Listing 7-14 into it.

***Listing 7-14.*** The login.module.css File

```
.contact {
    padding: 4rem 0;
}
.center {
    width: 80vw;
    margin: 0 auto;
}
@media screen and (min-width: 992px) {
    .center {
        width: 50vw;
        margin: 0 auto;
    }
}
```

```css
.contact label {
    text-transform: capitalize;
    display: block;
    margin-bottom: 0.5rem;
}
.contact h3 {
    text-transform: uppercase;
    font-size: 2rem;
    text-align: center;
    letter-spacing: 7px;
    color: var(--mainBlack);
    margin-bottom: 2rem;
}
.formControl,
.submit {
    width: 100%;
    font-size: 1rem;
    margin-bottom: 1rem;
    padding: 0.375rem 0.75rem;
    border: 1px solid var(--darkGrey);
    border-radius: 0.25rem;
}
.submit {
    background-color: var(--primaryColor);
    border-color: var(--primaryColor);
    text-transform: uppercase;
    color: var(--mainWhite);
    transition: var(--mainTransition);
    cursor: pointer;
}
.submit:hover {
    background: var(--darkGrey);
    color: var(--mainBlack);
    border-color: var(--darkGrey);
}
```

Update the `login-form.js` file to include these styles. The updated code is marked in bold in Listing 7-15.

***Listing 7-15.*** Styles in login-form.js

```
import React, { useState } from "react"
import styles from "./login.module.css"

const LoginForm = () => {
    const [name, setName] = useState("")

    return (
        <section className={styles.contact}>
            <h3>Login</h3>
            <div className={styles.center}>
            <form>
                <div>
                    <label htmlFor="name">Display Name</label>
                    <input
                        type="text"
                        id="name"
                        name="name"
                        value={name}
                        className={styles.formControl}
                        onChange={e => setName(e.target.value)}
                    />
                </div>
                <button type="submit" className={styles.submit}>Join Video
                Chat</button>
            </form>
            </div>
        </section>
    )
}

export default LoginForm
```

The web app now looks perfect, as shown in Figure 7-33.

**Figure 7-33.** *New and improved web app*

# Connect the App to Twilio

We need to do an API call to the Twilio endpoint, which contains our function. For this we will install Axios first.

Stop your gatsby develop and install Axios using the npm i axios command. Don't forget to restart your development server by re-running the gatsby develop command.

We will now use Axios to send the form data to our Twilio endpoint. Open the login-form.js file and create a form called onSubmit. It will call a function called handleSubmit and use the Twilio endpoint URL, and the data will be the name. The updated code is marked in bold in Listing 7-16.

*Listing 7-16.* Axios in login-form.js

```
import React, { useState } from "react"
import styles from "./login.module.css"
import axios from "axios"

const LoginForm = () => {
    const [name, setName] = useState("")
```

```
const handleSubmit = async event => {
    event.preventDefault()
    const result = await axios({
        method: "POST",
        url: "https://tan-cat-7689.twil.io/create-token",
        data: {
            identity: name,
        },
    })
    console.log(result);
}

return (
    <section className={styles.contact}>
        <h3>Login</h3>
        <div className={styles.center}>
        <form onSubmit={handleSubmit}>
            <div>

                        . . .
                        . . .

            </div>
            <button type="submit" className={styles.submit}>Join Video
            Chat</button>
        </form>
        </div>
    </section>
)
}

export default LoginForm
```

We get the Twilio endpoint in the code from the function page in Twilio (see Figure 7-34).

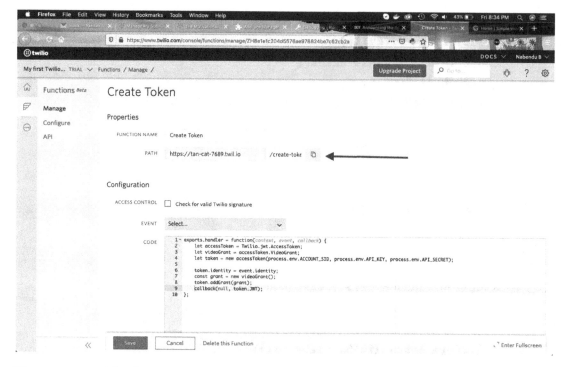

**Figure 7-34.** *The function page*

We also updated the code as per Listing 7-17.

**Listing 7-17.** Updated Twilio Function

```
exports.handler = function(context, event, callback) {
    let accessToken = Twilio.jwt.AccessToken;
    let videoGrant = accessToken.VideoGrant;
    let token = new accessToken(process.env.ACCOUNT_SID, process.env.API_
    KEY, process.env.API_SECRET);

    token.identity = event.identity;
    const grant = new videoGrant();
    token.addGrant(grant);
        callback(null, token.JWT);
};
```

Go back to the web app and open the console. After that, provide a name and log in.
We are getting a CORS error and are not able to log in (see Figure 7-35).

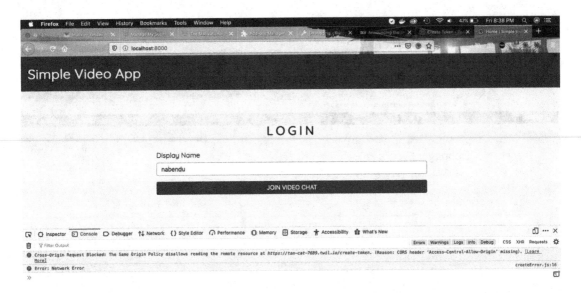

***Figure 7-35.*** *Logging in*

There is a very good way to check the actual error from inside the Twilio dashboard. Click the bug icon on the top-right side. After that, click the Go to the Debugger link (see Figure 7-36).

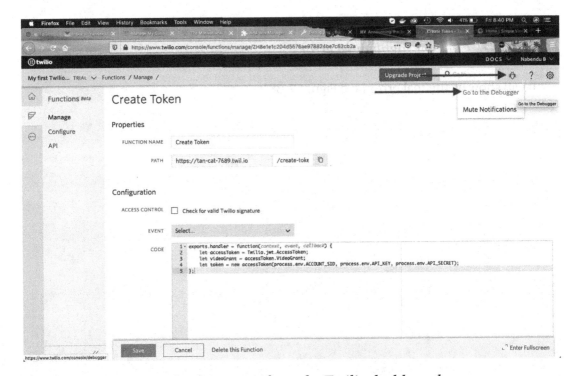

***Figure 7-36.*** *You can check an error from the Twilio dashboard*

The screen in Figure 7-37 will appear and will show the error. We need to click the highlighted error in this screen.

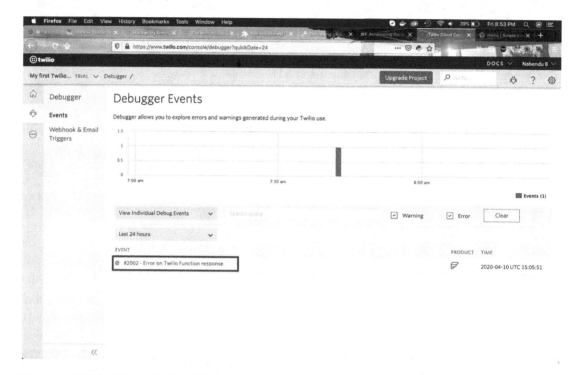

***Figure 7-37.***  *Click the highlighted error*

It will show us the real error (see Figure 7-38).

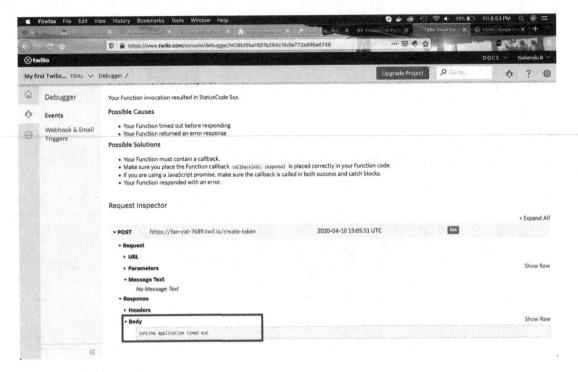

***Figure 7-38.*** *The real error*

After reviewing my function again, I realized that the four lines had not been saved from earlier. I added those lines again and clicked the Save button (see Figure 7-39).

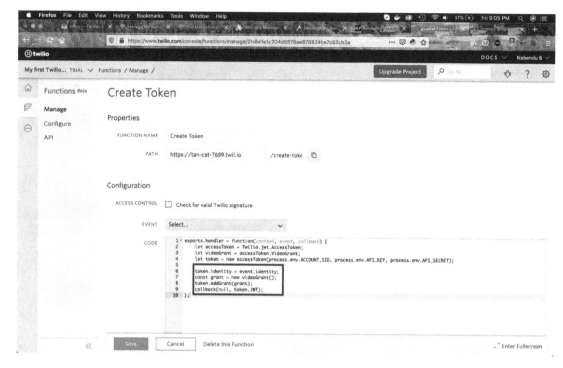

***Figure 7-39.*** *Added lines, added again*

After logging in again, I get the same error. By watching the YouTube[5] video, I realize
that we need to use the function as in the Twilio docs link[6] (see Figure 7-40).

---

[5]https://www.youtube.com/watch?v=KO2SnxY6c_O

[6]https://www.twilio.com/docs/runtime/functions/faq?code-sample=code-set-multiple-
http-headers-in-a-response-5&codelanguage=Node.js&code-sdk-version=default

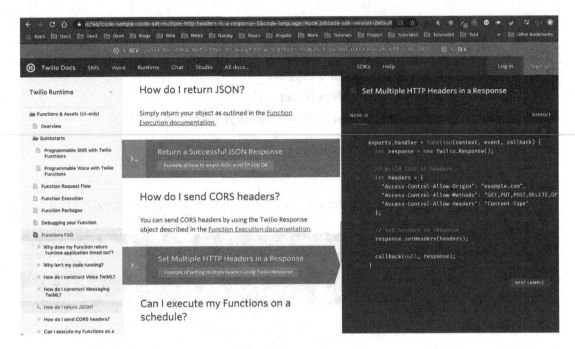

**Figure 7-40.** *Twilio docs*

Updating your function accordingly. Also, don't forget to click the Save button. The updated code is marked in bold in Listing 7-18.

**Listing 7-18.** Twilio Function Updated Again

```
exports.handler = function(context, event, callback) {
    let accessToken = Twilio.jwt.AccessToken;
    let videoGrant = accessToken.VideoGrant;
let token = new accessToken(process.env.ACCOUNT_SID, process.env.API_KEY,
process.env.API_SECRET);
    token.identity = event.identity;
    const grant = new videoGrant();
    token.addGrant(grant);

    let response = new Twilio.Response();

// Build list of headers
let headers = {
    "Access-Control-Allow-Origin": "*",
    "Access-Control-Allow-Methods": "GET,PUT,POST",
```

```
    "Access-Control-Allow-Headers": "Content-Type"
        };

        // Set headers in response
        response.setHeaders(headers);
        response.setBody(JSON.stringify(token.toJwt()));

        callback(null, response);
};
```

When we submit again, we will get the JWT back successfully (see Figure 7-41).

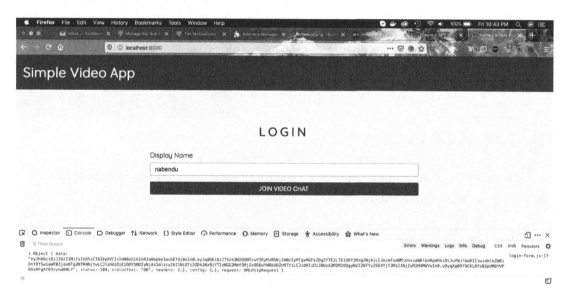

***Figure 7-41.*** *JWT back*

We can also check the validity of it by going to the site at `https://jwt.io/`[7] and pasting the returned JWT there. And, yes, it is valid (see Figure 7-42).

---

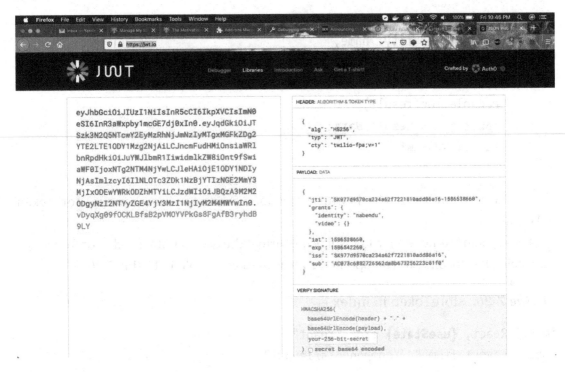

*Figure 7-42.*  *Valid JWT*

# Implementing the Video

It's time to store the result so that we can use it in the next section. Update the login-form.js file with a props storeToken and then save the JWT in it. The updated code is marked in bold in Listing 7-19.

*Listing 7-19.*  JWT in login-form.js

```
const LoginForm = ({ storeToken }) => {
    const [name, setName] = useState("")

    const handleSubmit = async event => {
        event.preventDefault()
        const result = await axios({
            method: "POST",
            url: "https://tan-cat-7689.twil.io/create-token",
```

```
        data: {
            identity: name,
        },
    })
    console.log(result);
    const jwt = result.data;
    storeToken(jwt);
}
```

Next, we will update index.js with a new state token and pass the props storeToken in LoginForm.

We are using ternary logic to display the form if the user is not logged in or for the time being has token text. The updated code is marked in bold in Listing 7-20.

***Listing 7-20.*** storeToken in index.js

```
import React, {useState} from "react"
import Layout from "../components/layout"
import SEO from "../components/seo"
import LoginForm from "../components/login-form";

const IndexPage = () => {
  const [token, setToken] = useState(false);

  return (
    <Layout>
      <SEO title="Home" />
      {!token ? <LoginForm storeToken={setToken} /> : <p>Has Token</p>}
    </Layout>
  )
}

export default IndexPage
```

It's time to test our code in http://localhost:8000/[8]. Upon opening it, we get the login form (see Figure 7-43).

---

[8]http://localhost:8000/

*Figure 7-43.  Login form*

When we provide a name and click Join Video Chat, we are taken to the screen in Figure 7-44.

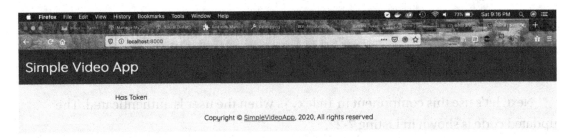

*Figure 7-44.  It was successful*

# Create the Video Component

Next, we will create the Video component. Create a new file called video.js inside the components folder. We are using a useEffect hook, which will fire when the token changes. The token comes as a prop and is used to connect to a room, using the twilio-video built-in method. The code is shown in Listing 7-21.

***Listing 7-21.*** The video.js File

```
import React, { useEffect } from 'react'
import TwilioVideo from "twilio-video"

const Video = ({ token }) => {
    useEffect(() => {
        TwilioVideo.connect(token, { video: true, audio: true, name: "SVA"
        }).then(
            result => {
                        console.log("Successfully joined room", result)
            })
    }, [token])

    return (
        <div>
            Video
        </div>
    )
}

export default Video;
```

Next, let's use this component in index.js when the user is authenticated. The updated code is shown in Listing 7-22.

***Listing 7-22.*** Video in index.js

```
import React, {useState} from "react"
import Layout from "../components/layout"
import SEO from "../components/seo"
import LoginForm from "../components/login-form";
import Video from "../components/video";

const IndexPage = () => {
  const [token, setToken] = useState(false);
```

```
  return (
    <Layout>
      <SEO title="Home" />
      {!token ? <LoginForm storeToken={setToken} /> : <Video
      token={token}  />}
    </Layout>
  )
}
```

```
export default IndexPage
```

We will again log in to our web app, by giving a display name and clicking the Join **Video Chat** button (see Figure 7-45).

***Figure 7-45.*** *Log in*

This will open a popup to ask for permission to use video and audio. We need to click Allow (see Figure 7-46).

**Figure 7-46.** *Choose Allow to continue*

It will successfully log you in and show Video (see Figure 7-47).

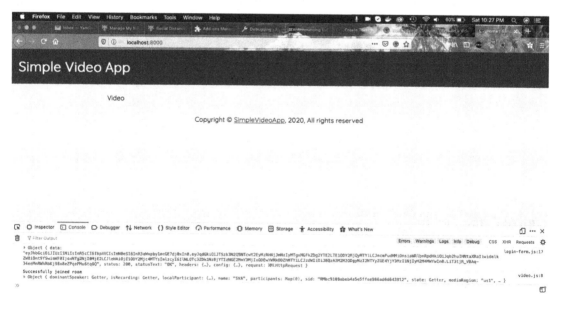

**Figure 7-47.** *Video*

We will now start showing the local webcam video. Open the video.js file and update the highlighted parts. Here, we are using useRef, as we want to attach the video to the div.

We are using a built-in createLocalVideoTrack() variable from Twilio to attach the video of the webcam to the div localVidRef. The updated code is shown in Listing 7-23.

***Listing 7-23.*** Local Video in video.js

```
import React, { useEffect, useRef } from 'react'
import TwilioVideo from "twilio-video"

const Video = ({ token }) => {
    const localVidRef = useRef()

    useEffect(() => {
        TwilioVideo.connect(token, { video: true, audio: true, name: "SVA"
        }).then(
            result => {
                        TwilioVideo.createLocalVideoTrack().then(track
                        => {
                            localVidRef.current.appendChild(track.
                            attach())
                        })
            })
    }, [token])

    return (
        <div>
            <div ref={localVidRef} />
        </div>
    )
}

export default Video;
```

Go to http://localhost:8000/[9] again and log in with any username (see Figure 7-48).

---

[9]http://localhost:8000/

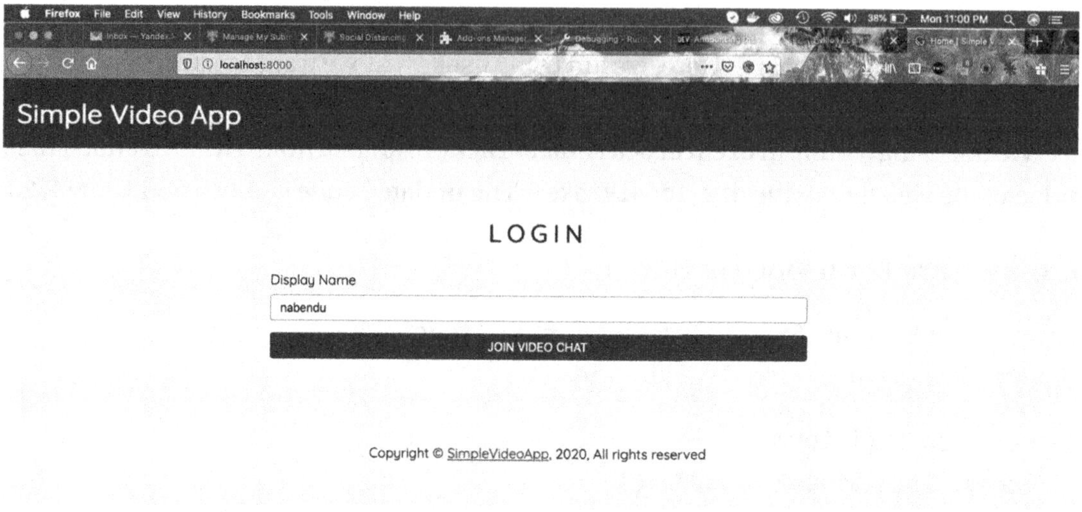

***Figure 7-48.***  *Log in again*

After that, allow the browser to use the camera and microphone (see Figure 7-49).

***Figure 7-49.***  *Allow the browser to use the camera and microphone*

You will be able to see yourself in the video (see Figure 7-50).

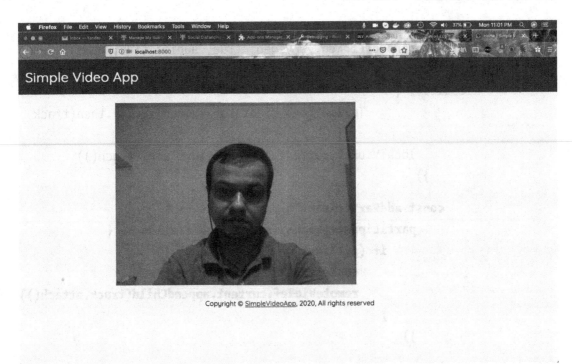

***Figure 7-50.*** *The video is working*

It's time to attach the remote participants. Update the video.js file as shown in Listing 7-24. We are adding another ref remoteVidRef to a div.

We then take the result and loop through each participant. Each participant can have one or more tracks (cameras), so we are looping through them as well. We then append it to remoteVidRef. The updated code is shown in Listing 7-24.

***Listing 7-24.*** Remote Video in video.js

```
import React, { useEffect, useRef } from 'react'
import TwilioVideo from "twilio-video"

const Video = ({ token }) => {
    const localVidRef = useRef()
    const remoteVidRef = useRef()
```

```
    useEffect(() => {
        TwilioVideo.connect(token, { video: true, audio: true, name: "SVA"
        }).then(
            result => {
                            TwilioVideo.createLocalVideoTrack().then(track
                            => {
                    localVidRef.current.appendChild(track.attach())
                })

                const addParticipant = participant => {
                    participant.tracks.forEach(publication => {
                        if (publication.isSubscribed) {
                            const track = publication.track
                            remoteVidRef.current.appendChild(track.attach())
                        }
                    })

                }

                result.participants.forEach(addParticipant)
            })
    }, [token])

    return (
        <div>
            <div ref={localVidRef} />
            <div ref={remoteVidRef} />
        </div>
    )
}

export default Video;
```

It seems to be working, as we are able to see two videos now (see Figure 7-51).

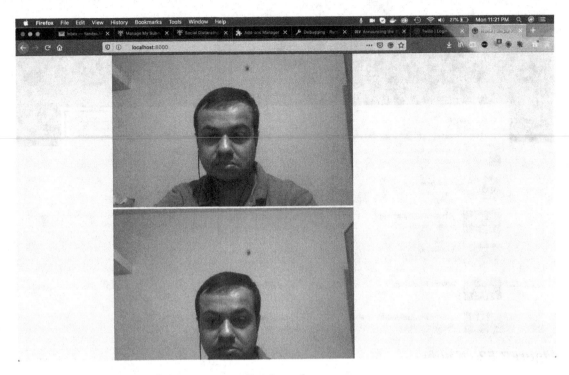

***Figure 7-51.***  *Two videos are now displayed*

# Deploying Netlify

It's time to deploy to Netlify, so that you can test from two devices. Open your Netlify dashboard and click the New Site from Git button (see Figure 7-52).

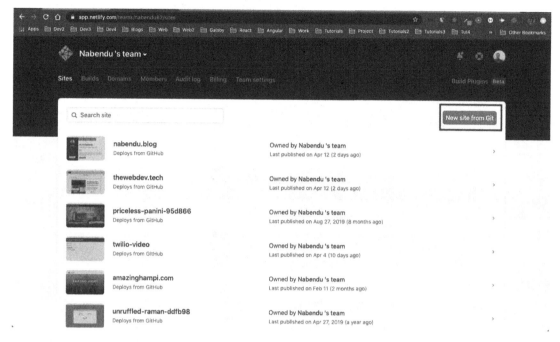

**Figure 7-52.** *Netlify*

Next, click GitHub (see Figure 7-53), as my code is in https://github.com/
nabendu82/SimpleVideoApp.[10]

---

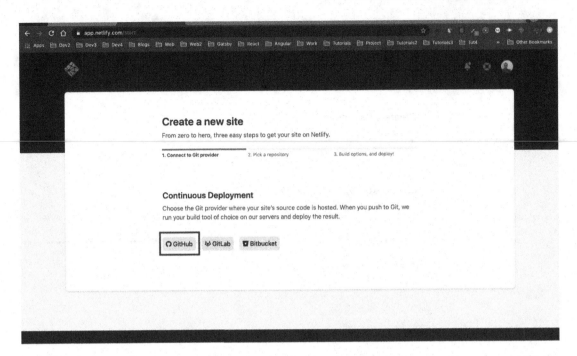

*Figure 7-53.* *GitHub*

After that, I need to search the repo, as I have a lot of them. After getting the correct repo, click it (see Figure 7-54).

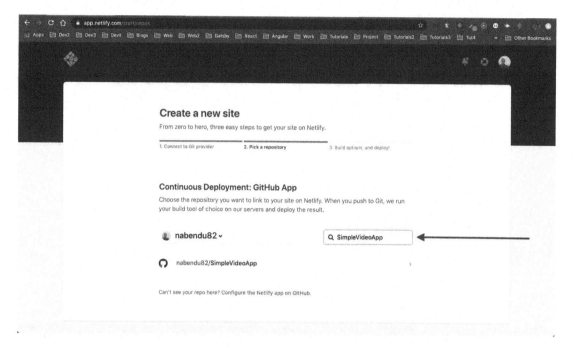

***Figure 7-54.*** *Searching for the correct repo*

After that, keep all the default settings and click the Deploy Site button (see Figure 7-55).

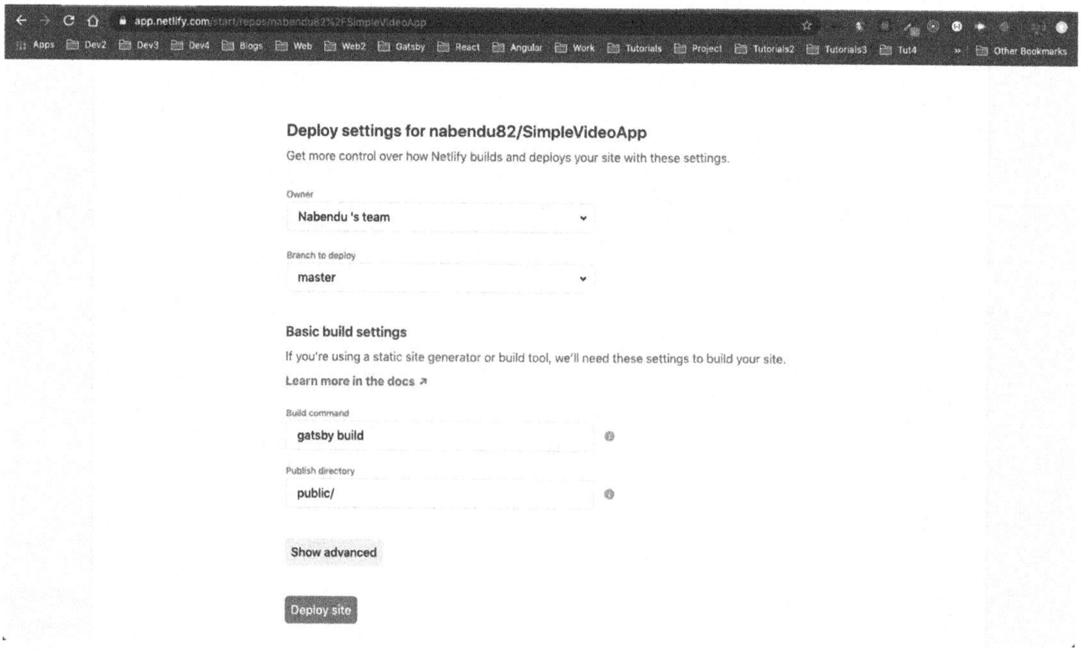

***Figure 7-55.*** *Deploy the site*

On the next screen, click the Site Settings button quickly (see Figure 7-56).

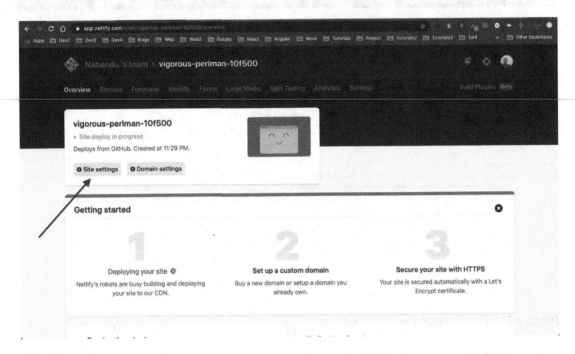

***Figure 7-56.*** *Site settings*

Next, scroll a bit and click the Change Site Name button (see Figure 7-57).

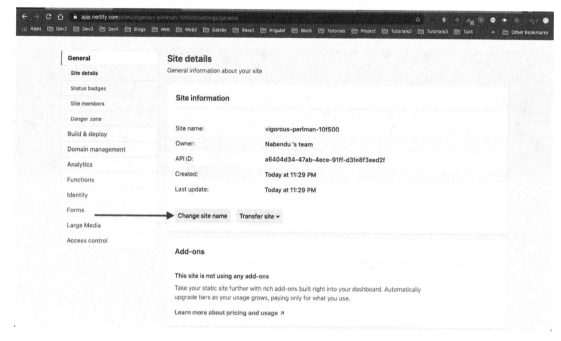

***Figure 7-57.***  *Change the site's name*

It will open a popup, in which you can change the random site name to something meaningful (see Figure 7-58).

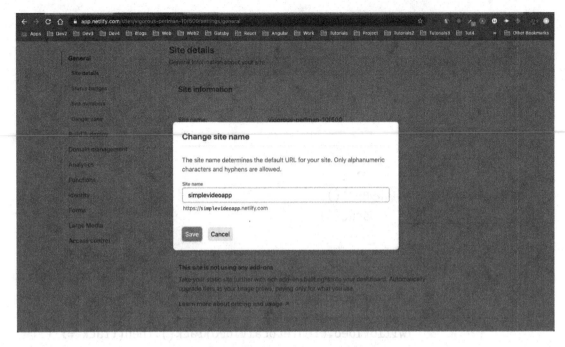

***Figure 7-58.*** *Choose a meaningful name for your site*

Finally, the site is deployed (see Figure 7-59).

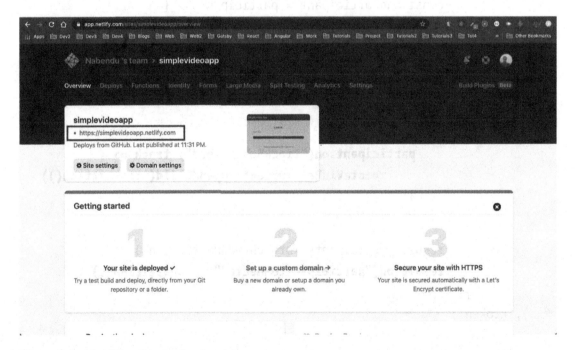

***Figure 7-59.*** *The site is deployed*

The app is deployed and I logged in from two machines, but I was not able to see both videos. Per the YouTube video, I realized I missed a part. We need to add the updated part to the video.js file. The updated code is shown in Listing 7-25.

***Listing 7-25.*** Fixes to the video.js File

```
...
...
const Video = ({ token }) => {
    const localVidRef = useRef()
    const remoteVidRef = useRef()

    useEffect(() => {
        TwilioVideo.connect(token, { video: true, audio: true, name: "SVA"
        }).then(
            result => {
                    TwilioVideo.createLocalVideoTrack().then(track => {
                    localVidRef.current.appendChild(track.attach())
                })

                const addParticipant = participant => {
                    participant.tracks.forEach(publication => {
                        if (publication.isSubscribed) {
                            const track = publication.track
                            remoteVidRef.current.appendChild(track.attach())
                        }
                    })
                    participant.on("trackSubscribed", track => {
                        remoteVidRef.current.appendChild(track.attach())
                    })
                }

                result.participants.forEach(addParticipant)
                result.on("participantConnected", addParticipant)
            })
    }, [token])
            ...
            ...
```

I then push the code, which automatically deploys to Netlify. I am able to log in from multiple devices and see the videos (see Figure 7-60).

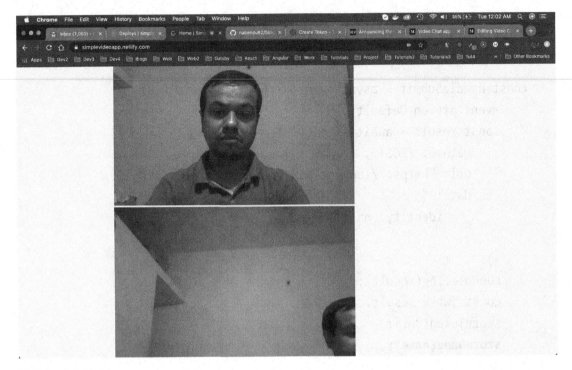

***Figure 7-60.*** *Working!*

There is some CSS and some other changes remaining, before I can submit my app to the hackathon.

# Making CSS Changes

Our web app is almost finished; only some CSS remains, so let's add it.

I also want to show the name of the organizer, so let's get it from `login-form.js`. We will use a callback function called `storeName`, which is similar to `storeToken`, to send the name back. The updated code is shown in Listing 7-26.

***Listing 7-26.*** storeName in login-form.js

```
...
...
const LoginForm = ({ storeToken, storeName }) => {
    const [name, setName] = useState("")

    const handleSubmit = async event => {
        event.preventDefault()
        const result = await axios({
            method: "POST",
            url: "https://tan-cat-7689.twil.io/create-token",
            data: {
                identity: name,
            },
        })
        console.log(result);
        const jwt = result.data;
        storeToken(jwt);
        storeName(name);
    }

        ...
        ...
```

Next, let's update index.js and use the logic similar to that of token. We are passing the name to the Video component. The updated code is shown in Listing 7-27.

***Listing 7-27.*** storeName in index.js

```
...
...
const IndexPage = () => {
  const [token, setToken] = useState(false);
  const [name, setName] = useState(false);
```

```
  return (
    <Layout>
      <SEO title="Home" />
      {!token ? <LoginForm storeToken={setToken} storeName={setName} /> :
      <Video token={token} name={name} />}
    </Layout>
  )
}

export default IndexPage
```

Next, let's update the Video component in the video.js file. Here, we are importing a video.css file. We will make it soon. After that, we are destructuring the name prop.

After that, in the video.js file, make the following changes. Change the enclosing div to a fragment and add Organizer and use the name prop.

Also add an h2 for remote participants. Lastly, add a className for remoteVideRef div, which we are going to style next. The updated code is shown in Listing 7-28.

*Listing 7-28.* Styles in video.js

```
import React, { useEffect, useRef } from 'react'
import TwilioVideo from "twilio-video"
import './video.css'

const Video = ({ token, name }) => {

        ...

        ...

    return (

            <h2>Organizer: {name}</h2>
            <div ref={localVidRef} />
            <h2>Remote Participants</h2>
            <div className="remoteVideo" ref={remoteVidRef} />

    )
}

export default Video;
```

Add a video.css file to the same folder and add the simple style shown in Listing 7-29.

***Listing 7-29.*** The video.css File

```
.remoteVideo{
    display: grid;
    grid-template-columns: repeat(auto-fit, minmax(260px, 1fr));
    grid-gap: 10px;
    justify-items: center;
}

video{
    width: 100%;
    max-width: 240px
}

h2 {
    margin: 1rem 0;
}
```

All the changes are done, so it's time to test it in `localhost`. It is working fine and I checked it in three different browsers (see Figure 7-61).

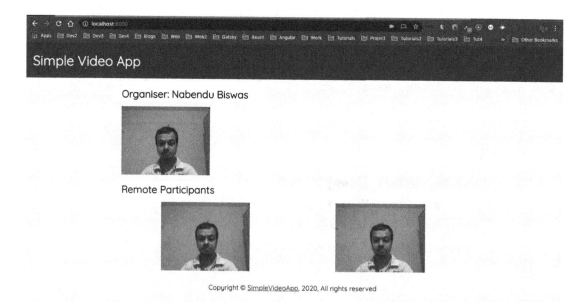

***Figure 7-61.*** *Tested in the localhost*

418

# Automatic Deployment

It's time to push the code in GitHub, to deploy it automatically. After it was deployed, I logged in from three different devices (see Figure 7-62).

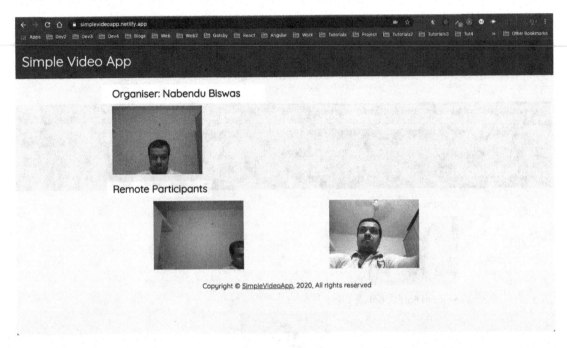

*Figure 7-62.* *Deployed*

It is working fine but I found a bug where, for remote participants, it will show their name in place of the word Organizer. Let's change the way it will look for each user. I am now showing the name in Connect, so it will be different for each user. The updated code is shown in Listing 7-30.

*Listing 7-30.* Bug Fix in video.js

```
return (

        <h2>Organizer</h2>
        <div ref={localVidRef} />
        <h2>Remote Participants</h2>
        <div className="remoteVideo" ref={remoteVidRef} />
        <p>Connected : {name}</p>

)
```

419

Let's add the code in Listing 7-31 to the `video.css` file.

**Listing 7-31.** The video.css File

```
p {
        margin-top: 1rem
}
```

It is now working fine for different users (see Figures 7-63 and 7-64).

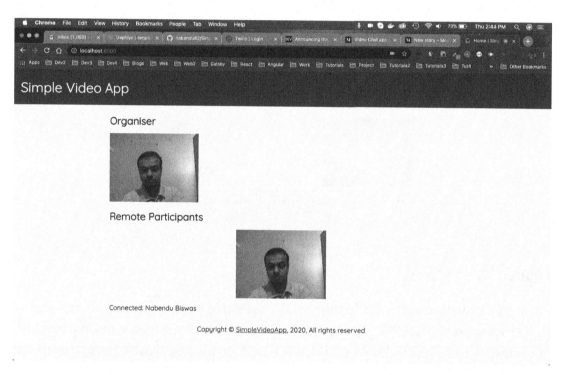

**Figure 7-63.** *Organizer*

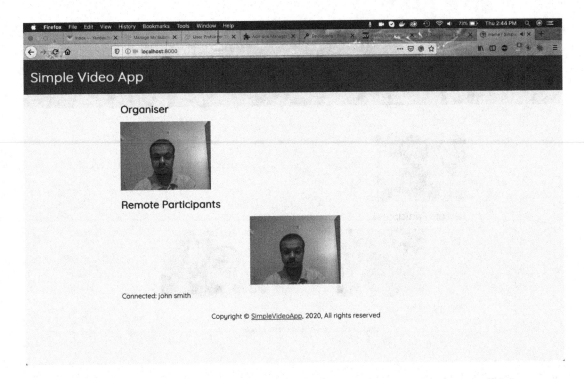

*Figure 7-64.* *Participant*

I will redeploy now and check the web app. I am testing with all three devices—two laptops and one phone (see Figure 7-65).

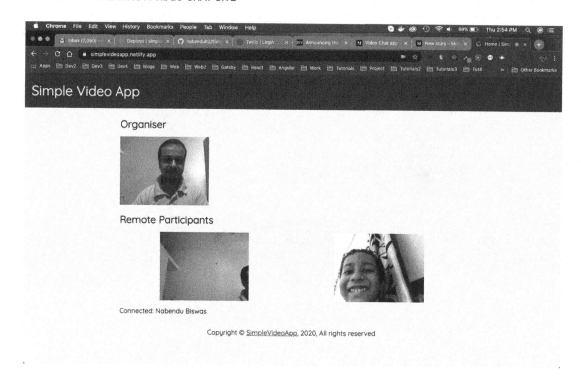

***Figure 7-65.*** *Working fine*

My app is complete and deployed. As I mentioned earlier, this is a very simple video app, which can be created with ease and deployed in no time with Netlify.

Share the link with your friends and enjoy video conferencing. We get $15 worth of free credits from Twilio and I used $3.24 while making this project (see Figure 7-66).

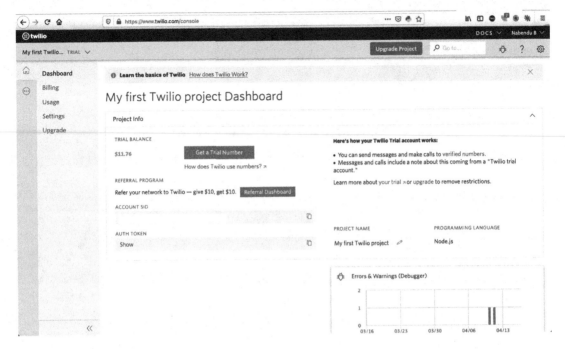

***Figure 7-66.*** *Twilio dashboard*

I am submitting the web app soon for the hackathon, so I had to add README and LICENSE files. I added both in my GitHub and joined the Twilio CodeExchange Community.[11] Details about the submission rules are found here[12]. You can also find the code for this project at this[13] GitHub link.

# Summary

I hope you liked the video chat app we created in this chapter. You can use it to create your own app. We covered the following topics in this chapter:

- Creating a video chat web app, using the awesome Twilio service

- Setting up the Twilio site

- Writing Twilio functions for the video chat app

---

[11] https://ahoy.twilio.com/code-exchange-community
[12] https://dev.to/devteam/announcing-the-twilio-hackathon-on-dev-2lh8
[13] https://github.com/nabendu82/SimpleVideoApp

# Index

© Nabendu Biswas 2021
N. Biswas, *Foundation Gatsby Projects*, https://doi.org/10.1007/978-1-4842-6558-1

# C

# D, E

# F

# G

# H

# I, J, K

# L, M

Printed in the United States
By Bookmasters